≡DEMOCRACY IN NAGALAND: TRIBES, TRADITIONS, AND TENSIONS

Edited by
Jelle J P Wouters and Zhoto Tunyi

≡ THE HIGHLANDER BOOKS

KOHIMA + EDINBURGH + THIMPHU

THE HIGHLANDER
BOOKS

http://www.highlanderbooks.org

Highlander Books – Kohima
The Kohima Institute
Kohima, Nagaland 797003

Highlander Books – Thimphu
Royal Thimphu College
PO Box 1122, Ngabiphu, Bhutan

Highlander Books – Edinburgh
C/o Arkotong Longkumer
New College, Mound Place, Edinburgh
United Kingdom EH1 2LX

ISBN: 9780692070314
Library of Congress Control Number: 2018934024

Cover Image: A picture of the Plebiscite of May 16, 1951
Source: www.nagajournal.com
Design and layout by Alina Ronghangpi

CONTENTS

ILLUSTRATIONS

TABLES

CONTRIBUTORS

A. Wati Walling is Assistant Professor at National Institute of Technology, Nagaland. His research focuses on the interface between religion and culture, political economy, corruption, and conflict studies. His previous publications include: 'The social construction of symbols, rituals, institutions, and folklores: its relation to worldviews' (2012, *The Tribal Tribune*), and the following two chapters in edited volumes: 'Customary land owning practices: the norm practitioners, land bearers, and the cocmmoners' identity in a tribal community in Nagaland' (2014, *Rawat Publications*), and 'Rethinking tribe, scientific knowledge based policies: a sociological analysis of bamboo development in Nagaland' (2010, *Serial Publications*).

Ankush Agrawal is Assistant Professor of Economics at Indian Institute of Technology, Delhi. His research focuses on Applied Econometrics and Development Economics.

B. Henshet Phom is Assistant Professor and Vice-Principal of Yingli College, Nagaland. He has authored the following books: *Socio-Cultural Issues in Nagaland* (2002, Yingli College), *Phom Naga customary laws* (2005, Longleng: customary law court), and *The Phom Naga indigenous religion* (2015, Heritage Publishing House).

Chothazo Nienu is a PhD candidate at University of Hyderabad. His research focuses on the communitisation of education in Nagaland. He recently published a book chapter titled: 'Institutional barriers to development in the state of Nagaland' (2017, *Springer*).

Dolly Kikon teaches Development Studies, Gender, and Anthropology at University of Melbourne. Her monographs include *Life and dignity: Women's testimonies of sexual violence in Dimapur* (2015, NESRC) and *Experiences of Naga women in armed conflict: Narratives from a militarized society* (2004, WISCOMP).

Jelle J. P. Wouters is Senior Lecturer at Royal Thimphu College. His research revolves around state, democracy, and development in Nagaland. He recently edited (with Michael Heneise) the book *Nagas in the 21ˢᵗ Century*

(2017, *Highlander Books*). His other recent publications include: 'The making of tribes: the Chang and Chakhesang Nagas in India's Northeast' (2017, *Contributions to Indian Sociology*), and 'Polythetic democracy: Tribal elections, bogus votes, and political imagination in the Naga uplands of Northeast India' (2015, *Hau: Journal of Ethnographic Theory*).

Kham Khan Suan Hausing is Professor at University of Hyderabad. His research interests include federalism, ethnic conflict, nationalism, and Indian politics with special focus on Northeast India. His publications include: 'Framing the North-East in Indian politics: Beyond he integration framework' (2015, *Studies in Indian Politics*), 'Symmetric federalism and the question of democratic justice in Northeast India' (2014, *India Review*), and 'Rethinking tribe identities: The politics of recognition among the Zo in North-East India' (2011, *Contributions to Indian Sociology*).

Michael Heneise is director of the Kohima Institute, and co-editor of the *Highlander*. His research generally focuses on the intersection between indigenous knowledge, sacred ecology, and modernity. In addition to his work with *The Highlander*, he is editor in-chief of the South Asianist, an academic journal published by the University of Edinburgh.

Moamenla Amer is Assistant Professor at Nagaland University. Her areas of expertise are gender studies, structural inequalities, and youth and democracy. Her publications include: 'Electoral dynamics in India: a study of Nagaland' (2014, *Journal of Business Management & Social Science Research*), 'Voting behaviour: A study of women voters in Nagaland' (2009, *Social Change and Development*), and 'Political Awareness and its implications on participatory behaviour: a study of women voters in Nagaland (2009, *Indian Journal of Gender Studies*).

Renchumi Kikon Kuotsu is Assistant Professor at Patkai Christian College. Her research concentrates on gender studies and electoral politics in Nagaland. She recently published a book chapter titled: 'Are women organisations in Naga Movement organisations? A brief study of the Naga Mothers Association, Naga Women Hoho Dimapur and the Miqlat Ministry' (2017, *Akansha Publications*).

Riku Khutso is a PhD candidate at University of Hyderabad. He works on language, public sphere, modernity, and culture in Nagaland.

T. Longkoi Khiamniungan is assistant professor at Central University of Haryana. Her work focuses on social inequality, development disparities, statehood demands, gender, and political representation. Her publications include: 'Inequality in Nagaland: A case study of "advanced" and "backward" tribes' (2014, *International Journal on Sustainable Development*), and 'Gender and democracy: disparity in women's political representation in Nagaland' (2013, *Eastern quarterly*).

Venusa Tinyi is assistant professor at University of Hyderabad. His areas of specialisation include logic, philosophy of religion, and moral philosophy, and he holds a long-term interest in Christian studies and Naga culture and identity. Tinyi jointly authored (with Paul Pimono and Eyingbeni) the book *Nagas: Essays for responsible change* (2012). His monograph *Politics of Naga nationalism: State and the Politicians* was published in 2014 by the Centre for Research, Interfaith Relations and Reconciliation.

Vikas Kumar is Assistant Professor at Azim Premji University, Bengaluru. His research focuses on Political Economy of Conflicts and Statistics, Law and Development, Economics of Religion, and Indian History

Zhoto Tunyi is Assistant Professor at Patkai Christian College. His current research concerns civil society, conflict resolution, and identity politics in Nagaland. He published the following article: (with Jelle J.P. Wouters) 'India's Northeast as an internal borderland: Domestic borders, regimes of taxation, and legal landscapes' (2016, *The NEHU Journal*).

PREFACE

This book grew from our long-standing interest and research on democracy and elections (and political life-worlds more widely) in Nagaland, and was inspired by the relatively dearth of scholarship on Nagas' actual experiences with democratic institutions, procedures, and politics. To address this lacuna, we sought to draw in a wide variety of scholars from different disciplines and asked them reflect on the form, functioning, and social substance of democratic politics in Nagaland. This resulted in 12 chapters, excluding the introduction, that engage democracy and elections in Nagaland from a variety of methodological approaches, historical and contemporary time-frames, and theories and themes. What these chapters show, both individually and collectively, is that any understanding of Nagaland's existing democratic politics must entail a critical appreciation of the dialectical relations that exist between modern ideals and institutions of (liberal) democracy, the politics of Naga insurgency, and the traditional predispositions, penchants, and prejudices of homegrown Naga political theory and praxis. Taken together, these produce a contemporary democratic sociality and structure of political morals that are both historically traceable and culturally contested, as well as enacted and evaluated afresh.

At *Highlander Books* we wish to thank Michael Heneise for his support and enthusiasm in seeing this volume through to print. We are also grateful to Edward Moon-Little, D.S. Teron, and Catriona Child for their careful editorial assistance and guidance, and to Alina Ronghangpi for typesetting and design. We also express our gratitude to *Economic and Political Weekly* for permitting us to reproduce here the following three articles: 1) Kikon, D. 2005. 'Engaging Naga nationalism: Can democracy function in militarized societies?' *EPW* 40(26): 2833-37, 2) Wouters, J. J.P. 2014. 'Performing democracy in Nagaland: Past polities and present politics' *EPW* 49(16): 59-66, and 3) Hausing, K.K.S. 2017. '"Equality as tradition": women's reservation in Nagaland', *EPW* 52(45): 36-43.

Jelle J P Wouters and Zhoto Tunyi
January 2018

01

INTRODUCTION: EXPLORING DEMOCRACY IN NAGALAND

Jelle J P Wouters

Every society arranges its political life and character in discrepant ways, based on what practices and principles it does, and does not, deem just and valuable. There are potentially infinite ways in which we can arrange our political lifeworlds, and our human archive reveals that we have attempted a good many. Broadly speaking, political systems are both designed by and benefit those that hold power. It is no coincidence that official histories are written by its victors. However, questions about political organisation, leadership, and legitimacy are not just about power; they are also about the material and moral actualization of social life. The question: 'what is the good political life?' or 'what makes a good politician?', thence, can hardly be answered in the abstract, but is subject to cultural and traditional values and a society's own conception of its political self, hopes, and aspirations.

While multiple waves of liberal democracy have made the globe more 'democratic' and, in some way, politically alike, than ever before, democratic lifeworlds continue to differ markedly between places and peoples. This is because democratic institutions, practices, and ideals find themselves here, there, and everywhere enmeshed and adapted into historically evolved contexts and circumstances, which, in the upshot, gives democracy everywhere distinct cultural hues. Lucia Michelutti (2007: 641) theorises this process as the 'vernacularization' of democracy:

> The moment democracy enters a particular historical and socio-cultural setting it becomes vernacularised, and through vernacularization it produces new social relations and values which in turn shape political rhetoric and political culture. Hence, an anthropology of democracy should study 'democracy' as both the product and the producer of different socio-political relations.

In this, Nagaland democracy is no different. The essays that make up this volume explore the political arrangements and values – both past and present – under which and within citizens in Nagaland live. It discusses what Nagas have done to the democracy 'imposed' on them by the postcolonial Indian state by way of adjusting it to their own traditional and tribal lifeworlds and uses, what democracy has done to Naga society, and the tensions that permeate Nagaland's post-statehood democratic domain.

Among modern democratic politics worldwide, postcolonial India draws special attention, not just for its status as the world's largest democracy but for the democratic and electoral enthusiasm reported all across the nation, the unprecedented political participation and emancipation democracy has offered the poor, lower castes, and other marginalised and oppressed rungs of the society, and its consistently high voter turnouts (Wouters 2015a: 215). India's polity and peoples however is large and varied; it is a country fragmented into myriad castes, tribes, and communities, with people speaking different languages, worshipping different gods and deities, tracing varying political histories, and articulating divergent identities, concerns, and aspirations. This social kaleidoscope shapes 'the political' differently in different parts of India, making it sensible to think about Indian democracy not in the singular, but in the plural, as *India's Democracies* (Ruud and Heierstad 2014), and of which democracy in Nagaland is one.

On multiple counts, the social and political substance of Nagaland's, what we might call, 'tribal democracy' differs from other places in India, and markedly at that. Absent in Nagaland are politics of caste relations and equations deemed so central elsewhere – 'politicians are obsessed with caste', writes Lucia Michelutti (2007: 645) for northern India – traditional, *Jajmani* inspired patron-client relationships scripted afresh unto the democratic playing field (Piliavsky 2014); politicians (even entire castes) identifying themselves with, or seen as avatars of, politically powerful gods and deities (Michelutti 2004, 008); or constituency-wise numerical assessments of Hindu versus Muslim vote-banks. Absent, too, are Dalit parties trying to unsettle upper caste dominance as is reported for South India (Gorringe 2011); or the unfolding of a 'silent revolution' with lower castes successfully seizing political power across Northern India (Jaffrelot 2002). These social dynamics are not part of the political landscape in Nagaland (cf. Wouters 2015a).

Among Nagas, instead, any understanding of elections and democratic networks must engage the history and sociology of clans, villages, and tribes, each of which, for better or worse, assume political significance, particularly in times of elections. If many in India's heartland prefer to vote their caste, most Nagas prefer to vote their clan, village, or tribe (usually in that order of priority), and so similarly privilege 'primordial', partisan, and parochial loyalties over broader civic considerations. Any understanding of Nagaland democracy must also engage the networks, economies, and moralities behind the 'trade' in votes, so widely reported across the state (e.g. Singh 2004; Dev 2006; Amer 2014; more below). It must further engage the authoritative presence of village, tribal, and church councils; and the ways these bodies influence voting-behaviour, as well as consider the wider and long lingering Indo-Naga conflict in whose volatile, bloodshed context modern democracy and elections unfold.

Nagas' experience with democracy, Charles Chasie (2001: 47) writes, 'has been complex, difficult, and painful'. It is 'complex' because of the 'disparate nature of the tribes' (ibid: 47). Rather than announcing a social rupture, or signifying a sharp disjuncture, the entrance of formal democratic institutions did not erase divergent past Naga political practices and principles, but amalgamated with them, making them occur in some kind of mix or blend. Besides 'complex', Nagas' experience with democracy, Chasie continues, is also 'difficult' because of the 'unresolved Naga Political Issue with simultaneous "insurgency" operating during the entire period' (ibid: 47). While democracy is often conceived as a harbinger, or protector, of peace and social harmony, in Nagaland modern democracy unfolds amidst protracted political turmoil, and this volatile context shapes and bends democratic politics locally. The experience has further been 'painful' because the arrival of democratic institutions and elections caught Nagas 'in a transition from the traditional to the modern' (ibid: 47). Few societies perhaps witnessed social change at such rapid pace as Naga society has over the past century or so, of which, in the domain of 'the political', the arrival of formal democratic institutions and competitive elections is both symptomatic and causative. I will engage these predicaments variously in this introduction.

Besides being complex, difficult, and painful, Nagas' experience with formal democracy and elections also remains comparatively recent. Seeing India as an invading and colonizing force, the Naga National Council (NNC) resisted and rebelled against Nagas' enclosure into postcolonial India and boycotted the first general elections in 1952. Nagas' participation in them, the NNC reasoned, would have communicated their acceptance of the Indian Constitution. In spite of the NNC boycott, Horam (1988: 50) recounts:

> The government went ahead with the election arrangements and the entire election paraphernalia was made ready, electoral rolls were prepared, polling booths were set up, ballot boxes were made and Returning Officers were stationed. Nagas, on the other hand, were indifferent to the goings on and went about their daily work with studied calm and the whole election show proved to be a mockery as a result of an election that never was.

India's second general elections, held in 1957, were similarly boycotted by the NNC. This time the boycott was less definite as three aspirant Naga politicians filed their nominations regardless. As there was no contest and very limited polling, the three candidates were elected unopposed into the Assam Assembly. One of them, Khelhoshe Sema, was appointed as Deputy Minister of tribal areas, thus becoming the first elected Naga Minister. But Nagas' delayed experience with modern democracy was not only the result of repeated election boycotts. Prior to India's Independence, during the colonial era, the (then) Naga Hills District was officially designated first as a 'backward tract' and then as an 'excluded area' to which 'privileges' of voting for the Imperial Legislative Council and Provincial Councils were not extended. Consequently, it was only in 1964 – a year after the enactment of Nagaland state as an envisaged (but failed) political solution to the Indo-Naga conflict – that political parties, politicians, voting slips, polling booths, and ballot boxes made their definite entrance into Naga society.

To be accurate, Nagas' first experience with voting preceded post-statehood elections, as in 1951 the Naga National Council, led by A.Z. Phizo, organised a plebiscite in an attempt to legitimise the Naga demand for independence (see cover image). In this first experience of 'voting', Naga historians record, 99% of those Nagas consulted offered their thumbprints in favour of Naga sovereignty. The ballot papers were duly transported to Delhi, along with an NNC delegation, but were instantly rejected as illegitimate and non-consequential by Jawaharlal Nehru and other early post-independence leaders of India, who instead claimed the Naga highlands as lawfully theirs.

A TRADITIONAL NAGA DEMOCRACY?

As a political idea, institutionalised democracy and its hallmark of free, fair, and participatory elections has travelled far and wide since its rudimentary inception in Ancient Greece (cf. Khilnani 2009). Most people alive today find themselves living in a democracy and during their life-time engage in voting, usually multiple times. But while some like to believe that modern, liberal democracy – as both a postulated model and a political ideal – can be reproduced similarly in different places, as though as Xerox copies of itself, the way democracy is understood and performed temporally and spatially is everywhere mediated by local histories, societal complexities, and pre-existent cultural traditions. In Nagaland, too, the past shapes the present, and an analysis of the form, inner-logic, and intricacies of contemporary politics must first explore the modalities and moralities of Naga 'traditional' politics. This section, in a much abridged form, discusses some traditional Naga political systems and sentiments, and which came to provide the traditional undergrowth on which post-statehood democratic politics unfolds.

As colonial officers first climbed the Naga highlands, they encountered, to their considerable astonishment, what to them seemed like an indigenous democratic bliss. British administrators reported about the 'democratic nature of the tribal arrangements' (Mackenzie 1884: 167) and how Naga villages were 'thoroughly democratic communities' whose customs were 'exceedingly democratic' (Davis 1891: 350). Mofatt-Mills (1854: xlii) could only agree, and concluded that Nagas' political actions and arrangements could only be typified as 'decidedly democratical', making for a form of democracy in its 'extreme' (Hutton 1965: 23). British officers perceived 'the village' as the locus of 'the political', but while this was true as a general principle, Riku Khutso, in Chapter 7, shows, by discussing the political system of the *Kuzha Netho Ketsii*, the existence of an annual assembly (*teakhe mepou*) in which cognate villages participated to deliberate customs and adopt new resolutions. In its form and functioning, Khutso explains, the *teakhe mepou* was meant to adapt customs and traditions to the exigencies of time through deliberation and consensus-making. Surmising above views, Colonial Butler wrote: 'Nagas possess a form of the purest democracy which it is very difficult to conceive of as existing even for a single day and yet that it does exist here is an undeniable fact' (cited in Hutton 1921a: 143). Naga villages and communities, which lived for centuries in relative seclusion, were, in the 19th century, 'discovered' as homegrown democrats.

But were they really?

Portraits of traditional Naga democracies remain an evocative part of popular Naga history, and may impel nostalgic yearnings for life in the prototypical and pristine 'village republic' (Wouters 2017a). But perhaps the past looks better as it recedes into the background, and in these images – of traditional Naga democracies – have crept a tinge of romanticism.

To begin with, Naga village polities were highly gendered in their political form and substance. Probably few, if any, Naga women alive at the time colonial officers frequented their villages and reported its democratic nature and customs had any notable influence in political decision-making. Even as Verrier Elwin (1961: 104) commended the status traditional Naga society bestowed on its women (compared to most other parts of the Subcontinent) – 'they hold a high and honourable position... and make their influence felt in tribal councils' – Naga women, in most cases, had little or no say in the political sphere, a predicament that reproduced itself in the post-statehood democratic domain. Politics in Nagaland, both past and present, has been a man's game, to the extent that, as Moamenla Amer notes in Chapter 3, Nagaland today earned itself the dubious reputation of being the only state in India that never elected a woman to its Assembly (although, with Rano Shaiza, Nagaland did elect a woman to the). This is hardly accidental, Amer argues, but a reflection of age-old values in which public and political domains were strongly male-dominated.

This is further illustrated by Renchumi Kikon Kuotsu and Wati Walling in Chapter 5. Through a detailed case-study of a Naga female politician, they show how patriarchy, traditional practices, and gender stereotyping thwart the rise of Naga women in the political sphere. Longkoi Khiamniungan, in Chapter 9, goes further still and applies Galtung's (1969) concept of 'structural violence' to describe the customs, traditions, and societal attitudes that 'hold back' Naga women from achieving their full potential in the political arena. She argues that these structures of 'violence' must be dismantled for democracy in Nagaland to become inclusive and flourish. Kham Khan Suan Hausing, in Chapter 13, draws specifically on the recent controversy about women reservation in Urban Local Bodies to show, among others, how patriarchally structured consultations an decision-making procedures adopted by both the Nagaland government and the judiciary fail to offer equal participation to Naga women.

Some of the phrases contributors to this volume use to portray the gender divide in Nagaland politics – both past and present (and future?) – are:

'Naga women as mute beings'
'Patriarchal practices of Nagas'
'Male-biased cultural milieu'
'Patriarchal systems of socialisation'

Besides the gender argument, the portrayal of Nagas as homespun democrats is also overtly generalised. A closer reading of the Naga archive reveals the presence of highly heterogeneous political structures and sentiments, often diverging from one village and tribe to another. While some Naga villages were guided by values of rough egalitarianism and functioned without permanent political offices, others followed political patterns that were clearly hierarchical and hereditary. Again, others possessed a mixture of both. This internal variation makes it analytically impossible to speak about a Naga political ethos in the singular, as Chasie (2001) also emphasises by discussing the contemporary complexities that arise from the disparate traditional political composition of Naga communities.

The Konyak Nagas, Fürer-Haimendorf (1969: 62) observed, while carrying out fieldwork amongst them in the 1930s, had a dual socio-political organisation. One section, known as *Thenkoh*, adhered to more-or-less democratic political norms, while another group, the *Thendu*, followed a hereditary kingship system headed by powerful kings. These kings, called *anghs*, enjoyed considerable political leverage, were often autocratic, and awarded (or demanded) privileges from their 'commoners' in terms of free labour, shares in meat, and excess sexual partners. Anghs, J.H. Hutton (1965: 23), former District Commissioner of the Naga Hills District, wrote, were 'sacrosanct and tabooed, often ruling several villages and with great authority'. 'Like other chiefs', Fürer-Haimendorf (1973: 9) observed, 'the Ang [sic] of Mon was an autocratic ruler who had power over life and death of his subjects'. But while angh-ship was hereditary, and clothed in sacred predestination, it was never absolute:

> At a ritual level, if a village did not prosper, the Angh might be held to blame, just as he was also held responsible for the village's prosperity. If his crops failed he would be unable to give the feasts that symbolized, and to some extent brought about, his power (Jacobs et al. 1990: 70).

The Sumi Naga similarly observed a political model of hereditary leadership with Sumi chieftain families making 'an aristocracy in the literal sense of the word' (Hutton 1965: 23). If inherited political hierarchies and dynastic leadership are deemed antithetical to democratic values (Dahl 1989), the figures of traditional Konyak kings and Sumi aristocrats clearly complicate straightforward and simplistic notions that all Nagas were indigenous democrats. Thence, if we wish to speak about traditional Naga democrats and republicans, we also need to talk about Naga aristocrats and kings.

Konyak and Sumi Naga political systems, however, were not characteristic of what might be deemed 'Naga society' as a whole. Colonial officers knew this, and contrasted these models with the 'extreme democracy' of the Angami village or the constitution of the Ao village council 'composed of elders representing various clans and kindreds for fixed, if fluctuating, periods' (Hutton 1965: 23). In most Naga villages, leadership was diffuse, impermanent, and flexible, and positions of authority, where they existed, were mostly nominal, as orders were 'obeyed so far only as they accord with the wishes and convenience of the community' (Hutton 1921a: 143). It was probably this absence of clearly demarcated and permanent positions of leadership in many Naga villages that made colonial officers to characterize Naga villages as inherently 'democratic'. The nonexistence of permanent village leaders, to be sure, was not accidental, but on purpose. It corresponded with political values and norms. Chasie (2005: 102) explains to us:

> Certainly, no leader was accepted on a permanent basis. The moment the person starts boasting, his downfall would begin. And soon, people would lose faith in him, discarding him, finally – while every person is considered valuable, no individual is also considered indispensable.

The early documentary accounts we have of Angami Nagas, then including Eastern Angamis (now Chakhesang), link their political philosophy to that of a 'debating society' (Hutton 1921a: 142), in which decisions were the cumulative outcome of prolonged deliberation and consensus-making, not through acts of voting or by raising hands in favour or rejection of motions proposed. A similar logic applied to the arbitration of disputes. Hutton (1921a: 143) wrote:

> Disputes, when settled at all, were probably settled by a sort of informal council of elders, who would discuss the matter under dispute with one another, the parties, and the general public at great length, until some sort of agreement was arrived at.

While achieving consensus could be a long-drawn exercise, and was not always successful, it was nevertheless widely regarded as cohesive as it reified a sense of community, avoided open competition and disputes, and skirted the public displays of division voting or raising hands invariably cause. Put differently, consensus-making reduced the risk of instigating disharmony and resentment within the village community.

Crucially, however, the essence of achieving consensus through public deliberation was not that everyone in the village must have the same opinion; the meeting's outcome, the resolution adopted, or the leader chosen for a particular purpose, was usually not the one to which the largest number of villagers agreed, but the one to which the least numbers vehemently disagreed. Interpreted thus, it was the 'tyranny of the majority in its reverse' (Wouters 2015a: 140-1). Or in the iconic phrase of T. Sakhrie: 'We believe in that form of democratic government which permits the rule not of the majority but of the people as a whole' (cited in Nuh 2002: 16).

If, in the modern democratic arena, consensus-candidates (in which individual and autonomous balloting is substituted with a collective village vote, as various contributors to this volume illustrate) are regularly agreed and publicly announced in Naga villages ahead of Polling Days, this, then, constitutes not just a malevolent electoral subversion, but can also be read as a resurgence of a pre-existent political ethos that revolved around public deliberation and consensus-making in which the collective ultimately took precedence over the individual.

This traditional disposition towards public deliberation, and the privileging of communal welfare over individual autonomy, is not saying that Naga villages were staunchly egalitarian, or that each voice counted equally. Social hierarchies existed, and mattered, and could lead to positions of political prominence. In the Chakhesang Naga village I call Phugwumi, and where I carried out extensive fieldwork, for instance, every villager traditionally had the right to speak and propose resolutions. However, the influence of one's political voice was subjected to the merit and virtue a person had accumulated in his (my usage of 'his' rather than 'her' is deliberate given the male-dominated public and political sphere) life-time. Such virtues were socially bequeathed and could result from acts of bravery and physical strength (by protecting the village and successfully raiding others). In a way, inter-village raids offered opportunities for individuals to rise in the village social hierarchy as every adult male was a potential warrior. But virtue also resided in wealth and generosity (by feasting the entire village through, what is known in anthropological annals as, the Naga 'feast of merit' (Wouters 2015b)), as well as through the privilege of ageing ('Age among Nagas has both prestige and power' (Horam 1988: 18)). As a general political norm, the views of elders superseded those of village youth, the voice of the village rich were louder than those of the poor, the opinions of the strong carried more leverage compared to those of the physically feeble, while, as noted, male voices topped female ones.

If reconstructed thus, this traditional Naga 'debating society' or 'purest democracy' may now connote a patriarchal autocracy of the old, male, wealthy, and meritorious, it was nevertheless one tested over time and treasured by not a few. What such reconstructions complicate, however, are claims that Nagas' political genius is democratic by traditional disposition. While there is much to learn, and appreciate, about Naga homegrown political philosophy and theory, classing it as intrinsically democratic appears an overstatement, or at best applicable to some Naga tribes rather than to others. All the same, the image of a Naga indigenous democracy shows a remarkable resilience in postcolonial scholarship in which Naga villages remain often typified as 'republican' (Vashum 2000: 59), 'ultra-republican' (Kumar 2005: 12), a 'democratic republic' (Bhattacharjee 1978: 263), even as the very 'symbol of the republic' (Singh 2004: 12).

Romanticizing are we?

What remains, however, is the observation that Nagas' post-statehood political arrangements and values, rather than dissolving with the arrival of modern democracy, reasserted themselves unto the new democratic playing field. Such changing continuities between traditional and modern Naga political practices are illustrated by Jelle Wouters in Chapter 6. He identifies and differentiates between four broad models of voting-behaviour in Nagaland (angh or chieftainship, village consensus candidate, clan, and household models), and argues towards a contextualised, culturally-embedded understanding of Nagaland's electoral processes, which renders bare the incongruence between modern (liberal) democratic ideals and the workings of traditional Naga polities. In the upshot, Wouters shows how different Naga tribes, instead of adjusting themselves to modern democratic ideals, adjust democracy to their traditional political practices and principles.

NAGALAND STATE, MODERN DEMOCRACY, AND THE 'UNDERGROUND FACTOR'

Besides taking stock of the form and substance of 'traditional' Naga politics, any thorough understanding of how democracy works, and what it is about, in Nagaland must also factor in an engagement with the protracted Indo-Naga conflict, and critically assess how elections, governance, and the politics of Naga insurgency interlace. To start with, it must account for the contested creation of Nagaland state, and its still disputed legitimacy with many viewing the state as 'a temporary arrangement pending a final [political] settlement' (A. Jamir 2002: 3).

Envisioning an independent Naga state, the Naga National Council (NNC), and later the National Socialist Council of Nagalim (NSCN) – in its various forms and guises – rejected and rebelled their enclosure in postcolonial India, insisting that Nagas historically flourished outside the ambit of Indian civilization, or *Bharat*. India's newly independent government disagreed with this narrative. When subsequent political talks, negotiations, and attempted treaties failed, Jawaharlal Nehru dispatched his armed forces. 'Troops moved into Tuensang by Oct. 1955', B.N. Mullick, then director of India's Central Intelligence Bureau recounted, 'and the war with the Nagas started from then' (cited in Vashum 2000: 137).

The NNC's Naga Army, in response, took to the jungle and adopted guerrilla tactics. Defying many odds, the Naga Army held out against Indian military and paramilitary forces despite being outnumbered many times over, although not without suffering significant casualties. After several arduous years suffused with incessant clashes, unforgivable bloodshed, and untold suffering, a group of so-called 'middle-ground' Naga leaders united as the Naga People's Convention (NPC) to explore a way out of the grim violence and misery engulfing the hills. Based on three conventions, held in 1957, 1958, and 1959, its members proposed the creation of Nagaland state within the Indian Union. Nagaland state subsequently became a state inhabited and governed by Nagas (although with the inclusion of several non-Naga indigenous communities and to the exclusion of Naga communities in present-day Manipur, Assam, and Arunachal Pradesh, besides those Naga tribes residing across the Indo-Burma border).

It was a demand acceptable to Jawaharlal Nehru, who envisaged Nagaland state as a political compromise to the NNC's demand for total sovereignty. Consequently, in December 1963, Dr. Radhakrishnan, India's then President, flew to Kohima to inaugurate Nagaland state. 'Friends', he began his speech:

> I have great pleasure in inaugurating the new state of Nagaland. It takes an honoured place today as the Sixteenth State of the Indian Union... [our] attempts to secure you the fullest freedom to manage your own affairs have culminated in the creation of Nagaland State... May I also express the hope that, now that the wishes of the Nagas have been fully met, normal conditions will rapidly return to the State, and those

Figure 1. Militarization of polling booths. Polling Day in Phugwumi.
(Photo by Jelle Wouters.)

> who are still unreconciled will come forward to participate in
> the development of Nagaland.

Members of the NPC agreed with this statement. S.C. Jamir (2016: 96) remarks: 'it is still a baffling proposition as to how a tiny district, the district of the Naga Hills of Assam province at first became Naga Hills-Tuensang Area and then a full-fledged state'. The NNC, and its loyalists, however mourned the new state as a divisive 'sell-out' and instantly rejected the new state's legitimacy to govern. Phizo himself was unequivocal in his judgment of NPC members: 'They are traitors. Every one of them. They have betrayed us and dishonoured the martyrs who died for our cause' (cited in Steyn 2002: 118).

In modern Naga political history, few events remain as controversial and contested as the creation of Nagaland state. It divided Nagas politically into two – the people of the new state and the people supporting Naga independence – although the boundaries between them had (and has) very many crossings. Not a few Naga 'overground' politicians nourish sentiments of sympathy towards the larger Naga political cause, while Naga undergrounds, or 'national workers' as they became known, routinely seek access to the treasures and benefits the new state puts on display.

Divergent political positions on the new state were also articulated in the post-statehood democratic domain. The Nagaland Nationalist Organisation (NNO), the political party that swept the first post-statehood elections in 1964, emphasised, in its manifesto, that the 'achievement of Statehood was a triumph of the people's will' (cited in Jimomi 2009: 49). Its later political adversary, the United Democratic Front (UDF) disagreed:

> People of no other state in India have made sacrifices like the
> Naga, so much so that the state of Nagaland is not considered
> by the Nagas as a gift, but as a state created for a price dearly
> paid; a sacrifice of over ten thousands lives (cited in Nibedon
> 1978: 282).

The UDF won the 1974 state elections. Once in power, however, the government it led was soon dismissed by the Centre which imposed Presidential rule, alleging that the UDF was 'indirectly encouraging the secessionist activities of the Federal Government of Nagaland [the NNC's political wing]' (Horam 1988: 149).

Nagaland's first elections (and all subsequent ones) were held under heavy security arrangements as the NNC staunchly opposed them, seeing them as Indian elections imposed on Naga soil. So dense was the militarization of polling booths that Sen (1974) dubbed Nagaland elections as 'operation election'. Dolly Kikon, in Chapter 2, approaches Nagaland's experience with democracy as shaped by a landscape densely militarised, noting the 'extremely undemocratic and militarised conditions under which electoral systems are introduced [in Nagaland]'. She goes on to argue that 'the initiation of democracy process through the processes of electoral politics has not contributed towards any solution in the Indo-Naga armed conflict'. The relationship between political conflict and democracy extends beyond a militarised landscape, however. In a rich and revealing ethnography, Michael Heneise, in Chapter 12, links conflict-induced displacement to contemporary ambiguities in citizenship as displaced Nagas may not fit into local clan genealogies. With the latter being paramount in political decision-making (as well as in other spheres of everyday life), those who do not 'belong' face a disjuncture between their citizenship, legally speaking, and their disadvantaged inclusion and participation in the public and democratic sphere. This not only applies to conflict-displaced Nagas but also to settler communities such as Nepali, Bengali, and Tibetan families. The relationship between clan and citizenship, Heneise shows, is an intricate one, including 'the impression that clan patriarchy – the dominant moral-political system – relieves itself of the responsibility of turning outwardly toward the broader citizenry'.

As a result of the political conflict, polling during the first Nagaland elections took place in a 'disturbed atmosphere', with NNC cadres issuing 'threats to candidates and the public' (Bareh 2001: 153). Nagaland's first elections subsequently became mired in polarities:

Ballots versus Bullets
Politicians versus Rebels
Manifestos versus Threats
NNO versus NNC
Operations versus Elections

It was the NNO that turned victorious and Shilu Ao, previously the Chairman of the Nagaland Interim-Government, was installed as Nagaland's first Chief Minister. Shilu Ao's tenure, however, was to be short-lived as a no-confidence motion was tabled against him in 1966 by his own party-men. He was made to resign, although not without the party presenting him 'with the handsome parting gift of a new car' (Dev 1988: 11). This revolt, within the NNO, was the first of many episodes of political intrigue that came to haunt Nagaland democracy as politicians and parties vied for power.

Nagaland's second elections, in 1969, took place amidst the first Indo-Naga ceasefire, which commenced in 1964. But even as the political climate was somewhat less volatile, the NNC sought to dissuade villagers from casting their votes, among others by 'intermittent firing at some of the polling booths' (Gundevia 1975: 199). Polling was nevertheless brisk with a

73.69% voter turn-out (Bareh 2001: 153), and which saw the NNO returned to power.

Over time, the political dynamic between 'overground' politicians and national workers grew more complicated than recurrent boycott calls and violent resistance by the latter. Increasingly, national workers interfered in electoral contests, applying their 'muscle-power' to influence the voting behaviour of villagers. What complicates matters greatly is the nascent fissuring of the Naga Movement into a myriad of factions and parallel governments – often identifying themselves with a confusing, near identical, set of abbreviations: NSCN-IM, NSCN-K, NSCN-KK, NSCN-U, NSCN-R, NNC-NA, NNC-A, GPRN, FGN-NA, FGN-A, and so on – each of which is today a powerhouse and political player in its own right.

If the overground / underground division within Naga politics was never plain and simple, after the factionalisation of the Naga Movement relations between politicians and national workers grew more complicated with different parties, politicians, and ruling governments cultivating divergent (often intimate) relations with different factions. About the 2003 state elections, for instance, Bhaumik (2009: 210) writes:

> The NSCN pushed Naga regional parties to cobble together a coalition with the BJP in a grand plan to oust the Congress. Its guerrilla fighters went into the villages, not asking Nagas to stay away from 'Indian elections', as they had done in the past, but asking them to vote for the Democratic Alliance of Nagaland (DAN) and oust the Congress from power. The NSCN said the coalition would be 'in the interest of peace and permanent settlement of the Naga problem', unlike Jamir's Congress, which was 'subverting the negotiations'.

Nagaland politicians, on their part, have been remarkably frank about their connections with Naga underground groups. A former Chief Minister, for instance, publicly criticised the former government's stance of 'equi-distance' towards Naga factions. His policy, on the contrary, he explained, would be one of 'equi-closeness' (cited in Baruah 2007: 14-5). Even as, in theory, Naga factions persisted in condemning Nagaland elections, in actual practice national workers are deeply implicated in electoral politics.

Commentaries on Nagaland democracy, both past and present, regularly invoke the 'unholy' alliances politicians and parties cultivate with Naga factions, allegedly for 'their own [political] survival and selfish gain' (L. Ao 2013: 3), by trading monetary donations and impunity in return for national workers' support during elections, with the latter flexing their muscles if they must to secure votes (Dev 2006). This 'muscle-power' is variously exerted to capture polling booths, intimidate candidates and parties, and to manufacture particular voting patterns. At other times, however, it is not politicians but national workers who seize the initiative and select and support 'inefficient candidates who often become their puppets and together they siphon off development funds' (Ezung 2012: 2).

Oftentimes, such allegiances are seemingly guided by mutual interests with politicians using national workers to win elections and stay in power, and Naga factions using politicians to gain access to lucrative state resources, which they use to sustain (and enrich) themselves and the wider Naga struggle. Such allegiances tend to assume distinct, if fluctuating, associations between particular politicians and Naga factions. As such, the post-statehood democratic arena has become further complicated through the remapping of factionalism on it. These linkages are well known locally: ask any Naga voter about the specific underground affiliations of a particular politician or party and most will offer a detailed account. Over time, the 'underground factor', thence, became an intricate part of Nagaland 'election talk': 'reports of insurgent groups having influenced the outcome of electoral politics', Amer (2014: 10) writes, 'have dominated popular discourse in the state'.

But even as the 'underground factor' became a sophisticated part of democracy and elections in Nagaland, it is nevertheless regularly emphasised that Nagas need a political solution, more than they need recurrent elections. In 1998, a year into the ceasefire struck between the NSCN-IM and the Centre, this sentiment revealed itself in the slogan: 'No election, but solution' and a call for the deferment of Nagaland elections. This demand was voiced both by the NSCN-IM and a conglomerate of Naga civil society organisations, among them the Naga Hoho (a pan-Naga tribal apex body). This boycott call, as Zhoto Tunyi argues in Chapter 10, exemplifies how Naga civil societies have, over time, variously resisted institutions, procedures, and laws of the Indian State in their attempt both to 'covertly' support the Naga Movement and to protect Naga culture, customs, traditions, and interests. When the Centre refused to postpone the election, a declaration was drawn up by the NSCN-IM and Naga civil societies, which they insisted Naga politicians sign. It read:

> The Naga people through their various organisations strongly oppose holding of elections in Naga-inhabited areas. As such I... candidate of... party will not file my nomination paper in the ensuing / state assembly elections in view of the ongoing political dialogue between the Government of India and the NSCN (I-M).

All Nagaland political parties heeded to this boycott call. That is, except for the Congress Party, which was the ruling government under the headship of S.C. Jamir. 'The NSCN(IM) adopted a very hard-line approach', S.C. Jamir (2016: 287-9) recalls the 1998 elections in his memoires. He narrates:

> Yet they had never hoped to meet their nemesis in me... The Commander-in-Chief and a Colonel of the NSCN(IM) met me in one house in Dimapur and at first requested me, then tried to intimidate me. Their point was that the Congress should also boycott the election... There was no way that I or the Congress would in any way succumb to their demand... Disappointed with my strong posture, the NSCN(IM) leadership thought to retaliate by sending its cadres to spread over to almost all the districts to prevent filing of nominations and these cadres did what they were instructed to do: resort to all kinds of means beginning from threats to intimidations to arm twisting.

But while Jamir (2016: 288) himself justified his stance by citing the Constitution of India he has sworn allegiance to, several commentators proposed a more political reading:

> For the Jamir Government, nothing could have been more advantageous [than the call for an election boycott by the NSCN-IM). The Nagaland chief minister is widely believed to have the backing of the other major faction of the NSCN led by Khaplang (India Today 16-02-1998).

Jamir's stance drew widespread criticism. 'We will ignore the state government', a spokesperson of the Naga People's Movement for Democracy stated, then continued:

> We have never really recognised it. We are in the process of discussing a solution to the Naga problem with the Centre, and the chances are that if the talks succeed, the government will be dismissed anyway (cited India Today 16-02-1998).

The 1998 elections took place regardless of the boycott, and, hardly surprisingly, resulted in the Congress Party capturing nearly all of the sixty constituencies, and in most of them without facing opposition.

Similar boycotts were deliberated for subsequent elections, but none of these came about in definite form, and in most constituencies a complex, multifaceted 'overground-underground' interconnection continues to influence election campaigns, as well as their outcomes.

THE POLITICS OF SMALL NUMBERS

Another corollary of Nagaland's contested creation is the state's small sized constituencies. A former Governor of Assam recalls:

> There were many efforts to pacify the Naga, and through concessions in 1963, the state of Nagaland was created. This state was for a population of barely 500,000 – less than the population of many of the colonies in New Delhi – and yet all the trappings that go with full statehood, a Legislature, Cabinet, Chief-Minister and later even Governor, went with this new status (Sinha 2001: 5)

What was already a small state (India's smallest at the time) came to be divided into sixty constituencies, up from an initial 40, thus making Nagaland constituencies small, much smaller compared to most states in India, so small that politicians know most of their voters (and opponents!) personally. This makes 'doing politics' in Nagaland often a highly personalised and intimate affair. Several constituencies, indeed, have been won or lost with only a handful of votes. Indeed, if a common democratic maxim holds that 'every vote counts', in Nagaland this is to be understood literally.

During the 2013 state assembly elections Nagaland counted 1,193,438 enlisted voters. This divided over sixty constituencies makes for an average of 19,890 votes per constituency. Among Nagaland constituencies 4-Ghaspani, located in the Dimapur foothills, constituted the largest with 58,269 voters whereas, with only 5788 electors, Mokokchung Town made the smallest. Given the presence of multiple MLA-hopefuls each constituency, a successful candidate, on average, requires roughly 6000 to 7000 votes to capture the constituency. In terms of voting behaviour, Nagaland constituencies shrink further still, as, among Nagas, the unit of voting, as a number of contributors to this volume illustrate, is often not the autonomous individual but collectivities of the household, clan, or village. These two factors combined, namely small constituencies and 'collective voting', is what makes electoral politics in the periphery of the world's largest democracy a politics of small numbers.

In comparison, in India's larger states such as Bihar and Maharashtra, the average size constituency towers over Nagaland constituencies – as much as ten times over. During the 2010 state elections in Bihar, to illustrate, in 60 of its 243 constituencies the voting margins of victorious candidates was already larger than the total tally of an average constituency in Nagaland. From a demographic perspective, then, Nagaland is an anomaly in India's democratic landscape.

While the electoral principle remains the same – the politician with the largest number of votes wins – this difference in size shapes the way electoral politics is played and lived out. Contrary to the noisy bustle of India's urban politics, its massive rallies, agitated processions, and brash sloganeering, in Naga villages electoral politics is deeply embedded in local histories and interpersonal relations; often glued by affective loyalties of family, clan, village, and tribe. Most Naga voters claim to be personally acquainted with the politician of their choice, and apply kinship honorifics by referring to him as 'brother', 'uncle', 'father', or 'grandfather', depending on the relative age-gap between them. Thus recast as a family member, Nagaland politicians are expected to take a genuine interest in the personal lives of their voters, including attending their weddings and funerals, hosting them for meals, and inquiring into their individual aspirations, expectations, and trials and tribulations. Naga voters, in turn, see it as a politician's duty to showcase personal care and commitment to them, and expect them to look after their individual material needs.

Enabled by this politics of small numbers, electoral politics in Nagaland revolves strongly around tight social bonds and parochial loyalties, as well as – it can hardly be denied – the material incentives and promises invariably offered by competing politicians (more below). As such, Nagaland democracy is not a politics of party manifestos, political ideologies, public platforms, or government policies, the political stuff most liberal political theorists would want voters to base their political affiliations on. Across Nagaland, villagers pledge their political support not based on party ideology and loyalty. Instead, they expect politicians, or their close aides, to accost them personally (not indirectly through manifestos and public speeches), and it is often in the relative seclusion of kitchens and living rooms that political alliances are made (or broken).

POLITICIANS, PARTIES, AND PORTFOLIOS

Adjudged by accomplishments of governance, Nagaland statehood can hardly be termed a success story. To most Nagas, the 'gift' of statehood soon came to taste like poisoned honey as Nagaland turned into a drain of corruption, misrule, and political volatility. After statehood, politicians and civil servants helped themselves freely to the lucrative budgets the Centre allocated for purposes of development (and for promoting the idea of India). Insurgency and violence continued, and elections had to be held under heavy security arrangements. Soon tribalism, too, was added to the political equation.

Tribalism of course

Of course tribalism

The structure of Naga society was already such that there was a pre-existent power struggle among the tribes, but it was during the new democratic arena that the political significance of tribal belonging augmented: most constituencies were delimited and divided tribe-wise, as were development allocations, government jobs, and other state projects, in the process pitching one tribe against the other in the struggle over access and ownership of state resources. Those politicians elected into power wanted not just to stay in power, but to expand their political clouts, and the most effective and simplest way for them to achieve this was to whip up tribal sentiments to their support.

This tribal competition in the new democratic arena had wide ramifications, including Nagaland's notoriously skewed population censuses. In Chapter 3, Ankush Agrawal and Vikas Kumar show convincingly how vastly inflated population censuses in Nagaland, especially the 2001 census, resulted from Naga tribes deliberately exaggerating their population numbers in view of the impending (but later postponed) delimitation of electoral seats, which is carried out every few decades based on demographic figures. Nagaland's inflated census figures, they argue, resulted from an inter-tribal contest over both protecting and increasing tribe-wise electoral seats and the associated leverages of political representation.

Modern democracy met the 'tribal psyche', if there was indeed such a thing, and in the post-statehood Nagaland history it was often educated politicians who proved to be amongst the worst merchants of tribalism. It is also here, in the 'tribal psyche' of Nagaland politics, that we encounter a Janus-faced manifestation of Nagaland politicians. While they became known – and criticised – for deriving personal wealth out of their privileged access to the state, Nagaland politicians also became known – and praised – for redirecting state resources to their respective clan, village, and tribe. Across Nagaland, Jimomi (2009: 399) writes, '[A Minister] forget[s] that he is the Minister of Nagaland, and he becomes the Minister of his own constituency, Minister of his own tribe, becomes the Minister of his own clan'.

The Ao Nagas, for instance, are today thought of as materially advanced in large part because one among their own ruled the state as Chief Minister for nearly two decades, and during his rule bequeathed Mokokchung District with manifold privileges, resources, and opportunities. The Angami Naga are said to be catching up given that, more recently, and for two consecutive terms, the Chief Minister belonged to them. 'Eastern' Naga tribes, on the other hand, partially ascribe their perceived economic 'backwardness' to the feat that no Chief Minister has ever hailed from among them. If the much noted 'miasma of tribalism' (Horam 1988: 23) has long been thought of in terms of headhunting feuds, communal antagonisms, linguistic incommensurability, as well as seen as the volatile source of recurrent splits in the Naga national movement, in the new democratic arena, tribalism reveals and reproduces itself through tribe-wise competition over discretionary allocations of government jobs and state resources.

Of course, amidst protracted political conflict, and with the NNC threatening the lives of Naga politicians (who they have regularly disparaged as traitors, reactionaries, and 'puppets' controlled from Delhi), it was never easy for post-statehood politicians to adopt legislation, implement policies, and serve the public good effectively. But this hardly seemed an excuse for the 'tribalism' and political corruption that flourished everywhere. This was much to the lament of the Federal Government of Nagaland (FGN), which publicly condemned 'the conduct of a few Naga mercenary politicians who are thriving at the nursery of India and have carnivorous appetites' (cited in Nuh 2002: 99). After Nagaland state, it was the old trade of self-interest that etched itself at the heart of the political scene.

That said, Nagaland politicians became corrupt not just because of their debauchery and decadence, but *also* because the post-statehood system and policies made corruption easy and profitable. With Naga insurgency failing to abate, the question how to run the new state, and to what end, soon emerged. It was in a bid to consolidate Nagaland state that the Centre offered monetary largesse, almost at once elevating Nagaland into the 'highest recipient of per capita expenditure of federal funds for any state in India' (Means 1971: 1016). This privileged treatment continued over subsequent decades as central assistance remained 'much higher than the national average' (S.C. Jamir cited in L. Ao 1993: 176). There was a clear political rationale behind this state largesse; Misra (2002: 54) writes: 'The Centre started pumping in massive sums of money in a clear effort to wean away sections of the Naga people from the politics of insurgency'.

State largesse, the countless crores that annually arrived and disappeared, then, made for an alternative mode of counter-insurgency (in the long run, monies, after all, often prove more effective than violence in altering peoples' political minds), one designed to 'soften up the Nagas' (Hazarika 2011: 241), to make them 'complacent about their struggle' (Longchari 2016: 236), and to increase the benefits for Naga leaders to *not* associate themselves with the Naga struggle.

In this process, accountability and transparency were soon sacrificed at the altar of national security. 'The immense funds' dispatched to 'pacify' Naga society, the historian Visier Sanyu (2003: 441-2) reflects, made for 'frequently floating easy money'. Naga politicians handling these monies 'became corrupt as they succumbed to the temptation of quick wealth'. If

Naga politicians, then, became corrupt *also* because of conditions put in place by the Centre, this would suggest that corruption might cease to be so widespread once corruption is made more problematic and difficult. This, in any case, is what many hope for.

When, in 1965, Charles Pawsey, the last serving British District Commissioner of the Naga Hills District returned to Nagaland, he expressed disgust at seeing Nagaland's politicians living 'like fighting cocks, smoke Player cigarettes, and consume vast quantities of spirits'. While the NNC insisted on the rolling back of Nagaland state structures, 'it is unlikely', Pawsey predicted, that Nagaland politicians 'will willingly renounce the sweets of Office' (cited in Steyn 2002: 137). This, indeed, they would not. Instead, elections turned into animated, often agitated, often divisive struggles for political power.

But while elections became ruthless scrambles for votes, post-election politics turned into scrambles for portfolios and ministerial berths, resulting in often fierce competition and contests between those elected into political offices. In this scramble, portfolios became ranked not based on their political mandate but on the access to state resources they promised, and over whose distribution politicians came to preside, often authoritatively so. Akin to places across India, Nagaland's offices and officers of government tend to be subservient to the whims of politicians (cf. Wade 1985) – even if often reluctantly so – and on very many occasions political considerations supersede detached, rational-legal policies, programmes, and practices, culminating, amongst others, in the polarising politicization of Naga society.

Within a decade of Nagaland statehood, the state functionary Dev (1988: 15), on deputation to Nagaland, observed the 'sordid ambitions of some members of the Naga Nationalist Organisation who felt no scruple to tarnish the image of the party... [in their] hankering after the loaves and fishes of office'. Such ambitions led to rumblings within the ruling government. When the NNO lost their political mandate in 1974 to the United Democratic Front (UDF), this was, certainly in parts, because of 'jealousy' and conflicting 'political ambitions' among party members (Dev 1988: 18).

The UDF government faced similar political infighting. The trouble, Dev narrates, began with the Minister of Civil Supplies 'when the party bosses began to pressurize him, seeking appointment as handling agents for cement, sugar, corrugated iron sheets, rice, etc., and for construction and other contracts'. The Minister was unable to meet the demands of so many. This 'disgruntled' his colleagues, for the 'simple reason that he did not help them to make money'. The UDF Government, consequently, did not survive long, and was substituted by an Naga National Democratic Party (NNDP)-led government headed by Jasokie. But while the Council of Ministers was enlarged, it 'was not big enough to accommodate all the aspiring politicians. So, defections began'. Eleven days in, the government was brought down (Dev 1988: 19).

As politicians vie over power and portfolios, the politics of defection comes in handy for those who feel underappreciated or left out. By the 1970s, (Zhimomi 2004: 124) writes, 'politics of defection was the order of the day in Nagaland'. Throughout the 1980s, too, defections remain in 'full swing', over time including 'almost all Naga politicians' (Murry 2007: 65). The anti-defection law India adopts in 1985, while changing the rules of the game, fails to quell continuing defections in Nagaland. A former MLA explains:

> Judging from political events and developments ever since the Anti-Defection Law came into operation, the legislators of Nagaland have learnt the practice of defection under the provisions of the Law, reducing themselves to gain opportunism at any opportune time (cited in Singh 2004: 155).

this makes the then Nagaland Governor lament:

> Those who are already Ministers wanted so-called better portfolios and those who were MLAs wanted to be ministers... Why is it that the Government changes so frequently in Nagaland, that is, with average tenure of about two years and some with as little as few days? People elect MLAs on the basis of party's ideologies, objectives and programmes, and the MLAs defect and re-defect for personal aggrandizement, how can stability by achieved in any government? (cited in Zhimomi 2004: 127).

While motivations of 'personal aggrandisement' are certainly part of the puzzle of Nagaland's politics of defection, the Governor is misinformed in asserting that Naga voters elect their politicians based on party ideology. True, a broad ideological distinction is generally made between regional and national parties, but over the past five decades, political parties in Nagaland have come, split, and gone in the wake and aftermath of elections, often so without leaving behind a distinctive ideological footprint. Very few Nagaland politicians, indeed, remain faithful to their political parties. Henshet Phom, in Chapter 11, notices how party-hopping has always been widespread in Nagaland with most politicians portraying 'no inhibition to switch his loyalty in favour of another party'. Taking the case of Phom politicians, he explains that they do so 'either in the interest of the community he represents, as to increase his position in the power-hierarchy, or for sheer personal gains'.

But not just for Naga politicians. For most Naga electors, too, party ideologies and manifestos are merely the obligatory humdrum behind which actual politics operate. It is to their evaluations and expectations of politicians that I now turn.

THE TRADE IN VOTES

While Naga politicians stand accused of abusing democracy into 'an industry to earn through malpractice' (Kiewhuo 2002: 61), Naga electors reciprocate by turning 'campaign inducements [into] a sort of industry' (Amer 2014: 4). Consequently, election expenses sky-rocketed, and by the late 1980s it was alleged that were Nagaland elections computed they might well constitute India's costliest per capita (Misra 1987). On this, Amer (2014: 9) details:

> It is widely believed that elections in Nagaland are considered among the most expensive in the country... Issues are often subdued by money and the dispensation of favours by the candidates during election campaign. Some of the electorate sees payment of money for votes as reparation for public funds that politicians are assumed to have stolen. Some voters may succumb to campaign inducement due to poverty... The scale and pervasiveness of these abuses has created widespread public scepticism about all electoral exercises.

For some Naga electors, the opportunity to vote, no doubt, conjures first and foremost a lucrative economic transaction. 'I am a poor man. I will cast my vote for the highest bidder', Keho, a Phugwumi farmer, tells me as I inquire about his political inklings in the wake of the 2013 elections. Keho has grown cynical of electoral politics. In the past, he actively campaigned on behalf of a certain politician, who promised him a government job in return. The MLA Keho supported won the election but Keho remained the farmer he no longer wanted to be. 'I don't trust politicians anymore', Keho concludes. 'This time I want prepaid cash for my votes, not postpaid promises'. Keho's usage of the telecom language of 'pre-' and 'post-paid' packages is part of a wider electoral vocabulary with most villagers preferring the certainties of prepaid monetary incentives and gifts in return for their votes over the uncertainties of post-paid promises. Future promises, they had learned, were not just subject to their politician winning the election, but ran the risk of being forgotten once a politician ascended into elected office. Keho had learned this the hard way, and now refuses to be 'tricked' into supporting any politician for 'free'.

During election seasons, cash becomes the electoral staple. 'I don't have small change anymore', a village shop-keeper apologises as I try to break a five-hundred rupees note at his counter. 'During elections everyone pays with big notes'.

For other villagers, elections offer a lucrative, temporary inversion of the status quo. They know that many politicians vastly enrich themselves while in office, and decide that now it is 'our turn', and demand large amounts – Restitution? Reparation? Revenge?

And yet, even as pundits on elections in Nagaland regularly report (and revile) the flow of monies and gifts typical of election seasons, there is more to this than mere electoral chicanery. I propose here (tentatively so) a more culturalist and moral reading of what is often called 'vote-buying', clientelism, and corruption in Nagaland. I do so not to absolve both politicians and electors of occasional greed and gluttony, but to account for the observation that in 'traditional' Naga politics the capacity to act as a generous 'provider' and 'repository' of social life was deeply intertwined with expectations attached to political leadership.

This argument is also pursued by Venusa Tinyi and Chothazo Nienu, who argue, in Chapter 8, that political corruption in Nagaland is not just a reflection of 'dirty' electoral politics, particularly the trade in votes, but also persists as a contested remapping of the past communitarian ethos of the Naga 'village republic', in which leaders were expected to 'help' their own people. In the modern democratic domain, this expectation, they argue, reveals itself in Naga electors expecting their politicians to be partial in allocating government jobs and state benefits. They therefore argue that 'ensuring a clean election will not ensure good governance. We have to look at our social norms and values carefully in order to tackle the problem of [political] corruption'.

Let us explore this argument further. In the political ethos of the Naga past, it was often the capacity and commitment to 'provide' (or 'help' as Tinyi and Nienu frame it) that invested meaning in political leadership, and that made it useful to have village leaders in the first place. Summing up the qualities expected of village leaders, Hokishe Sema (1986: 168) wrote:

> These rulers have some personal distinction acquired by them through their performances of sacrifices and good judgments. They also have a great economic power and their capacity to help the poor and the needy in the village is greatly appreciated. They provide food, shelter, and clothing for the needy in an

emergency. It is a great shame for the rulers if their subjects go to other villages for food. It is the duty of these rulers to ensure the security and welfare of their subjects.

An election, of course, is no 'emergency', yet most Naga voters expect, as did their fathers and forefathers, aspirant political leaders to be generous 'givers'. After statehood, however, it was no longer primarily 'food, shelter, and clothing' that, as Hokishe Sema wrote, defined 'security and welfare', but spoils of state:

From food to government employment

From shelter to state contracts

From clothing to development schemes and subsidies

Politicians offering cash for votes, in this view, is not just amoral vote-buying, not just political corruption, but is also communicative of a politician's care and capacity to qualify as a leader.

To illustrate this, let us take a step back to the 1960s and to a by-election called in Mokokchung district. Temsula Ao (2013: 181) recalls her life being transformed after her husband entered the election fray:

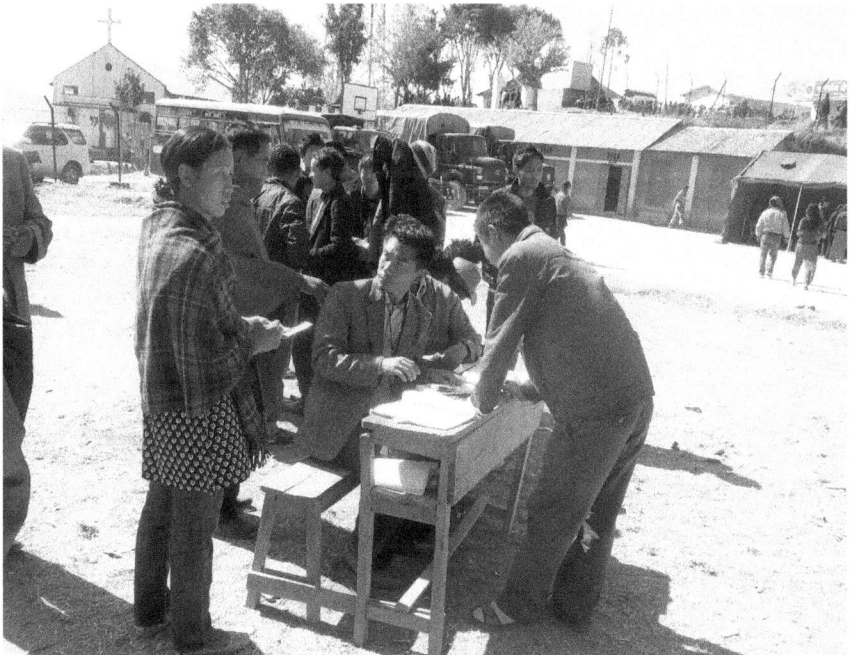

Figure 2. Polling Day in Phugwumi.(Photo by Jelle Wouters.)

> And suddenly from a placid existence, the campaign took
> us by storm... The house was turned into a free-for-all arena,
> where all kinds of people came and went at all times of the day
> and night. All our resources went into feeding and pleasing
> these so-called supporters... Success only made things worse;
> our life was not our own anymore, and there was no end to
> the 'demands' of the so-called 'supporters' as we pawned our
> souls to the great fraud of our times called electoral politics.

What Temsula Ao laments as incessant 'feeding and pleasing', most Naga electors evaluate in a different moral frame. They see it as a political leader's duty to host, feed, and look after their individual material needs. In fact, his capability and commitment to do so is what, in their eyes, defines him as a politician worthy of the name. What, in the end, is the point of electing a leader who cannot act as a redeemer of social and material life? Phizo (1951), long ago, captured this by the relational principle of *mhoso*, which roughly translates as 'to excel, to be of service to others'.

Take 'feeding'. In the material and moral world of the village past, wealth communicated virtue, but for an ambitious villager to climb the social ladder, to expand his sway, and to have his voice heard more loudly, he had to dispense generosity through the provisioning of paddy to the poorer (even if, at times, against interest) and, more crucially, through feasting, resulting in an elaborate social institution known as the Naga 'feast of merit'. With a communal basis of political life, it was through hosting lavish and ritualised feasts that a rich man absolved his material wealth but accumulated material symbols (among them, a specifically embroidered shawl, the right to decorate one's house with X-shaped boards and carvings, to ultimate monoliths being erected in one's honour) that communicated social ascendancy (Wouters 2015b).

On a tour through the Eastern Angami (now Chakhesang) hills in the 1930s, Fürer-Haimendorf (1976: 9) stumbled onto a large open compound with houses on two sides. He wrote:

> Cross barge boards rose from the gables of one of the houses,
> like the enormous antlers of some proud stag. Proud, too,
> must have been the owner of these wooden horns, for they
> showed that he had given several of those expensive Feasts
> of Merit whereby the Naga rises in social prestige and in the
> esteem of his neighbours.

Such acts of generosity were not just morally incumbent on leaders, but produced social hierarchies and notions of leadership in the first place, making pre-state village leaders not 'servants' but 'providers' of their people. To be sure, the majority of villagers never found themselves in the position to host even a single feast, but relied on the wealthier to now and then indulge them in meat and rice-beer. Fürer-Haimendorf (1939: 47) observed thus:

> The wealth of the ambitious was employed to provide food and enjoyment for the less prosperous members of the community, for at a Feast of Merit there was meat, rice, and rice-beer, for every man, woman, and child in the village.

While there usually existed no mechanical linkage between becoming a feast-giver and becoming a village leader (wealth and wisdom, both then and now, are known to be two different things altogether), the village influential were nevertheless often also known as feast-givers. Unfortunately, the feast of merit was amongst the first sacrifices Christian missionaries demanded from their new Naga converts, and, as a social institution, it has long ceased to exist (Wouters 2015b).

That said, can we not recognise odds and ends, or remnants and leftovers, of this traditional Naga practice in contemporary election feasts, as they are hosted by aspirant politicians from one Naga village to the next? True, unlike feast-givers in the past, politicians do not feast the whole village but only their followers (yet another manifestation of the divisive nature of post-statehood politics?), while the wealth necessary to host such feasts is no longer derived from the sweat and toil of agriculture (but from acts of 'corruption'? Does that make the meat taste differently?). Yet, do we not see in these election feasts, with politicians displaying generosity and accumulating social status and standing in return, not some of the expectations and moral values that shaped traditional feasts of merits reappearing?

Not just in terms of feasting, however. More broadly, it is a Naga politician's capability to 'provide' his followers that often remains the yardstick by which villagers evaluate his political successes and failures. Note the following judgment a village elder in Phugwumi made about a certain politician:

> I don't appreciate his ideology. For many times, I campaigned on his behalf. But what has he done for my family when he was in power? Nothing much! He held such big portfolios but see the condition of our village. Hardly has he made anyone rich.

The village elder then drew a comparison with the (then) Nagaland Chief Minister, telling me:

> You should go and visit his village. All houses are made of concrete and there is plenty of development. After he became Chief Minister he made not less than twenty-five of his fellow-villagers first-class contractors, giving them charge over big contracts. Others he provided with government jobs. And not just small jobs, cut those carrying the ranks of officer. He has a good ideology.

In the vocabulary of Nagaland politics, 'ideology' clearly does not refer to political or party ideology, spanning a left-centre-right spectrum, but is evaluated by a politician's ability to secure material welfare for his followers. It is this, the supplying of government jobs and state resources, what many Naga electors think of as a politician's prime responsibility for his constituency, not, say, the implementation of rational-legal policies and programmes in a detached, impersonal manner.

On the flipside, such expectations make politics and governance in Nagaland constituencies sectional and highly personalised, as many politicians tend to reserve government appointments and state benefits for those who voted for him. 'For the past three elections I campaigned on behalf of the wrong [losing] candidate', a Phugwumi villager explains, while also divulging his poor material standing. The implication here is that because he has not voted for the sitting MLA, he is debarred from accessing the state and its resources. Post-election politics in Nagaland constituencies, then, is often a politics of reward and punishment with MLAs exerting considerable discretion in the allocation of state resources.

What about the democratic principle of secret balloting? Does this not prevent politicians from knowing who voted for and against them? And is this not meant to preclude partialities and paybacks by politicians once polling is over? Not so in Nagaland. Because of the politics of the small numbers, the highly personalised relations that exist between politicians, party-workers, and voters, any politician usually knows his supporters and opponents personally. Villagers themselves, moreover, are hardly secretive about their votes (to the contrary, they may declare their votes in local dailies (see Chapter 6)).

It is in the aftermath of the 2013 elections, in a constituency close to Phugwumi, that a victorious politician goes on record promising – in a thanksgiving feast he hosts for his party-workers – that 'he would not accept any member from other political parties for the next four years but purchase them in the fifth [election] year if needed' (cited in Hoshi 2013). In local political lexicon, this promise not to enlist any new members to his party-unit (but to 'purchase' their votes if needed close to the next election) is easily understood by his voters as his pledge to reserve all government allocations to the constituency for his supporters alone. Whoever had voted against him, the politician now makes it clear, have not just lost on polling day but need to prepare themselves for a prolonged spell of state marginalisation.

To be sure, most Naga electors themselves opine that an MLA should privilege his supporters once elected into office, rather than focusing on the public at large. In fact, a politician's failure to allow his party-men and voters access to lucrative echelons of state instantly reduce his political life-expectancy, and renders him vulnerable to accusations of 'corruption'.

When, for instance, an 'educated unemployed' youth in Phugwumi was shortlisted for the final interview that would adjudicate induction into the Nagaland Police, he immediately called on the constituency's MLA, for whom he had actively campaigned during the previous election. He told him the date of the interview, as well as his roll-number, anticipating that the MLA would apply his authority to recommend his appointment. When, to his utter disappointment, all the MLA replied was 'May God bless you in your efforts', the village youth (who subsequently failed to make the cut) declared the MLA as 'corrupt' and campaigned against him during the next election. Read thus, political corruption in Nagaland is not just an objective judgment, but also a term used to criticize a politician for not fulfilling the personal promises he makes to voters during election times, for not exerting his political authority to help his supporters, and for not giving his voters a share in the spoils of state.

Among Nagas, put differently, a great deal of ideology is invested in a politician's commitment and capacity to act as a provider and repository, resulting in a set of contemporary political practices and moral values that depart from projections of 'clean elections' and 'good governance' but whose antecedents lie in the pre-state 'village republic'. Thence, if elected politicians vie for plump portfolios (as argued above) this is, certainly in parts, because any politician's political standing in his constituency hinges crucially on the access to state resources he can secure, and his expediency in accumulating and redistributing these to his followers. In Nagaland's political milieu, then, the public good habitually finds itself substituted, or certainly mediated, by a struggle between politicians for the discretionary powers to allocate state resources to their constituents, who, in turn, expect such largesse from their MLAs.

This tracing of contemporary political practices and principles to a pre-existent Naga political ethos may not justify the many 'back-door' appointments, vote-buying, and nepotism, but it does suggest that there is more to such political acts than mere venality and corruption. Even those who disagree (for justifiable reasons) with this culturalist reading of election feasts, vote-buying, nepotism, and even 'corruption', must nevertheless accept that vote-buying, in most cases, is not devoid of moral standards and considerations. Put differently, the 'trade' in votes does not operate in a moral void but is itself subject to moral yardsticks.

To start with, money is seldom asked for randomly. For the village poor, the amount demanded for their votes is often calculated based on objective need-assessments, which may include educational and medical bills, and which they expect their politician – as a true caretaker – to settle for them.

There are other considerations too. For instance, villagers may be ready to settle for a lower amount if the politician belongs to their own clan or village (or tribe in Nagaland's urban settings), compared to a politician with whom they share no such bonds, usually on the moral ground that they should 'help' a clansman or fellow villager. The demands levied on a politician may also be subject to the perceived economic position of a candidate. A seasoned politician, who is known for his riches, is often expected to be more 'generous' compared to a political novice. And, in any case, the richest or most 'generous' candidate does not mechanically win the election. Clearly, there are other factors at play than money alone.

But no matter the amount demanded and received, it is considered outright immoral to accept money from two rivalling politicians in the same way as it is considered unethical to eat lunches and dinners in more than one political camp. These are acts no morally upright villager is expected to indulge in.

SALVAGING DEMOCRACY: PASTORS ON A MISSION

The previous section showed how the rational-legal values of a 'modern', impersonal system of political representation has not made significant inroads into the interstices of Nagaland democratic politics. Politicians know this and appeal to their voters not in a Weberian frame of policies and programmes but through invoking clan, village, and tribal sentiments and loyalties, as well as by dispending patronal generosity in an often Godfather-like fashion.

But even as the above ethnographic, culturalist reading of vote-buying, nepotism, and even 'corruption' complicate simple and straightforward judgments of Nagaland's democracy as hopelessly and amorally corrupt, many in Nagaland opine that the contemporary motivations, moods, and moralities of democratic politics and elections leave much to be desired. They are now calling for change, for clean elections, 'front' instead

Figure 3. Clean Election Campaign in Phugwumi.(Photo by Jelle Wouters.)

Figure 4. Confiscation of liquor as part of the Clean Election Campaign.
(Photo by Jelle Wouters.)

of 'backdoor' appointments, and overall corruption-free governance. Democracy and elections, they lament, adversely impact Naga society; a past sense of community, they say, descended into greed and selfishness; 'humble' leadership swapped with proud and self-serving politicians; notions of communal welfare replaced with exaggerated individualism; genuine deliberation substituted by aggressive electioneering; and honesty by deceit and deception. These observations have resulted in both a Christian and culturalist critique of Nagaland democratic politics. The next section discusses the substance of this culturalist critique. Here I focus on the Christian critique that has emerged.

Twilight has fallen, the sun vanishes into a spur of jungle-clad hilltops. In Phugwumi, *Athe* (a classificatory term for 'grandfather') switches on the radio, as he does every evening to listen to the news. 'Did you hear that?', he asks after the bulletin ends. I nod. A Reverend, also the principal of a leading Nagaland theological college, has announced his candidature for the 2013 State Assembly Elections. Athe sighs: 'He stands no chance. No righteous person can win an election in Nagaland'. In his inaugural speech, the pastor turned politician pledges to abstain from using the three 'M's' ubiquitous to Nagaland elections:

Money

Muscle

Malt

Instead, he wants to contest and win his constituency fair and square, upholding both Christian ethics and the rules and regulations set out by India's Election Commission.

Athe, and most elders in Phugwumi, however, think the pastor would best confine himself to his pulpit. Not because he is not a good man, but precisely because they think highly of him and worry that his Christian teachings and lifestyle will soon prove incompatible with contesting an election, hence Athe's comment: 'a good man cannot win an election in Nagaland'.

Well into his eighties, Athe has participated in all Nagaland's post-statehood elections and, in his judgement, electoral politics has already moved beyond redemption:

> Elections make villagers worse. It makes them greedy, dishonest, and selfish, and there is no unity. I have seen it happening with my own eyes. Even if Jesus Christ would descend from Heaven and contest an election in Nagaland, he will not be voted in. Then, what chance will a pastor stand? He will just end up embarrassing himself.

For the pastor-politician it is, however, precisely this negative evaluation of politics, the cynicism that shrouded it, that arouses him into joining politics. In a newspaper interview, he explains that he wants to 'change the way things are':

> People know how Naga politicians at the helm of affairs accumulate wealth at their cost. They are building palaces with public money. They have created the haves and the have-not ... I sense an awakening in the people that the way politics has been played in Nagaland is not producing good fruits... politics is not dirty by a sacred and divine institution which people [then] pollute[d].. I am entering politics without money. I want to set the trend that good and young people who do not have money can also enter the poll fray (cited in *The Telegraph* 18-01-2013)

That Nagaland democracy and elections need reform is also propagated by the locally commanding Nagaland Baptist Church Council (NBCC), which characterises elections as 'the biggest force that is eroding the moral foundations as well as the future of the Naga people' (NBCC 2012). To counteract this worrying trend the NBCC launched, in the wake of the 2013 state elections, a Clean Election Campaign (as it had done during previous elections with varying degrees of success) aimed at fighting 'the ugly face of the election'. This the NBCC perceived as its 'prophetic moral duty'. The campaign took off with the publication and distribution of a booklet titled: *Engaging the Powers: Elections – A Spiritual Issue for Christians*. It read:

> We know that the Election Code of Conduct laid down by the Government of India itself is good enough to conduct a clean and fair election. More so, as [a] Christian dominated State, Nagaland could have shown to the world the conduct of election in a much better way based on Biblical principles. The Church has raised this issue during every election in the state but we have gone against God whom we worship. Should we continue and invite the wrath of God?

For the NBCC, the 'trade' in votes, and the temporary moral void elections seemingly effectuate, is not just evidence of perverse and dissolute politics but, more significantly, constitutes an abomination before God. During sermons I attended in the months and weeks preceding Polling Day, as well as in private conversations with Naga theologians, the right to vote was presented as a person's birth-right, a divine gift, the selling or otherwise misusing of which connotes a grave sin. To illustrate this, they invoked the Biblical episode of the brothers Esau and Jacob. When Esau, one day, returned home after tending to his cattle, exhausted and famished, he begged his younger twin brother Jacob to feed him. Jacob obligated but in exchange demanded Esau's birth-right as the first-born. Too hungry to appreciate the sacredness of being the first-born, Esau consented. 'So Esau despised his birth-right', the book of Genesis says. Selling one's vote is similarly interpreted, as wrongly privileging worldly and immediate pleasures over divine rights.

To achieve clean elections, the NBCC framed a set of guidelines, which pastors and deacons across the state were instructed to impress upon their congregations. Among these:

To avoid tampering with one's date of birth

To possess only one voter identity card

To abstain from collective voting decisions

To honour the individual right and freedom of choice

To keep one's vote secret

To not impersonate another person

To not cast proxy votes

To desist from indulging in feasts politicians throw

To stay clear from substance abuse and sexual immorality

To not use one's vote as a commodity

That these practices were highlighted, of course, indicates that these have been commonly witnessed during previous elections.

But while, in the wake of Polling Day, the NBCC expressed optimism about the success of their campaign, some local pastors expressed scepticism; not about the rationale of the clean election campaign, but about its effectiveness. As Polling Day drew closer, Phugwumi's church premises was decorated with a banner, which read:

> Clean Election Campaign – Buying Votes, Selling Votes, Booth Capturing, Proxy Voting, Etc. are against the law and against moral and spiritual ethics. 'Dzieyha ze mu khrü cuha kephouma zo' [selling and buying of votes is a sin].

The pastor, who had pinned the banner against a wall, however, expresses his hopelessness. 'During elections villagers forget about God', he remarks gloomily. 'They can no longer distinguish between right and wrong. Just watch. The church attendance will dwindle in the weeks before Polling Day. That says everything'. The pastor's prediction proves to be correct, and as Election Day draws closer fewer and fewer villagers congregate for Sunday service.

Although the NBCC campaign could count on widespread support from tribal apex bodies and Naga intellectuals, at the village level the church's interference also draws up occasional resistance. It is a week prior to Polling Day when a party-worker invites me along to a nearby administrative town where the Chief Minister is to arrive by chopper to speak in support of his party's candidates in the district. It is also the day the Women Department of the Chakhesang Baptist Church Council (CBCC), affiliated to the NBCC, sets aside to check vehicles for the presence of liquor. Little do I know that the party-worker in whose car I travel has stacked his trunk with bottles of liquor (which he intends to distribute to party-workers in the town). The bottles are duly confiscated by the church's Women Department and stalled out on the road as a display of the party-worker's (and mine!) immorality. As we drive on, without liquor, the party-worker grumbles: 'The church should confine itself to praying and fasting for the election, not checking vehicles like this'.

As for the pastor-politician. He did not just lose the election, but polled the lowest number of votes in his constituency.

A CULTURALIST CRITIQUE

This Christian critique against local democratic politics is coupled by a Naga culturalist critique, which links the corrosion of a past communitarian ethos with the advance of electoral politics. However, instead of 'healing' democratic politics through an injection of Christian ethics, this critique insists that modern democratic institutions and competitive elections are fundamentally at odds with homespun Naga political practices and principles. They therefore seek to reform democratic institutions and processes in Nagaland altogether.

In boycotting newly independent India's first general elections, the NNC rejected not just Nagas' inclusion into the Indian Union but also communicated the cultural incongruity of political parties and competitive elections with Naga traditional lifeworlds. 'There is no political party in Nagaland. We don't need it. Nagaland need not intimate or adopt foreign institutions in matter of political organisation', Phizo (1951) argued polemically. In Phizo's view, Nagaland was already democratic by traditional design: '[it] is the very spirit of our country'.

'Nagas', Misra (1987: 2193) wrote, 'always prided themselves as honest and straightforward people', then diagnosing: 'Anyone even marginally acquainted with the politics of Nagaland would agree that this idyllic picture has undergone a radical transformation'. Subscribing to this observation, the Chakhesang Public Organisation (CPO) expressed its deep concern about electoral politics destroying the traditional fabric of Naga society:

> It is time to realize that the evil practices associated with electoral politics are destroying the good traditional system of our Naga Democracy, the system, which would regard the opponents as worthy and the integrity of everyone would be safeguarded even as the rival groups disagree with one another (CPO 2013).

This, so-declared, 'good traditional system' of 'Naga democracy' invoked the communitarian ethos of the pre-state Naga village; a time when 'the collective life took precedence over the individual' (Sema 1986: 10). Contrary to communitarianism, liberal democracy has long been associated with social processes that promote individual autonomy, freedom, and self-expression. It is a political system, De Tocqueville (1969: 506) recognised long ago: 'which disposes each citizen to isolate himself from the mass of his fellows and withdraw into the circle of family and friends; with this little society formed to his taste, he gladly leaves the greater society to look out after itself'. This privileging of individual autonomy over the shared ends of community, as liberal democracy seemingly promotes, is where, for many Nagas, the apprehension lies.

Not just Misra (1987), but several scholars observed the corrosive and corruptive influences electoral politics unleashed across Naga society. 'Contemporary politics and the party-system', Dev (1988: 27) writes, 'have done great damage to the village, dividing many villages along party lines'. 'Party politics', Nuh (1986: 201) agrees, 'has destroyed the harmony of Naga society'.

It is the perceived disruption of community life caused by electoral politics that made a Nagaland Minister propose, on the floor of the State Assembly, that the election system be reformed as it undermined and undercut 'the Naga way of life' (cited in L. Ao 1993: 211). This realisation also made at least two Nagaland Chief Ministers publicly espouse that 'Indian elections' would best be done away with (more below). The NNC, in its Manifesto, had long warned against the havoc political parties and elections would effectuate on Naga society. Its Manifesto read: 'In a country like Nagaland, particularly at the present time, party system could never accomplish anything except leading to ruination' (cited in Horam 1988: 321-22).

What could accomplish things, Phizo insisted, was the continuation of public deliberation and consensus-making, an (Angami-inspired?) political vision he captured as *mechü medo zotuo*, or 'the binding will of the community'. As a case in point, Phizo refrained from introducing himself as a Naga leader, insisting that he was merely their spokesperson:

> I can only say what my people want and what they have decided... The position of a spokesman and a leader is often confused. Like a pilot, a spokesman shall have to follow direction (cited in Nuh 1986: 95).

On another occasion, Phizo clarified that he himself was 'not a politician as the word is understood in the West'. He continued: 'I am neither a capitalist nor a socialist. I am a Naga from inside out. Firstly, because there is no alternative, secondly because I am a son of the soil, thirdly because there is no better social, political, and economic system than the way a Naga lives' (cited in Steyn 2002: 133). Phizo was to persist in his rejection of electing leaders, and in adopting a non-Naga political system. When one Mr. Tarkunde, a former Chief Justice, once asked him how the NNC elected its leaders, Phizo's reply was telling: 'Mr Tarkunde, we do not elect our leaders, we select them'. He then explained:

> The selection process goes on for several years beginning from the village level where people know each other thoroughly and only people with virtue of integrity and character are accepted to become leaders. Then on the basis of these observations the leaders of the various villages select the most competent person to be the leader. The same is followed through to the national level. Thus a national leader emerges after so many years (cited in Mishra 2004: 4).

This traditional and moral vision of selecting leaders was also adopted by the Naga People's Convention (NPC) that brokered the creation of Nagaland state. When in preparation of the new state to be enacted an Interim Government had to be formed, Naga tribes and villages selected its members 'by their own traditional methods' (Ramunny 1993: 162). And when the first post-statehood elections were scheduled, Hokishe Sema appealed for cultural wisdom: 'I strongly felt that it was too early for the Nagas to fight elections on the basis of political parties...The system of Tribal Representatives was doing very well and could have continued' (Sema 1986: 104).

The first post-statehood elections were nevertheless fought along party-lines. The contest was over 40 assembly seats, added by 6 seats (increased to 12 in 1969 and 20 in 1974) for Nagaland's (then undivided) Tuensang District, which, on account of its purported 'backwardness', was given a ten-year respite from 'voting'. Instead, the Tuensang Regional Council, made up of clan and tribal leaders, selected amongst its ranks 6 members to serve in the Legislative Assembly. While many votes were cast, not a few Naga villages opted for consensus-building and selected their politicians, rather than electing them through free and autonomous balloting. In as many as fourteen constituencies candidates were returned unopposed as 'village leaders had met earlier and by consensus had decided who would be their representative and discouraged all opponents' (Ramunny 1993: 161).

And while, in Nagaland's first elections, the Naga Nationalist Organisation (NNO) swept to power, in the political discussions and skirmishes that followed, including the resignation of all members of the opposition (made up of the Naga Democratic Party), by-elections, and the manoeuvring of independent candidates, all 46 politicians became part of the NNO Government, making Nagaland's first Legislative Assembly a house without opposition, functioning, instead, on the basis of internal deliberation and consensus-making. This absence of opposition should not be construed as an absence of debate and disagreements within. In 1966, as noted, a no-confidence motion within the ruling government led to a change in Chief-Minister. As such, the first post-statehood elections and subsequent government was a blend or mixture of a pre-existent communitarian ethos based on consensus-making and competitive elections, including the idea of individual voting.

The decades following witnessed the rise and fall of several Nagaland political parties, many of which were seemingly 'non-ideological in their character' (Amer 2014: 5). This apparent absence of party ideology showed itself, once more, in 2015, when the benches of Nagaland's Opposition – made up solely of the Congress Party as all other political and Independent Candidates had joined the NPF-led Government through pre- and post-polling alliances – resolved to merge with the ruling Democratic Alliance of Nagaland. 'It will be a party-less government in Nagaland', the Chief Minister concluded with delight, then adding that with party-divisions done away with the Government would work collectively and through consensus-making to facilitate the on-going peace negotiations between the National Socialist Council of Nagalim (NSCN – IM) and the Central Government, as well as to bring material welfare to its citizens.[1]

---

[1] In this case, too, this creation of a party-less government should not be read as the absence of debate and divisions within. In fact, this 'coming together' of all

While celebrated as a sign of political unity by some, the idea of a party-less government also drew criticism. Political commentators lamented the demise of meaningful opposition, animated assembly debates, and the discontinuation of question hours. To make their point, they highlighted the duration of a particular Assembly Session, which had taken a record-low of 25 minutes (as all possible disagreements had been defused and decisions settled prior to the actual Assembly). The high-Commands of the BJP (which had a pre-polling alliance with the NPF) and the Congress Party, too, objected to Nagaland's party-less government. In view of nation-wide ideological and political antipathies between both parties, the BJP leadership issued a statement saying: 'There can never be the BJP and Congress in the same camp or government' (cited in *Hindustan Times* 09-05-2015). The Congress leadership judged likewise and summoned the 'defaulting' Nagaland Congress MLAs to Delhi and issued them a suspension order. This decree did not stop the Congress MLAs from joining Nagaland's consensus-based, party-less government; as one of the suspended Congress MLAs responded 'We would continue to remain as Congress members in the Assembly though *we will have nothing to do with party affairs*' (cited in *Indian Express* 11-05-2015; emphasis mine).

If some saw in the abolishment of party-divisions a step towards restoring traditional democratic values, and the communitarian ethos in which such values were steeped, a further culturalist critique advocates the discontinuation of competitive elections altogether, as its premises and procedures run counter to Nagas' sense of communal harmony, complimentary coexistence, and consensus-making. 'Traditionally', writes Chasie (2005: 102), 'we did not elect our leaders...the notion itself would have been a scandal'. He explains:

> When you 'go to the people', [as contemporary politicians do and must] you are telling them that you are the best person they could possibly have as their leader! This in a [traditional] society where even a majority or consensus nomination, to be part of a delegation, is often refused several times by the persons concerned, pleading that they are unworthy. In traditional society, such arrogance and absence of fear of God could result in immediate beatings and social ostracism.

---

parties was preceded by intense bickering over positions of leadership and portfolios within the NPF-led DAN Government, and some accused Nagaland's Chief Minister of 'power-politics', of only inviting the Congress MLA's into his government to strengthen his own position, which some of his own party-men had started to undermine.

To attune modern democracy to traditional Naga cultural and communitarian values, a (then) Chief Minister declared, as recently as 2011, that 'election is not suited for Nagas', then elucidating that 'selection of leader[s] would best suit Nagas' (cited in Solo 2011: 67), thus recognising that 'the idea of "an elected leader" was not in the scheme of life in the Nagas' (Solo 2011: 68). Years earlier a former Chief Minister had already published a political treatise that advocated the abandonment of political parties and elections, not in order to undermine Nagaland's democracy but to strengthen it. What Hokishe Sema envisaged was the adoption of a state-wide selection system. This system would start at village levels with villagers selecting, through consensus-making, council members based on their capacity, integrity, and accumulated merit and wisdom. Council members would then confer and amongst themselves select area representatives. These, in turn, were to select a Regional Council. Hokishe Sema (1986: 171-2) continued:

> In Nagaland, even the members of the State Assembly, which is the final level, can be selected by the Regional Councils. This system will reduce the increasing expenses of elections and minimize the corruptions. This is necessary for a good society based on faith in each other and in common values. This does not in any way hamper the power of the State Government, rather helps the progress and thereby good government.

Critics may argue that much has changed since Naga life-worlds were first and foremost centred in 'village republics', and that, in today's complex, cosmopolitan world, traditional political norms and values simply no longer do. Others highlight the marginal position of Naga women in traditional politics, which can no longer be condoned. Yet, many I spoke to across Nagaland argued along the lines of Nuh's (1986: 184) evaluation that 'Unless the present election system is changed, it will not serve the [Naga] people well', and that this change must be in accordance with 'traditional and customary practices'.

■ ■■ ■■

02

ENGAGING NAGA NATIONALISM: CAN DEMOCRACY FUNCTION IN MILITARISED SOCIETIES?

Dolly Kikon

INTRODUCTION

The North-Eastern region of India is not only an important cartographic reality in Indian politics but also a space where physical power plays a dominant role in constructing a political discourse of citizenship and peoplehood. This region does not find itself within the narrative and memory of the nation, yet continues to occupy a central position regarding the territorial integrity of India. In this context, the Naga struggle for right to self-determination has been considered a threat to the territorial integrity of India. Despite several attempts at resolution of the Indo-Naga conflict in the past few decades, the demand for self-determination has continued to fuel relations between the government of India and the Naga people. Of late, the demand for a sovereign Naga nation 'seems' to have accommodated the idea of an autonomous, unified homeland within the republic of India.

The population of Naga people according to the 2001 India census stood at 1.9 million.[1] However, there are disagreements. If myths and legends gave rise to imagined communities, modern dynamics continue to construct nationalistic solidarities through number games. Naga political and civic organisations put the total Naga population at around 3-4 million,[2] which includes Nagas both in India and Myanmar.[3] British colonial surveys of the 19th century, and British administrators like Mackenzie, while charting out the unadministered frontiers of north-east India in 1835 referred to the Burmese Nagas as 'Patkoi Nagas'[4] and cited their population as 'under 5,000 souls' without specifying the number of tribes (Mackenzie 1995: 88-89). However, during the creation of the state of Nagaland in 1963, the Naga population stood at 12.5 lakh with the total number of Naga tribes quoted at eight. Today, an official document published by the state of Nagaland asserts that 16 Naga tribes inhabit Nagaland.[5] The Naga insurgents, with a far greater stake in consolidating the people, quote 43 Naga tribes as constituents of the Naga nation.[6] However, Naga civic organisations like the Hoho and Naga Peoples Movement for Human Rights (NPMHR) state there are 3.5-4 million Nagas and consists of 42 different tribes.[7] Leading us all thus into an obscure conclusion, Julian Jacobs summed up the numbers game as a subjective matter (Jacobs 1990: 172). It is easy to get lost in the catacombs of colonial and Naga nationalist construction that have informed the debate on Naga identity. However, such factors have paved the way for Nagas to develop a strong sense of nationalist consciousness. Thus, identity formations along with Naga nationalism are ongoing projects in the Naga political discourse.

[1]But this accounts only the Nagas of Nagaland. There is no break up for Nagas in other states because the census is conducted on the basis of scheduled caste/tribe of particular states.

[2]See http://www.nscn.com (accessed on December 12, 2004).

[3]This is a rough estimate since there has never been an attempt to bring out a joint census of the Nagas residing in India and Myanmar. Yet, the Naga civic and political bodies frequently use this figure. In such instances Naga nationalist myths not only circulate around one blood / one people theory, but also graft onto modern nation state practices of censuses and number games to mobilize and demand for a homeland.

[4]'Patkoi' refers to the Patkai hills situated between India and Myanmar.

[5]Government of India Census Report 2001.

[6]See http://www.nscn.com (accessed on December 12, 2004).

[7]For a detailed text see: www.npmhr.org (accessed December 12, 2004).

MODERN POLITICAL DECISION-MAKING TOOLS AND NAGA EXPERIENCE

The Naga plebiscite of 1951 constitutes a landmark in Naga national history. Did Nagas trek down from the Patkai range in present-day Myanmar responding to a clarion call for the Naga Nation? Does it even matter if they did not? The call for Naga plebiscite was carried out in the Naga Hills, an administrative unit within the state of Assam. The administrative, territorial and political character of the Naga inhabited areas have drastically changed since then, but the 1951 Naga plebiscite has become a modern legend in the struggle. The plebiscite was held around two basic issues. First, whether they (Nagas) wanted to remain in India or establish a separate independent state. Second, to repudiate the Indian government's view that the call for sovereignty was the work of a few misguided Nagas under Phizo and the Naga National Council. Modern Naga historians claim with certainty that 99 per cent of the people voted for freedom (Yonuo 1974: 202). The following year (1952) the Naga people boycotted the first Indian parliamentary election and decided to continue the Naga 'freedom struggle', which aimed at achieving a sovereign Naga homeland'.[8] These two events are the building blocks of a modern Naga national project and are reiterated to emphasise the legal continuities of the struggle of oppressed peoples and the process of decolonization.

The Nagas claim that their demand for the right to self-determination is based on a different historical background from India. Emphasising this point, Wati Aier says:

> ...There was a cohesive understanding among the Nagas that we are different historically and politically, and this made our earlier leaders take a stand... (while) our struggle is a legitimate one, the question of what is self-determination is a big question.[9]

Protracted struggles for right to self-determination show that notions of sovereignty, self-determination and nation not only get interpreted and re-interpreted during the transition of power from one generation to another,

---

[8]The present term used for a sovereign Naga homeland is Nagalim (Lim means land), a term used by the Naga armed opposition in their manifestos. I use Nagaland because the documents referring to the Indo-Naga conflict use this term.

[9]Personal interview held in Dimapur, Nagaland on January 7, 2004.

but also engineer negotiation processes with centralised governments and redefine priorities of the people. In this context, Smith (2001: 20) points out:

> It is true that we are dealing here with long-term constructs, but these are not essences or fixed quantities or traits... national identities change, but this is a process that occurs in every generation, as external events and internal realignments of groups and power encourage new understandings of collective traditions.

Articulating a similar position, an official in the Naga armed opposition shared his personal view:

> (In) the 1950s, we felt that it was practicable to demand for sovereignty according to the international situation with the changes going around the world. We felt that the Nagas had a case at hand. However, according to me, the demand for Naga sovereignty in today's context has become a problematic issue. The reason being that it is not possible for us to manage without the support and backing of a power nation... for the moment we have kept aside the demand for sovereignty. In this present political process, we are looking at how we can have a peaceful and a working relationship with India.[10]

This view establishes some thoughts on nationalism and what practical attitude to adopt towards it. Historical studies acknowledge that the national identities change with time, that the demands and needs that first gave rise to national consciousness may give way to others without a radical rupture in identity itself (Miller 1995: 4). Another Naga interviewee describes the 'shift' in the Naga struggle as follows:

> ... Right now the shift that is taking place is about the sovereignty of the Nagas as a people. So, the sovereignty has shifted from the state to the people. It is the people who will decide how the system of governance, and how the Naga people will organize themselves. So, even if it means forming a Naga

---

[10]The interviewee (name omitted) is an official in the Naga-armed opposition. The interview was held in Dimapur, Nagaland on January 4, 2004.

state (as part of the present Indo-Naga political settlement) it may not be a 'state' going by the existing definitions of what a state is. It may be a form of state that may emerge out of indigenous values and principles and not so much in terms of its rigidity. For example, doing away with rigid structures and boundaries and more in terms of sovereignty that deals with inter-dependence (sic). And the question of inter-dependence again emerges out of the idea of the people being sovereign, so that the people themselves decide the areas in which they want to have a relation of inter-dependence with a particular nation or to what extent. So it is the people (Nagas) who will decide and not the Indian state.[11]

IMAGINING DEMOCRATIC INDIAN MECHANISM

For the Nagas, the image of democratic India is through the Indian electoral process. Samaddar argues that the electoral system and the process of voting is a rite of political theatre and a protocol in national life (Samaddar 2001: 160). However, the process of imposing legitimacy through the electoral system as a strategy has failed to address issues of governance. Between 1946 and the early 1950s, Naga villages and tribes came together under indigenous village institutions like the councils, women's societies and various youth forums to mobilise and resist army operations and also to keep alive politics of dissent in the region. But these institutions were either banned under the prevailing state laws or integrated into the state machinery.[12] Nonetheless, Nagas continue to mobilise themselves and politically participate in organisations and institutions which are often seen as anti-state entities by the administration. Often, indigenous institutions like the Hoho,[13] student bodies and human rights organisations are tagged as fronts/mouthpieces of armed opposition groups.[14]

[11]The interviewee (name omitted) is a research student. This interview was held in Dimapur, Nagaland on January 8, 2004.

[12]For instance, the traditional village guards were employed by the state and transformed into a tool for governance. They were often used by the Indian military forces as spies or guides to track down Naga nationalists and their sympathizers.

[13]The Naga Hoho is the apex tribal council of the Naga people.

[14]The SATP portal indicates such allegations frequently in their publications. For reference see http://www.satp.com.

Thus, it is within such a militarised context, that even while the Indian security forces launched development initiatives in the early 1990s, the union home ministry of India blacklisted 82 Naga non-governmental organisations operating in Nagaland for suspected links with militant outfits in 2003. According to the official report, the blacklisted organisations were cited as pro-militant groups masquerading as service providers in the economic, healthcare and education sectors (*Eastern Mirror* 25-05-2003). The Indian state manifested its presence in the north-eastern region mainly through military expeditions and operations. Continued militarisation has reinforced people's views that the government is not committed to protect the rights of citizens especially during civil conflicts. Baruah states that such state policies are not new for the government of India. One of New Delhi's containment policies has been the paternalistic carrot-and-stick approach routine with the use of military force interrupted by lavish doles of development money – whose source and targets are often couched in secretive deals – in the backward region (Baruah 2002: 1).

The attempt of Naga independentists has been to negotiate at the level of the most basic, yet the most fundamental point, i.e. where people can have the choice to decide what system of governance they prefer. Ironically, the growing campaign for transparent and democratic governance has failed to take into consideration the extremely undemocratic and militarised conditions under which electoral systems are introduced. The initiation of democracy process through the processes of electoral politics has not contributed towards any solution in the Indo-Naga armed conflict. Electoral mechanism have not only been unresponsive but have systematically destroyed existing indigenous institutions and created a group of parasitic elite 'managers' for New Delhi. A Naga social worker highlighted his concern by saying:

> When people do not know the system and are not comfortable with it they are bound to get confused (within such systems of governance). However, as far as the participation of the Naga people in electoral politics is concerned, they do that because they have no other option.[15]

Political participation of the electorate is necessary (though not sufficient) indicator of democratic practice in a democratic society because it is through participation that the public can choose and decide their options

[15]The interviewee is a human rights activist, social worker and a student advisor. This interview was held in Guwahati, Assam on December 20, 2003.

and interests. However, what are the underlying bases of electoral choice for people in militarised society? Can democratic mechanisms function under conditions where state agencies either coerce or bribe the electorate to cast their vote? To begin with, there is an inherent difference in the manner in which the nation state and the people choose to define political participation. In Naga politics, the introduction of electoral system significantly defined the language of 'political participation'. Electoral system became one of the significant acts of 'political participation' and also a duty to become a 'good' citizen. In this manner, politics became state patronage politics. For instance, Hokishe Sema, chief minister of Nagaland during the early 1970s warned Nagas of protecting and supporting 'anti-social' elements. He issued stern warning to the Naga public that if the guerrillas were given protection and it came to the notice of the government, police and the army, the consequences would be severe (Yonuo 1974: 160-161). Such democratic policing also defined the 'anti-national'. In militarised zones like the north-eastern region of India, construction of these definitions severally restricted civil and political rights as the discourse of participation and 'rights' was entrusted to security institutions armed with regulations like the National Security Act, the Armed Forces Special Powers Act 1958, the Nagaland Security Act 1962, and the Disturbed Areas Act 1955.

Ironically, lawmakers who constituted, framed and reviewed regulations that conferred enormous powers at the hands of military forces[16] acknowledged that mere possibility of abuse could not be counted as a ground for denying the vesting of powers or for declaring a statute unconstitutional.[17] On November 27, 1997, the Supreme Court of India, while upholding the Armed Forces Special Powers Act, 1958 (AFSPA) stated that, 'The powers under the act are not arbitrary or unreasonable and are subject to sufficient safeguards, such as binding instructions on the Armed Forces, to prevent

---

[16]Amnesty International report on the Indian military operation in Oinam, a Naga village, recorded mass torture, rape and murder of the villagers. Major General P L Kukrety, the officer in command at the time of the Oinam operation stated: '... we shall bash on regardless and not rest until we recover ever single arm... we have not spared those whom we suspect of being involved with the underground move-ment'. He acknowledged that, 'villagers and suspected informers were interrogated and some them beaten to extract the truth'. (India: "Operation Bluebird" A Case Study of Torture and Extrajudicial Executions in Manipur: Amnesty International, October 1990: AI Index ASA 20/17/90 Distr: sc/co/gr)

[17]On December 16, 2003, the Supreme Court upheld the Prevention of Ter-rorism Act which has been highly misused across the subcontinent. Victims of this Act area as young as 23 years old and old as 81 years old. (http://www.sentinalon-line.com/ (dated January 13, 2004).

misuse and abuse. Therefore, the powers do not violate any constitutional rights'.[18] The consequences of state policies where the language of rights and justice are abused, unresolved political conflicts are handed over to the army, and people are collectively clubbed under anti-democratic laws and regulation does not yield in the end, sustainable meaningful political settlements. It is under such existing structures, that people's choices are severely restricted. But shrinking political spaces does not mean a decline in resistance. It may well indicate that one needs to readjust and look at the situation to adequately probe further into the efforts of the invisible population in north-eastern region who continue to mobilise against state and address a centre that has encouraged in a sycophancy culture based on client-state relations and policies. In this context, development projects initiated by security agencies to bring an end to violence results in lack of popular participation[19] and further limit the role of official civic bodies.

SHRINKING DEMOCRATIC SPACES IN INDIA

It is within such rigid processes that the government of India often contradicts the Constitution which spells out a cultural diversity and a pluralistic political system. As a result, such processes expose cleavages and strains within state-centre relations in India. Therefore, the present political discourse as outlined above points to the circumstances in which Naga nationalism generally evolved, these have not been those in which the state itself was lacking, or when its reality was in serious doubt. The state was only too conspicuously present. It was, as Gellner states 'its boundaries and the distinction of power, and possibly of other advantages, within it which were represented' (Gellner 1983: 4). This reality underlines the shrinking democratic spaces, within which notions of rights and justice are re-constituted.

Existing political circumstances have conditioned Naga political

[18]Naga People's Movement for Human Rights vs Union of India (1997). ICHRL 117 http://www.worldlii.org/int/cases/ ICHRL/1997/117.html.

[19]Hannum points out that a broad definition of popular participation might simply require the involvement of citizens in public affairs with the fullest respect for human rights, without any discrimination and giving special attention to groups which have so far been kept apart from genuine participation. For text see Hannum, Hurst, Autonomy, Sovereignty, and Self-Determination (University of Pennsylvania Press, 1990: 114).

strategists to redefine their actions and functions, which in turn continuously reinforce political mobilization. In this manner, ideas evolved from everyday lives become vital in reconstituting the social and political voice of the people. In this context, and interviewee defined what freedom meant for him:

> It would mean being able to exercise the truth that I believe in without being intimidated, without being obstructed, without being coerced or threatened... I mean being able to manifest my humanness in different spheres of life like political, social, economic and cultural fields...[20]

The interviewee's vision and understanding of freedom can be categorised as a general human rights need, but not a definition for 'freedom' in a political sense. However, this ambivalence reflects the fact that the right to self-determination has continuously been redefined in the last 300 years. Scholars and jurists continue to argue whether there exists a right to self-determination in customary law and the definition of who constitutes a definite 'peoples' remains disputed between nation states and peoples' movements. At the same time, Hannum (1990: 27-49) points out that while the meaning and scope of the right to self-determination continues to remain vague and imprecise, the principle of self-determination will continue to be a major political force both internationally and domestically.

An ambiguous language of rights has also shaped and defined the rhetoric of what actually constituted 'rights'.[21] In the interviewee's response, freedom and self-determination are synonymous. Thus, for him, it comprises fundamental rights like the right to create and participate in one's own internal political, social, cultural and economic systems. Ironically, it is only through such basic demands that the Indian democracy's failure to recognise

---

[20]The interviewee is a Naga student and a human rights activist. The interview was held in Dimapur, Nagaland, on January 8, 2004.

[21]States justify gross human rights violations by shifting the focus from addressing rights to that of defending the state's sovereignty and its territorial integrity. But many non-violent movements are subjected to state repression. States often refuse to 'compromise' and give into demands not realising that many existing frameworks of states fail to chalk out rights of its people, especially so in cases of ethnic minorities and indigenous people. Thus, inflexible nature of the state and its coercive nature of addressing such voices not only leads to violent retaliations from people's movements but has also exacerbated these conflicts into long drawn bloody armed conflicts. Ironically, by the time states are willing to 'give in' and 'compromise' the situations tend to become much more complex.

and address people's movements becomes evident. Electoral politics in India often glosses over critical political issues raised by its marginalised electorate.

One may then argue that no democracy is perfect. What then is the difference experienced by Naga people, especially when compared to other marginalised groups within India? To being with, there is the ubiquitous conflict and processes of militarisation of the region. Besides, as Deng (1987: 69) argues, if the concept of political participation has to be equated to electoral politics, liberal democracy has to presuppose a framework characterised by a broad consensus on the fundamental principles of nation-hood, the structure of government, and the shaping and sharing of power, wealth, and other national resources. Where consensus on these fundamentals is lacking, parliamentary democracy becomes the rule of a numerical majority imposed on an alienated minority, whether numerically determined or otherwise marginalised. This means that we must address the pending fundamental issues of nationhood before we can legitimately invoke majority votes as justification for imposing any decisions on the minority.

To understand whether electoral politics ensures a reasonably meaningful participation, one has to understand the schizophrenic character of politics in the north-east region. Baruah observes that the political parties in the region re-align themselves with the existing national ruling party. He says that this underscores a dependency syndrome related to the north-eastern states' structurally weak position in India' constitutional architecture. Such political equations with mainland Indian political parties are critical for establishing the conduit of nebulous funds from New Delhi (Baruah 2004: 1). After the 2004 elections in Nagaland the Democratic Alliance of Nagaland (DAN)[22] seemed hard pressed to re-align itself with the Congress Party. The (then) chief minister of Nagaland, Neiphiu Rio, stated that his party might support the Congress-led alliance in the centre, and declared, 'everything is possible in politics'.[23] There was also speculation whether the Congress-led government in New Delhi would show any enthusiasm for the ongoing Indo-Naga peace process, and whether financial packages released by the previous NDA government would be sanctioned by the new government in Delhi. Thus, even solemn affairs such as electoral alliances and political ideologies are undermined or determined by an omnipresent

[22]The Democratic Alliance of Nagaland ((DAN) is the current coalition government that consists of the Naga People's Front (NPF), Bharatiya Janata Party (BJP) and other groups.

[23]The reason for this re-alignment, according to the chief minister was suggested so that the peace process between the government of India and the Naga armed opposition does not get derailed (http://www.telegraphindia.com/1040518/asp/northeast/story_325969) (accessed on October 12, 2004).

need to continue with the economic packages extended from the centre to the states.

Nagaland was granted statehood in 1963, solely on political grounds without any consideration for financial viability. While it was a strategic consideration to appease certain sections of the Naga armed opposition, it served only to intensify the armed struggle and 'garrisoned' a section of the Naga people within a territorial unit that was created without the consent of all the Nagas. Notwithstanding democratic mechanisms like regular elections following the granting of statehood, Naga political practices seem to reiterate the position of the Indian state as s hegemonic power structure located in New Delhi. Therefore, addressing the issue of losing out in the Indian electoral numbers game for the Naga people is academic and irrelevant. Irrespective of which coalition is in power in New Delhi, the significance of India's territorial and political sovereignty over Nagaland continues to define the relationship between the government of India and the Naga polity. While justifying coercive state mechanisms and policies, patronage politics catering to a small section of Naga elites has become a ready substitute for institutionalizing civic tensions over almost all political issues. Hence, even though there are few instances of regional Naga parties who form the state government, their failure to effect changes in the structure adds to their powerlessness and invests greater importance to centralizing actors within Naga politics. Thus, the vicious cycle of dependency on the central government ends up reducing even well-meaning Naga regional political parties into 'managers' for an agenda emanating from New Delhi – an agenda with little resonance in the 'lived politics' in Naga areas and which is almost totally divorced from local concerns.

CONCLUSION

Why does a multicultural democracy like India lack a framework to tackle demands of ethnic groups and nationalist movements, other than a coercive one? Despite obvious tensions between minority rights and multiculturalism on one hand and citizenship and civic virtue on the other, India's republican history has accommodated both trends. Naga political discourse on self-determination and nationhood could be read by constitutionalists as a manifestation of a minority rights debate that recognises that justice is no longer defined in terms of difference-blind rules and institutions. Developing concepts of human rights, minority rights and indigenous rights may contribute directly to strengthening the principle of self-determination, even as state-developed law seeks to minimize its post-colonial impact. It is important to recognise that a successful Indo-Naga negotiation will open up positive pathways to address questions such as autonomy and right to self-determination claims voiced by different groups in north-east India.

It is necessary to find a ground to restore mutual trust and initiate a process of democratization that provides a system to address social, political and economic justice for the people. Finding a common ground, one that appeals to both the negotiating parties can be a settlement whereby Naga people can decide to choose a system of governance. Instead of following the existing Indian electoral system of politics, Nagas can work out an association with their indigenous forms of governance thereby bringing all the Naga inhabited areas into one administration. But such representation should ensure equality and gender balance because Naga customary law and indigenous institutions continues to remain a strong patriarchal domain.

In accordance with the Indo-Naga ceasefire agreement, the talks have remained outside the ambit of the Constitution. Ironically, Article 371(A) of the Constitution which grants rights and concessions to the Nagas has remained silent over issues of political rights. In this context, the constitution of Jammu and Kashmir points out that a discourse about a Naga Constitution is in itself, not a scandalous suggestion. The reason being that if the Indo-Naga negotiation finds a solution, it is most likely that the settlement will be ultimately 'within' the Constitution. The settlement would require a parliamentary ratification and constitutional amendments for it to be effectively implemented. Such a settlement would require the participation of jurists, policy-makers and an effective third party to monitor the agreement. Any shortsighted negotiation between the government of India and the Naga representatives will not only exacerbate the Indo-Naga conflict but also set a poor precedent to ethnic and nationalist conflicts willing to negotiate for peace in the north-east. Thus, for a long-term solution, India needs to reflect on its principles of federalism. Such a step would not only enable India to come out with a framework that will translate peace processes and political negotiations in the subcontinent but also give up its knee-jerk reaction to ethnic and nationalist movements in the north-east. However, such a solution cannot turn into a reality without engineering the existing Constitution, which at present grants enormous power to the central government.

Demilitarisation is the most important issue that needs to be addressed. Indian policy-makers have never hesitated to impose un-democratic and coercive force to settle political differences with its citizens. Notions of equality and respect are not immediately the first principles that come to mind in the relations between the Naga people and the Indian state. The Indo-Naga ceasefire negotiation is an apt example. In it, the formal demilitarisation of Naga areas has not been discussed. The Armed Forces (Special Powers) Act, 1958, continues to be enforced throughout the Naga inhabited areas of Nagaland, Assam, and Manipur. This raises uncomfortable questions about the psychological advantage enjoyed by Indian security personnel in a region where a citizen's political rights can be revoked according to the whims of non-commissioned officers. A political dialogue where justice and peace are desired goals would seem impossible under such circumstances. Policymakers in India have defended such draconian regulations in the interest of security. Yet, in the last five decades, leave aside involving an adequate response to the Naga national question, this militarised environment has only seen the creation of more armed conflicts, hence more insecurity for the citizens of the north-east.

Democratic mechanisms such as electoral politics do not spell out democracy, nor does it guarantee to preserve and address democratic participation. Unless nation states are willing to negotiate with people's movements on terms of equality, centered on people's rights, measures such as equality and rights remain mere tools which do not ensure people's empowerment and participation to address questions of rights in different spheres of their lives. These measures are not an end in itself. The burden of proof now lies with the defenders of Indian national (and territorial) interest, who must show how retaining the status quo is the best way to engage with Naga nationalism.

■ ■ ■ ■ ■

03

COMMUNITY, NUMBERS AND POLITICS IN NAGALAND

Ankush Agrawal & Vikas Kumar

INTRODUCTION

Statistics have an intimate relation with modern statecraft and, indeed, with the very ways in which modern states are popularly imagined. This close relationship is reflected in, among other things, the origins and spread of modern democracy and state-sponsored human population censuses. The United States, where decennial delimitation linked modern democracy and census in the late 18th century, is an early exemplar of this relationship.[1] Over the following two centuries, the deep and multi-faceted relationship between demographic statistics and politics emerged as one of the defining features of modern states.[2] While the planning and evaluation of state interventions

[1]The Voting Rights Act, 1965 that called for fair representation of minorities further strengthened the relationship between elections and census in the United States (Kertzer and Arel 2002: 17).

[2]The journey of South Sudan, the latest member of the United Nations, toward independence was marked by controversies over census and delimitation (Santschi 2008).

(related to federal redistribution, trade, employment, migration, health, education, and law and order, among others) necessitate recourse to a variety of demographic statistics, the principle of *one person one vote* perhaps best exemplifies the relationship between state and statistics in democracies.

This longstanding relationship between state and statistics notwithstanding, government statistics of most developing countries are often not free of errors. Errors may result from definitional and measurement problems, as well as from bureaucratic incompetence and corruption. Developed countries may face similar problems, though to a lesser extent because of a longer history of engagement with modern statistics, greater availability of skilled personnel and resources to build reliable databases, better quality of general administration, and greater non-state capacity to critically assess government statistics and build alternative databases.

Demographic statistics are additionally susceptible to errors because of potential political interference insofar as *whom to count* and *how to count* are inherently political choices. This is particularly true when communities are locked into ethno-political competition over public resources under weak public institutions, as is the case in Nagaland.[3] This chapter examines the possible manipulation of population censuses in Nagaland. Such manipulation, to be sure, is not restricted to Nagaland. For Nigeria, Adepoju (1981: 29) observes thus:

> population issues play dominant roles and are largely responsible for major landmarks in the contemporary Nigerian political scene: it precipitated the constitutional crisis in the country in 1962; it played a major role in the crisis in the old Western Nigeria in 1965; was largely responsible for the military take-over in 1966; contributed greatly to the fall of Gowon's regime in 1975 and still looms large in the minds of Nigerians with the recent demand for the creation of even more states in the country; and revenue allocation among existing states soon after the return to civilian rule.

[3]Even in the absence of ethno-political competition, demographic statistics can be unreliable if the data collection exercise has been designed keeping in mind the dominant community resulting in, for instance, the under-enumeration of tribes in the United States (Lujan 1990) and blacks in South Africa (Lipton 1972) or the misreporting of land use pattern among tribes in the North East (Nongkynrih 2010) and the undercounting of tribes in Uttar Pradesh (Verma 2013).

In other words, statistics impact politics and policy-making, even as the latter intervene at various stages of production, dissemination, and consumption of statistics. However, the mutually constitutive relationship among statistics, politics, and economy has received insufficient scholarly attention in the Indian context. The manipulation of census data in Nagaland during 1981-2001, for instance, did not attract the attention of either policymakers or academics. This chapter clears the ground for building a better understanding of the relationship between statistics and politics in Nagaland and in ethnically divided societies more widely. It discusses why standard demographic factors are insufficient to explain Nagaland's *demographic somersault* — decades of very high population growth (1971-2001) followed by a sudden contraction (2001-11) that was essentially a correction of the over-count of earlier censuses[4] — and, therefore, establishes the need to examine non-demographic explanations in greater detail.

The present chapter contributes to the literature that explores the interface between politics and statistics.[5] It deals with coverage error (error in overall headcount) rather than content error (error in sub-classification of headcount).[6] This chapter also relates to contributions on Nagaland that have explored anomalies in statistics pertaining to area (Agrawal and Kumar 2017a, 2017c), population (Agrawal and Kumar 2013, Kumar and Agrawal 2016), and sample survey (Agrawal and Kumar 2017b, 2014). This chapter further explores the interaction between electoral competition and statistics that is associated with systematic and growing errors in the headcount of Nagaland, and in doing so contributes to the literature on electoral politics in Nagaland (Wouters 2015a, 2014). Wouters (2014) outlines four broad models of voting in Nagaland that differ in terms of the level or point of aggregation at which voting/political choices are made – household, clan,

---

[4]The word somersault is used to highlight the deliberate choices of various actors both during the decades of abnormal population growth as well as the decade of contraction/correction of headcount.

[5]This chapter relates to the literature on the political economy of conflicts (Horowitz 2000) and political economy and sociology of statistics (Begum and Miranda 1979; Wade 1985, 2012; Jerven 2013). Bose et al. (1977) and Barrier (1981) are among the early and comprehensive discussions of the quality of Indian census data. Contributions in the Indian context have examined colonial censuses (Barrier 1981; Cohn 1987; Peabody 2001; Guha 2003) and caste (Chaudhury 2009), tribe (Kulkarni 1991; Verma 2013), language (Brass 1974, Gill 2007), and religion (Bhagat 2001; Bhat and Xavier 2005; Gill 2007) in post-colonial censuses.

[6]While Nagaland's census suffers from both coverage and content errors, the former is a bigger problem in the state. We examine content errors in Nagaland's census with regard to various identity markers elsewhere.

village, and hereditary chiefs. Each of these four models implicitly assumes ethnically homogenous villages and explores an intra-village mode of aggregation of political preferences. Even Wouters' exceptional cases are intra-tribal in character. Our discussion is different as it relates to choices at

The remainder of this chapter is organised as follows. We first draw attention to the abnormal growth rates of Nagaland and discuss the sustained discrepancy between actual and projected populations of Nagaland. We then examine the plausibility of the census population estimates by looking both into their internal consistency and by comparing them with other sources of demographic information. This is followed by an examination of political-geographic and political-economic explanations of population changes in Nagaland. We end with a reflection on the implications of Nagaland's demographic somersault for our understanding of the social and political lives of statistics.

ABNORMAL GROWTH RATES

Nagaland registered the highest growth in population amongst all Indian states between 1981 and 2001 (Table 1). However, in 2011 it became the first state to register a negative population growth in the postcolonial period.[7] What makes Nagaland's case particularly intriguing is that its population contracted between 2001 and 2011 in the absence of epidemical diseases, famines, natural calamities, major political disturbances, wars, changes in its political status, and any major change in socioeconomic conditions.[8]

---

[7]In the past, a few other states/union territories have also recorded a contraction in population, but only in the first or second post-colonial census. Punjab and West Bengal recorded negative population growths between 1941 and 1951 (GoI 2011a), a decade which overlaps with the colonial period. The 1941 Census over-enumerated the population of Punjab, where communities anticipating the religious partition of the country tried to boost their numbers. The over-count was corrected in the 1951 Census (Natrajan 1972, p. vii; GoI 1954, p. 5). Other reasons for the decline in Punjab's population include unprecedented bloodshed during the partition of British India. The case of Bengal is similar, except that during this period it also suffered one of the worst famines of the 20th Century. Also, two union territories, the Andaman and Nicobar Islands (1941-51) and Daman and Diu (1951-1961), reported negative growth rates in the decades following independence (GoI 2011a) possibly due to out-migration to other parts of the country.

[8]Key socio-economic correlates of fertility include income, literacy, urbanisation, female work participation, and access to public health services (Barro and

trend of population growth for Nagaland, where about 90% of its people profess Christianity and belong to tribal communities, is abnormal even in comparison to tribal and Christian populations in other states (Kumar and Agrawal 2016).

Table 1: Decadal Population Growth Rates (in %), 1951–2011[9]

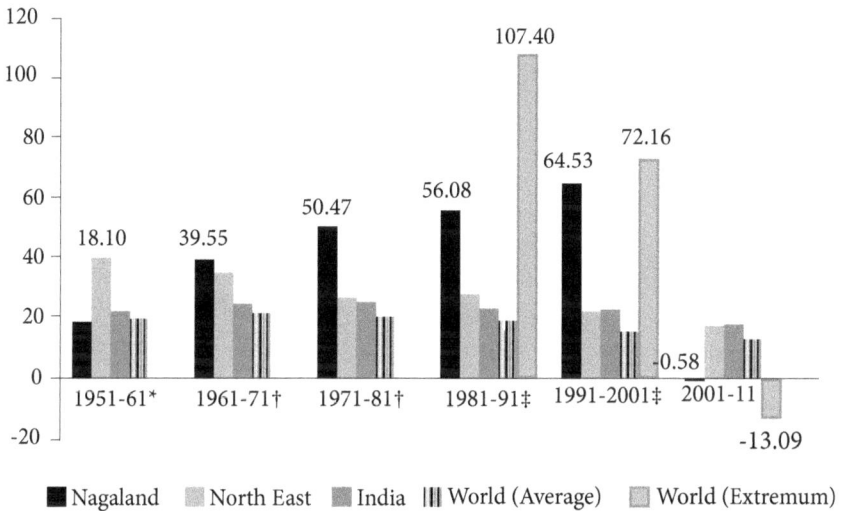

The Sala-i-Martin 2004, 407-408). Nagaland's human development rank has improved steadily over the past four decades, which should, in principle, be associated with a steady reduction in fertility (Agrawal and Kumar 2012). This does not agree with the sustained increase followed by an abrupt decline in Nagaland's population growth rate.

[9]Notes: (i) * The growth rates for Nagaland, North East (viz., Arunachal Pradesh, Assam, Nagaland, Manipur, Meghalaya, Mizoram, Tripura), and India (viz., All states/Union Territories) for the period 1951–61 have been computed after excluding Tuensang, where only a small fraction of the population was enumerated in the 1951 Census. (ii) † The growth rates have been further adjusted for the periods 1961–71 and 1971–81 to take into account the change in reference period in 1971. This adjustment could not be carried out for 'North East India' because the 1981 Census did not cover Assam, which accounts for about 70% of the region's population. (iii) ‡ The growth rate of Nagaland was the highest among the states of India. (iv) World (Extremum) is shown only for the period 1981–2011, i.e. the period during which Nagaland's population grew at abnormal rates compared to the

During the past three decades Nagaland's population repeatedly defied projections (Table 2), but without attracting the attention of the administration and academia. The Expert Committee of 1974 under-projected the 1991 population by about 21%. This implies that the dynamics of population growth between 1981 and 1991 were inconsistent with the trends in fertility and mortality prevailing in the 1960s and 1970s. In the decade following, the Technical Group of 1988 similarly underestimated the 2001 population by as much as 14%. The underestimation for 2001, despite the use of an inflated baseline (i.e. 1991 Census) means that population growth between 1991 and 2001 was abnormally high. Moreover, the census, which recorded progressively increasing growth rates of Nagaland's population until 2001, did not agree with studies based on the census data, which indicated a declining trend in crude birth rate (GoI 1997c; Guilmoto and Irudaya Rajan 2002). These developments should have raised red flags and the administration should have adopted preventive measures ahead of the 2001 Census. This did not happen until 2009, however.

The direction of forecasting errors reversed after 2001. Unlike the forecasts for 1991 and 2001, which were underestimates vis-à-vis the corresponding censuses, the forecasts for 2011 proved to be over-estimates. While the Technical Group on Population Projection (1988) overestimated the 2011 population of Nagaland by 10%, the 2001 Technical Group overestimated the population by 14%, and the Population Reference Bureau and Population Foundation of India (2007) over-projected the 2011 population by 23%. The projection errors for 2011 grew over the years, i.e. projections made closer to 2011 were more erroneous compared to those made earlier. This is counter-intuitive because the errors should in principle

---

country as a whole. Until 2001 the growth rate of Nagaland was positive so 'World (Extremum)' shown in the figure corresponds to the maximum population growth rate in the periods 1980–90 and 1990–2000 recorded by any territory listed in the World Population Prospects 2010. However, during 2001–11 the growth rate of Nagaland was negative and 'World (Extremum)' in the period 2000–10 corresponds to the minimum population growth rate. There were six territories (Qatar, United Arab Emirates, Equatorial Guinea, Djibouti, Saudi Arabia, and Oman) in 1980–90 and two (Afghanistan and United Arab Emirates) in 1990–2000 whose population grew faster than Nagaland's population. During the period 2000–10 the number of such territories increased to more than 150 in 2010 (United Nations 2011). A comparison of Nagaland's growth rate with growth rates of provinces of other countries, which would have been more appropriate, could not be carried out for want of data. Sources: (i) 1951–61 Nagaland, 1951–61 and 1991–2011 North East: Authors' computations, Agrawal and Kumar (2012); (ii) 1961–2011 Nagaland and 1951–2011 India: GoI (2011a and 2013a); (iii) 1961–91 North East: Sharma and Kar (1997); and (iv) World: United Nations (2011).

decrease as the forecast horizon narrows.

Four other points need to be noted in this regard. First, Nagaland's boundary dispute with Assam provided a clue regarding potential errors in Nagaland's population estimates. In 2001, Assam's population estimates for 62 villages in the disputed territory were 'consistently' lower than that of Nagaland (GoI 2005, p. 24).[10] Second, soon after the 2001 Census, leading political figures, including Nagaland's (then) Chief Minister Neiphiu Rio and Manipur's former Chief Minister Radhabinod Koijam, provided population estimates that did not agree with the 2001 Census estimates. Koijam suggested that in 2001 Nagaland's population was about 16 lakhs (Koijam 2001). Rio suggested that the state's population must have been about 14 lakhs (Hazarika 2005). Third, in 2005, the Chief Secretary of Nagaland informed the Registrar General of India and Census Commissioner of 'the decision of Govt of Nagaland rejecting 2001 Census Report' (Chakhesang Public Organisation & Ors. vs. Union of India & Ors., W.P. No. 67 of 2006). Fourth, the 2001 Census was challenged in the court soon after the data were released (ibid.).

Table 2: Actual and Projected Populations of Nagaland, 1981–2011[11]

Year	Source	Population (in '000)		Error (per cent)*
		Projected	Actual	
1981	Expert Committee (1974)	714.5	774.9	-7.80
1991	Expert Committee (1974)	957.9	1209.5	-20.80
2001	Technical Group (1988)	1721	1990.0	-13.52
2011	Technical Group (1988)	2185	1980.6	10.32
2011	Technical Group (2001)	2249	1980.6	13.55
2011	PFI-PRB (2007)	2426-2439**	1980.6	22.49-23.14**

[10]We are not suggesting that Assam's estimates were correct, only that the discrepancy should have raised an alarm.

[11]Notes: (i) * 'Error (%)' is the excess of the projected over actual population as a share of the actual population. (ii) ** PFI-PRB (2007: 6, 11) provides two projections, corresponding to low and high fertility scenarios. Sources: (i) Expert Committee (1974); GoI (1978: 158-59) (ii) Technical Group (1988); GoI (1996 : 64) and (iii) Technical Group (2001); GoI (2006 : 35).

So, the erroneous projections of the 2001 Technical Group and the Population Reference Bureau and Population Foundation of India, which were finalised after the above became known, are difficult to explain because they not only wrongly estimated the total population, but also misjudged the direction of change of the reported population.

The sustained abnormality in Nagaland's growth rates did not receive administrative attention until after the 2001 Census. Researchers, too, did not wake up until after the 2011 Census. Also, while the state government eventually took note of the problem, when it rejected the 2001 Census (GoI 2011b: viii), various government organisations and researchers continue to uncritically use these flawed population statistics. The Economic Survey of 2010-11 (GoI 2011d: A125), for instance, used the flawed population series for Nagaland. Similarly, other surveys, including those conducted by the National Sample Survey Office (NSSO), used the uncorrected figures from the 2001 Census of Nagaland (Agrawal and Kumar 2017b). The High Level Committee on Socioeconomic, Health and Educational status of Tribal Communities of India, whose report has not been formally released, casually notes the following, which seems to suggest that Nagaland's tribal population is shrinking in absolute terms and that this possibly has something to do with the deteriorating health of the people: 'Health of the ten crores vulnerable people should become an important national concern. At the same time negative Scheduled Tribe population growth in Nagaland and in the Great Andamanese tribe in Andaman & Nicobar is a concern'.

We now turn to a few examples from academia. Gulimoto and Rajan (2013: 59) tersely highlight the 'apparent stagnation [of population] in Nagaland' without giving any explanation, even though they discuss in some detail the possible anomalies driven by non-demographic factors in the case of Jammu and Kashmir. Kundu and Kundu (2011) argue that 'law and order in many of the border states (impacting coverage and quality of data) could explain their sluggish growth' and, in addition, 'the *tendency* of the people in the so-called heartland to go to these states to grab employment and business opportunities *seems* to have weakened' (emphases ours). Likewise, Chaurasia (2011) suggests that the decrease in population can be explained by a 'very heavy out-migration (almost 14% [of population]) between 2001 and 2011'. However, contrary to these perceptions, Nagaland witnessed unprecedented peace in the last census decade, at least compared to the earlier decades of political violence, and this was also a period during which local people routinely and increasingly complained against the influx of outsiders.

The state government eventually decided to clean up the mess. A sample survey conducted in six districts of Nagaland in 2009 found fewer people compared to the 2001 Census (*Nagaland Post* 2009). In a consultative meeting held on 30 September 2009, the State Government canvassed the support of political parties, a wide range of civil society organisations, church organisations, student organisations, tribal bodies, and village elders to make a fresh start. The participants unanimously agreed that 'previous censuses conducted in Nagaland were defective and inaccurate' and that the next census 'should be conducted properly' (GoN 2009, emphasis ours). It is noteworthy that the consultative meeting not only questioned the reliability of the 2001 Census, but also the preceding *censuses*.

PLAUSIBILITY OF CENSUS ESTIMATES

This section analyses the plausibility of Nagaland's population figures using information on births, deaths, and lawful migration into the state. The state of Nagaland came into existence in 1963. The pre- and post- 1963 decennial censuses cannot be compared directly because of the sustained increase until 1963 in both the reach of census operations (GoI 2011b) and the area of the Naga Hills (the precursor to the state of Nagaland) (GoI 1975: 4). Moreover, the population figures for areas covered fully before the 1961 Census were in many cases based on estimates rather than direct enumeration (GoI 2011b: xii). The discussion in this section is, therefore, restricted to the 1971–2011 period. Before examining births, deaths, and migration, the three main demographic determinants of population change, we will briefly examine certain factors specific to Nagaland of the 1990s.

Nagaland-specific factors

In our conversations with people in Nagaland, we encountered three kinds of explanations of population growth linked to insurgency. These are the deployment of armed forces, the return of insurgents to the mainstream, and a reduction in fatalities due to the 1997 ceasefire. Political developments in the late 1990s, when the government and the largest insurgent faction (the NSCN-IM) entered into a ceasefire, are important in this regard. Additionally, we will discuss the possibility of HIV/AIDS being a factor underlying the negative population growth during 2001-11.

Changes in the extent of deployment of armed forces cannot explain the abnormally high growth rate reported in 2001 for at least two reasons. First, insurgency-related fatalities dropped significantly in the aftermath of the ceasefires between the government and insurgent groups in the late 1990s (SATP nd1, nd2), which must have resulted in a reduction rather than an increase in the numbers of troops posted in Nagaland. Second, the 1999 Kargil War necessitated the relocation of forces from across the North East to the western border (Jamir nd1: 69, Jamir nd2: 14, Kumar 2003). If anything, the population of armed forces is likely to have declined in Nagaland in the run-up to the 2001 Census.

Likewise, the return of underground fighters to the mainstream cannot explain the high growth rate recorded in 2001 and the dramatic decline thereafter. Given what we know about the strengths of different factions, the number of people staying permanently in insurgent camps is unlikely to have been in excess of ten thousand. Hence, even if we assume that all those who 'returned' were not counted in the earlier censuses and were recorded as non-immigrant natives in the 2001 Census, the return of insurgents to the mainstream can at best account for a little less than one per cent of the growth of Nagaland's population.

Likewise, the drop in death rate after the ceasefire agreement can also not explain the high growth rate reported in 2001 and the subsequent reversal in 2011. At the time of the census, the effect of the ceasefire was limited to only four years of the 1991-2001 decade, and, if anything, this effect should have grown in the following decade and contributed to an increase rather than dramatic decrease of growth rate in 2011. In any case, in the 1990s, in the run-up to the ceasefire, the overall insurgency related death rate, including insurgents and civilians, was less than one per 1000 persons per year (authors' calculation based on SATP nd1, SATP nd2). Therefore, the effect of ceasefire can at best account for less than half a per cent of the population growth.

Yet another explanation for the decrease in population during 2001-11 relates to HIV/AIDS. There are several reasons why this explanation is implausible, even if we assume that the government underestimates HIV/AIDS related deaths. First, the population of Manipur did not shrink despite a much higher HIV/AIDS prevalence rate compared to Nagaland (1.4% in Manipur vis-à-vis 0.78% in Nagaland) (NACO and NIMS nd, GoI 2010). Second, despite a comparable prevalence of HIV/AIDS Nagaland's population grew rapidly during the 1990s. Third, population growth was positive in districts with high HIV/AIDS prevalence – e.g., Dimapur and Tuensang, where the population grew by 23.13% and 5.81% respectively – and negative in districts with low HIV/AIDS prevalence – e.g., Mon, which registered a 4% decline in population (Bachani et al. 2011, GoI 2011b, 2011c). Last but not the least, while Nagaland is among the six worst HIV/AIDS affected states in India (GoN 2010: 121), the resultant deaths (564 deaths between 1994 and July 2011) are too few to explain any dramatic changes in Nagaland's population (Nagaland State AIDS Control Society 2011).

To conclude, the Nagaland-specific explanations discussed here can at best explain a minor fluctuation in Nagaland's population. We now turn to the standard demographic factors that govern demographic changes.

Birth and death rates

We can estimate the natural growth rates (NGR), the rate at which a population grows in absence of migration, using the National Family Health Survey (NFHS) and the Sample Registration System (SRS) estimates of birth rates for two scenarios – one, assuming zero death rates (NGR(0)), and the other, assuming death rate is equal to the SRS death rate (NGR(SRS)). For the post-1971 census decades, the observed population growth of the country as a whole lies within the range spanned by NGR(SRS) and NGR(0), whereas in Nagaland's case the crude birth rates (CBR) cannot support the observed population growth even when the crude death rate is assumed to be zero (Table 3). Also, changes in birth and death rates between 1991–2001 and 2001–2011 reported by NFHS and SRS rule out the possibility that the transition to a low birth-and-death rates regime explains the decline of Nagaland's population between 2001 and 2011.

The inferences based on large datasets provided by NFHS and SRS are supported by sources of information for small areas. Bhowmik et al. (1971: 74-75) found that CBR among the Zeme Nagas of Benreu village (Peren) was 49.77 per 1000 population in 1961, which compares favourably with the national average during 1951-1960, i.e. 41.7 per 1000 population. More recently, Murry et al. (2005) found that CBR among the Lothas in a village in Wokha was 28.35 per 1000 population, which is close to CBR estimates for Nagaland (30.4 for 1996-98, NFHS-2) and rural India (29.4 for 1995-97, SRS).

In short, the census is not consistent with other sources of information on births and deaths in Nagaland.[12] Since births and deaths are insufficient to explain the changes in Nagaland's population we turn to other determinants of demographic change.

[12]Nagaland's population estimates are also inconsistent with estimates based on school enrolment data and electoral rolls (Agrawal and Kumar 2012).

Table 3: Birth, Death and Natural Growth Rates[13]

Period	Data Source	Nagaland				India		
		Birth rate	Death rate	NGR (0)	NGR (SRS)	Birth rate	Death rate	NGR (0)
1971-1981 (Census decadal growth rates: 50.05 (Nagaland) and 24.66 (India))								
1976–181 (average)	SRS	21.88	6.87	24.16	16.07	33.67	13.67	39.26
1981-1991 (Census decadal growth rates: 56.08 (Nagaland) and 23.86 (India))								
1983–1991 (average)	SRS	21.41	5.02	23.60	17.65	28.82	10	32.86
1991-2001 (Census decadal growth rates: 64.53 (Nagaland) and 21.54 (India))								
1991–94 (average)	SRS	19.45	4.02	21.24	16.54	24.65	8.95	27.57
1990–92	NFHS-1	31.3	NA	36.10	30.88	28.7	NA	32.71
1996–98	NFHS-2	30.4	NA	34.91	29.74	24.8	NA	27.76
2001-2011 (Census decadal growth rates: -0.47 (Nagaland) and 17.64 (India))								
2004–11 (average)	SRS	16.57	4.05	17.87	13.26	22.96	7.37	25.49
2003–05	NFHS-3	28.5	NA	32.45	27.07	23.6	NA	26.27

Migration

Migration is widely held responsible for abnormal changes in the population of the North East, including Nagaland. If migration is indeed the primary factor driving demographic changes in Nagaland then it has to be assumed

[13]Notes: (i) 'Birth rate' is the number of live births per 1000 population and 'Death rate' is the number of deaths per 1000 population. (ii) NGR stands for natural growth rate arrived at by calculating compound growth rate. NGR (0) denotes the decadal NGR of 'closed' (no migration) population assuming zero death rate and NGR (SRS), assuming SRS death rate for the corresponding decade. (iii) The figures for 1976–81 for Nagaland are based only on the rural sample, which does not severely affect our estimates because the share of rural population in the state's population was 90% and 85%, respectively, in 1971 and 1981. (The share of rural population dropped in 1981 as four new towns were recognised that year. Before this reclassification the share of rural population was about 89%). (iv) We could not retrieve the SRS data on Nagaland for 1995-2003. (iv) 'NA' indicates non-availability of data. Sources: (i) Srivastava (1987) (ii) GoI (1999 and 2011b) (iii) IIPS and MI (2007, p. 78 and 2009, p. 36) and (iv) SRS birth and death rates have been compiled from SRS Bulletins for the respective years.

that there was massive net in-migration between 1981 and 2001 and net out-migration during 2001-11. Chaurasia (2011: 15) implicitly assumed that there is no abnormality in the 2001 Census and used SRS (2004–09) birth and death rates to estimate the 2011 population of Nagaland. He overestimated the actual population by 14%. He attributed the discrepancy between the projected and actual figures to 'very heavy out-migration (almost 14%) between 2001 and 2011', but without giving any evidence in support of the migration hypothesis. While interstate migration data for 2011 are not available yet, out-migration is unlikely to explain the absolute decline in Nagaland's population after decades of very high growth, as the number of out-migrants during 2001–11 would have to far exceed 83,083, the total number of out-migrants during the entire 1971–2001 period (GoI 1977: 84-85; GoI 1988a: 318-19; GoI nd1; GoI nd2). Kundu and Kundu (2011), in turn, attributed the low growth rate to a drop in in-migration. However, it is not clear why the population growth rate would turn negative due to a slowdown in in-migration unless, say, the birth rate of the native population is less than its death rate, which is certainly not the case in Nagaland.

So far, we have argued that (lawful) migration recorded in the Census alone cannot explain *both* very high population growth rates in Nagaland during 1971-2001 and the negative growth during 2001-2011. But, can in-migration from other states and countries at least explain high growth rates during 1971-2001? Statistics on migration (Table 4) indicate that even this restricted explanation is implausible. First, migrants constituted about 5% of Nagaland's population in both 1991 and 2001, and only 40% of these migrants were from outside the state. Therefore, the migrants from outside Nagaland constituted nearly 2% of its population in both years.[14] Second, the share of in-migrants from other states and countries in Nagaland's population has been *falling* over time, making in-migration an unlikely cause of *increasing* population growth rate during 1981–2001. We will return to the issue of migration when we discuss political-geographic explanations (*infra*).

[14]A proper accounting of internal migration in the state that eliminates double counting of settlers from villages in urban areas will force a downward revision of population growth rates. However, double counting is insufficient to explain the ab-normal population growth rates as the adjusted growth rates remain high (Agrawal and Kumar 2012, 31).

Table 4: Share of Migrants in Nagaland's Population (in per cent), 1971–2001[15]

Type of migration	1971	1981	1991	2001
All in-migrants*	12.64	15.33	5.74	4.36
*Intra-state**	*48.29*	*62.38*	*61.96*	*59.24*
*Inter-state**	*42.16*	*34.00*	*35.31*	*38.74*
*International**	*9.56*	*3.62*	*2.73*	*2.02*
In-migrants from outside the state*	6.54	5.77	2.20	1.78

Births, deaths, and migration

Statistics on birth, death, and migration can be combined to check if together these factors can explain the changes in the census population estimates for Nagaland. The change in population between two years is captured in the literature on demography using a fundamental equation, which is an identity that equates the change in population between two years to the number of births net of deaths and in-migration net of out-migration (Preston et al. 2001: 2). For the sake of analysis, the population can be divided into two groups, namely, 0-9 year and 10+ years. Note that there is no birth in the 10+ years age group. Table 5 estimates the number of deaths in the '10+' years age group to balance the fundamental equation. If the population figures reported by the Census since 1971 are assumed to be correct, then until 2001 the number of deaths among those aged 10 years and above must have been *negative* for Nagaland as a whole as well as for the state's rural and urban areas and male and female sub-groups separately.[16]

For Nagaland as a whole, the discrepancy, defined as the ratio of the unaccounted population to the end-of-the-decade population, increases from

[15]Notes: * as proportion of state's total population ** as proportion of in-migrants. Sources: Computations based on GoI (1976, 28, 24; 1977, 84-85; 1985, 34, 48, 50; 1988, 318-19; 1997a, 52-53; 1997b, 6, 40, 52; nd1, nd2).

[16]The sharp deceleration in Andhra Pradesh's population growth between 1991 and 2001 (Kumar and Sharma 2006) was incommensurate with the changes in the socioeconomic correlates of fertility. We carried out a similar exercise for Andhra Pradesh and found the number of deaths in the 10+ years age group to be greater than zero during 1971-2001.

4% in 1971–81 to 18% during the 1991–2001 period (Table 5). Therefore, three successive censuses between 1981 and 2001 overestimated Nagaland's population. Note that the discrepancy figures, reported here, are arrived at under the implausible assumption of zero deaths in the '10+' years age group. The actual discrepancy in, say, 1991 will be 125,657 plus the total deaths between 1981 and 1991 in the '10+' years age group. So, Table 5 provides the lower bounds for discrepancies in Nagaland's population. Having ruled out demographic explanations, we are now only left with political explanations. It is to these that we presently turn.

Table 5: Decomposition of Population Changes[17]

Population/change	1971-81	1981-91	1991-2001
The end of decade population	774930	1209546	1990036
Total population change, all ages	258481	434616	780490
Net in-migrants, all ages	38227	13797	-16511
Population change, net of net in-migrants	220254	420819	797001
Birth-Deaths, 0-9 years	189739	295162	445190
Birth-Deaths, 10+ age group	30515	125657	351811
Deaths in 10+ age group	-30515	-125657	-351811
Discrepancy (%)	3.94	10.39	17.68

POLITICAL-GEOGRAPHIC EXPLANATIONS

After ruling out migration as the cause of Nagaland's population change, this section examines a sub-class of migration-based explanations, which focus on the political aspect of the problem at hand. Political-geographic explanations suggest that people migrate to adjust to arbitrary colonial

[17]Notes: Discrepancy is calculated as the ratio of excess deaths required in the 10+ years age group to the end of the decade population. Sources: GoI (1976: 24, 28; 1977: 84–85; 1985: 34, 48, 50; 1988: 318–19; 1997a: 52–53; 1997b: 6, 40, 52; nd1; nd2).

and post-colonial boundaries. On the one hand, these boundaries divide communities, but, on the other, enclose unwilling partners within the same territorial jurisdictions (Agrawal and Kumar 2017a). Several Naga and other related tribes are distributed across Myanmar and different states of the North East, including Nagaland, Manipur, Assam, and Arunachal Pradesh. Can the otherwise unexpected shifts in the population dynamics of Nagaland be explained by conflicts rooted in colonial (between Myanmar and India) and post-colonial (between North Eastern states) boundaries that generate demographic gradients redistributing Naga, and even non-Naga, population of the region?[18]

In the decades preceding 2001, the levels of conflict and economic development did not vary considerably between Nagaland and its neighbouring states to be able to support an influx into Nagaland on a scale that would explain the increase in Nagaland's population. The Naga-Kuki conflict in Manipur and Kohima and Peren districts of Nagaland during the 1990s is an exception, but it pushed Kukis *away* from rather than towards Naga-dominated areas. Even if it is assumed that an influx can explain the abnormal increase in population in 2001, the complementary assumption that there was a reverse flow in the run-up to the 2011 Census is highly implausible as Nagaland witnessed a significant de-escalation of conflict in this period. If anything, in-migration should have increased during 2001–2011 as the geographical scope of ceasefires was limited to Nagaland.

Moreover, if only intra-national boundaries are considered, the number of potential settlers belonging to the Naga tribes and related tribes of Arunachal Pradesh and Assam are too few to account for any major demographic change in Nagaland. In Assam, such population is limited to a few villages. (The recent Naga settlers in the disputed territory along Assam-Nagaland border are already included in Nagaland's headcount.) Arunachal Pradesh's native Naga population is limited to a few comparatively small tribes in the districts along the border with Nagaland. If these districts had seen large-scale outmigration to Nagaland, their population should have registered lower growth rates between 1991 and 2001, which was not the case. The migration of northern and western Manipur's large tribal population could possibly account for a part of Nagaland's unaccounted population.

---

[18]A related hypothesis explores the contribution of the changing political boundaries of Nagaland and the growing reach of census in Nagaland to changes in the population of the state. A detailed discussion of this hypothesis will require a detour into the history of formation of Nagaland and the history of census operations in the state. Briefly, the nature of these changes in case of Nagaland is such that they can at best explain an increase in the earlier decades but not a steadily growing population growth rate until 2001 followed by a precipitous drop in 2011.

But the relevant districts of Manipur—Senapati, Tamenglong, and Ukhrul—recorded extremely high growth rates despite the out-migration of Kuki tribes due to ethnic conflict. Moreover, we have not come across any report referring to large-scale movement of tribes from Manipur into Nagaland. In fact, since 2010, Nagaland has witnessed a growing Nagaland-for-Nagas-of-Nagaland sentiment in the state in response to the purported threat posed by the *possible* in-migration of Nagas from Manipur after the settlement of Naga political problem. Since 2007, quit notices have been served to Manipuri tribal settlers in Nagaland on several occasions. The major Manipuri tribes under focus in this regard include Tangkhul, Rongmei, and Mao, but these developments postdate the 2001 Census by at least a decade.

In short, political-geographic explanations of the abnormal demographic changes in Nagaland can also be ruled out. However, the census cannot help us check if *undocumented* migration from Myanmar and (popularly referred to as 'illegal' migration in case of) Bangladesh explain the high growth rates.[19] While documented international migration into Nagaland reported in censuses has always been very low (Table 5), most Nagas believe that the illegal/undocumented immigration is a major contributor to abnormally high growth rates. Successive chief ministers have publicly supported this hypothesis (Jamir nd2: 12-13; Rio 2010). However, alleged undocumented international migration cannot be a major determinant of demographic changes in Nagaland as the available evidence does not support the claim that there was substantial international in-migration on a scale that could explain the demographic anomalies observed in Nagaland (Agrawal and Kumar 2012). Also, if indeed international migration is responsible for abnormal changes then we have to assume that such migration grew until 2001 and then dropped in the subsequent decade even though the post-2001 period provided a more conducive atmosphere for in-migration.

More importantly, we will have to assume that over five lakh international migrants left Nagaland during 2001-11. We have not come across any report

[19]It is noteworthy that in-migration of Myanmarese Nagas is not seen as problematic as the alleged Bangladeshi immigration because the dominant discourse within the state does not recognise the artificial colonial era border between India and Myanmar that divides Naga tribes. Myanmarese Nagas come to Nagaland to access better educational and health services and also to escape religious persecution and military operations in Myanmar. There has also been some permanent migration from Myanmar, but the number of migrants is small and distributed across several census decades and cannot explain the abnormal shifts in Nagaland's growth rates, except perhaps in Khiamniungan Naga areas around Noklak in Tuensang district and some parts of Konyak dominated Mon district. Details have been omitted for want of space.

referring to out-migration on such a scale. Out-migration on such a scale also does not agree with consistently growing complaints against outsiders stealing jobs and land from locals.[20] Last but not the least, if we assume that the drop in population during 2001-11 can be explained by massive out-migration of illegal settlers, then it is not clear why Nagaland's indigenous tribal population contracted in absolute terms and why the drop in the tribal population accounts for most of the drop in the state's population.

POLITICAL-ECONOMIC EXPLANATIONS

We have so far ruled out demographic and political-geographic explanations of Nagaland's demographic somersault. Kumar and Agrawal (2016) argue that a combination of political-economic factors — competition over development funding, government jobs, and political representation in legislative assembly; demands for new districts; boundary disputes with other states; and assimilation of outsiders on the sly to access cheap labour and presumably to add favourable voters to one's village or constituency — triggered inter- village / tribal / district contests leading to widespread competitive manipulation of the census (Agrawal and Kumar 2012).[21] In this section, we will outline and briefly examine some of the major political-economic explanations.[22]

[20]Often insiders fearing influx of 'outsiders' call for increasing the fertility of the daughters-of-the-soil (Horowitz 2000), but we have not come across such calls in Nagaland.

[21]Note that while job quotas are a source of never ending inter-tribal squab-bling in Nagaland and it is widely believed that politicians and bureaucrats help job applicants from their own communities, we have not come across anyone who directly linked the manipulation of headcount to quotas.

[22]There are several other political-economic hypotheses that have not been discussed here for want of space. For instance, Alesina and La Ferrera (2005) discuss the negative impact of ethnic competition on the quality of public goods. Census statistics that feed into government planning process can be seen as public goods and we can say that the quality of these statistics will be poor in ethnically divided societies. Nagaland is among the most diverse states of India and, more importantly, its diversity is ethnically and geographically delineated. Other hypotheses focus on factors such as population density, government's tax collection capability, inter-departmental struggle over government budget, inter-state politics within the Naga community, etc.

Nearly everyone we interviewed suggested that Nagaland's rural population statistics are unreliable because villagers deliberately overstate their headcount to attract more development funds and add to their electoral strength, which in turn strengthens their bargaining power vis-à-vis prospective and elected legislators (see, for instance, Wouters (2015a) for a firsthand account).[23] While this village centric manipulation does not overtly invoke the delimitation of constituencies as a threat, it ultimately feeds into the larger politics of delimitation which influences the distribution of legislative seats according to population share of districts.[24]

Demands for creation of new administrative units was suggested by the then Director of Census Operations Hekali Zhimomi (personal communication, Kohima, June 25, 2013) and several interviewees, including a civil society leader in one of the newly formed districts, as a factor behind high population growth reported in the census.[25] Two factors drive the demand for new districts in Nagaland: the lack of development of remote administrative circles and the desire for aligning district and tribal boundaries. The Phoms of Longleng, Zeliangs of Peren, and Sangtams of Kiphire are examples of communities that earlier inhabited remote parts of multi-tribal districts but managed to get their own districts between 2001 and 2011. Khiamniungan and Yimchunger tribes of Tuensang and Rengmas of Kohima continue to struggle for new districts (Khiamniungan-dominated Noklak was recently granted district status in December 2017).

Foremost among the political-economic explanations is former Nagaland Chief Minister Neiphiu Rio's claim that the population was inflated in the 2001 Census, which was conducted under the shadow of

[23]There is perhaps an older inter-village contest that complements the more recent contest for resources and political power within constituencies. Jelle J.P. Wouters drew our attention to the relationship between the standing of villages in an area and their number of households. So, perhaps pre-modern solidarities and sentiments are being harnessed to achieve modern goals. This agrees with the findings of Wouters (2014), who suggests that Naga tribes have entered the modern democratic space armed with their respective pre-modern modes of organisation and mobilisation.

[24]Except Sumis and Kukis, all other recognised indigenous tribes of Nagaland live predominantly within one district. These two tribes are divided between their 'ancestral' districts and Dimapur. On the other hand, except Tuensang and Dimapur, all other districts are overwhelmingly dominated by one of the recognised tribes.

[25]See, for instance, Debroy (2017) for a discussion of the factors driving district formation in India, including population, area, and the distance from district headquarter.

the impending delimitation, due to the competition for greater political representation:

> All this is because of competition among the tribes, between districts. So we have been told that if we go for a review, then it will be more. *The delimitation commission process* [of distributing seats in proportion to population] *is also creating problems because some districts are losing seats and Dimapur is gaining five seats.* Mokokchung seats are dropping by three, Phek will have one less and so on. In the plains, the constituencies are large, Dimapur I has 50,000 voters but the hills have smaller voting numbers, between 12,000 and 20,000. Now these seats are distributed on tribal lines but the ones which the hills are losing are being added to Dimapur which has a three lakh population. And Dimapur has a lot of non-tribals (Hazarika 2005, emphasis added).

The high growth in population during 1991-2001 can, therefore, be explained by tribal competition for greater political representation, which in turn is linked to access to public resources including allocations of development funds, government contracts, and government jobs because political connections are usually needed to secure these.[26] S.C. Jamir, who was the Chief Minister of Nagaland when the 2001 Census was conducted, offered a related explanation of high growth rates in Wokha. He suggested that the people of Wokha over-reported their population to make up for the assembly seat they 'lost' in the last delimitation in the 1970s (personal communication, Bhubaneshwar, August 27, 2013). Phek also 'lost' a seat in the last delimitation, but its population growth rate was low by Nagaland's

---

[26]Given the strong sense of belonging to one's village and tribe, leaders are expected to privilege their 'own' people in the distribution of state resources and government jobs rather than pursue the common good. Nagaland's newspapers and social media abound in allegations of favouritism against those who hold positions of responsibilities. A simple game-theoretic exercise will show that such expectations feed a kind of security dilemma that would push the society toward the collectively worst outcome. This phenomenon is akin to what is known in the literature as patronage-democracy, 'a system in which the government monopolises access to basic goods and services valued by a majority of the population, and in which government officials have individualised discretion over how these basic goods and services are distributed', in which 'voters decide between politicians, not by assessing their policy positions, but by assessing whether a candidate will favour them in the distribution of patronage' (Chandra 2009).

standards. In any case, the election-census link is not unique to Nagaland. Horowitz's survey of ethnic conflicts draws attention to the inter-linkages between ethnic conflict, election, and competitive manipulation of population census in different parts of the world.[27] Horowitz suggests:

> As an entitlement issue, *the census is a splendid example of the blending of group anxiety with political domination*. On the one hand, it is common to encounter anxiety-laden perceptions of fecundity or illegal immigration of competing groups; these produce considerable overestimates of the population of outgroups . . . On the other hand, since numbers count in the quest for political domination, the hope of a group is to enlarge its relative share of the population . . . The census is therefore no dreary demographic formality to be left to experts. *Disputes over census results in ethnically divided societies are common* . . . The census shows nicely the capacity of ethnicity to stand ordinary processes on their head. In a severely divided society, we have seen that an election can become an ethnic head count. *Now it is clear that a census needs to be "won." So the election is a census, and the census is an election*. (Horowitz 2000: 194-196, emphases added)

In other words, in ethnically divided societies, elections are reduced to 'racial censuses' ('tribal censuses' in the context of Nagaland) in which a person's vote is pre-determined by ethnic identity (Horowitz 2000: 326).[28] As a result, instead of facing the uncertainty of elections, communities try to skew the contest in their favour by over-reporting their headcount that in turn determines electorate size and the allocation of seats. The Naga Hoho, the apex tribal council, admitted as much when it noted that 'the Census has been a much misunderstood exercise in Nagaland with the people equating it with the electoral roll listing' (*Eastern Panorama* 2011). Census officials also complained that the government practice of cross-checking electoral rolls with census population estimates contributes to the general belief that

[27]Political-economic considerations have, in fact, influenced censuses and, more generally, modern government data collection exercises right from the earliest phase of colonialism (Cohn 1987, Peabody 2001, Guha 2003).

[28]Others have equated census in such settings with 'plebiscite' and 'political campaign' (Kertzer and Arel 2002: 28-29), 'opinion polls' (Abramson 2002: 178), and 'show of strength' (Hekali Zhimomi, Director Census Operations, Nagaland, personal communication, Kohima, June 25: 2013).

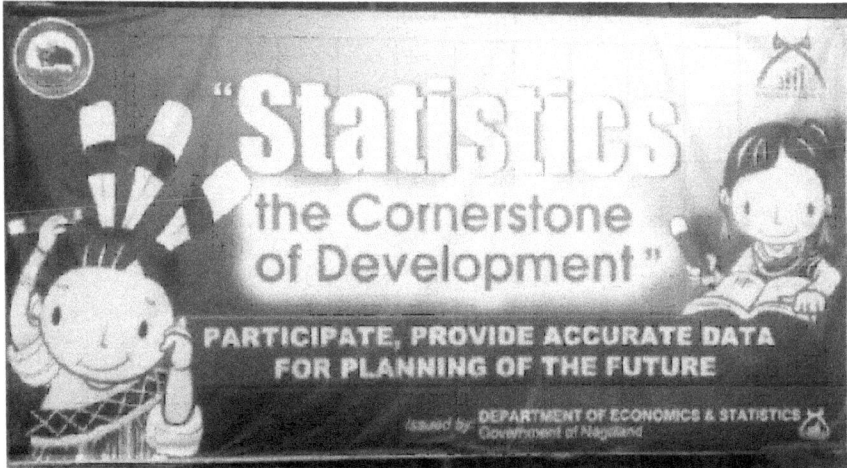

Figure 5. Government promoting accurate statistics (Photo by Vikas Kumar)

both census and electoral rolls have to be manipulated.[29] The Directorate of Census Operations, Nagaland explains thus:

> Many equate it with electoral rolls and saw the decennial Census exercise as an opportunity to . . . increase [the] vote bank . . . [The d]evelopmental model followed in the state in which allocation of funds . . . is made on the basis of population . . . naturally led many to try and increase the fund flow into their villages by showing non-existing population and households in the Census records. (GoI 2011b: viii)

The remainder of this section examines a political-economic hypothesis that divides the state into two broad parts, Dimapur and 'the Hills', which are coterminous with the hills–plains and Naga–non-Naga[30] dichotomies

---

[29]See Wouters (2015) for a discussion on the role of bogus votes in Nagaland's elections.

[30]Statistically speaking, Dimapur is a Naga district because the Nagas of Nagaland account for a majority of its population. However, Naga settlers in hot, humid, and mosquito-infested Dimapur continue to view themselves as members of their respective tribes and ancestral villages in the cooler hills. Moreover, when the hill-based politicians and civil society leaders expressed their resentment against the potential transfer of seats to Dimapur from the hills, they consciously focused their attacks on

in the state, for the purpose of analysis.[31] During the last delimitation of electoral constituencies in the 1970s, two assembly seats were transferred from the hill districts to Dimapur. Since then, the disparity in the sizes of constituencies has grown tremendously. In 2003, the last assembly election before Hazarika (2005) interviewed Rio, the largest constituency Ghaspani I (Dimapur district) had 54,453 voters, whereas the smallest Mokokchung Town (Mokokchung district) had 4,971 voters.[32] This disparity indicates the excessive political power wielded by voters in the hills, which can be attributed to the skewed distribution of political and human capital during the formative years of Nagaland in the 1960s. Since most tribal communities are geographically concentrated, the disparity in voting power gives an idea of the scale of inter-community disparity and the potential for conflict due to delimitation between the groups favouring status quo and those demanding rectification of imbalances. Following the former Chief Minister, one could, therefore, argue that the conflict between Dimapur, which was bound to gain seats, and the hill districts was the driving force behind the manipulation of census in 2001. Our analysis shows that based on the 1991 Census, the 2002 Delimitation would have transferred four seats to Dimapur (Table 6).[33]

'outsiders' in Dimapur completely overlooking the fact that Dimapur-based tribes would be the main beneficiaries. A discussion of the origins of this schizophrenic perception of Dimapur in the Hills is beyond the scope of this chapter.

[31]We have restricted the following discussion to the delimitation-based explanation at the level of Dimapur vs the rest of the state. In a state generally lacking in economic development, Dimapur, the only plains district of the state, was the locus of competition because historically it has been the most developed district and the sole transport hub of Nagaland. For want of space we have omitted assembly constituency, administrative circle, and tribe level analyses of the larger class of political-economic hypotheses discussed elsewhere (Kumar and Agrawal 2016).

[32]There is enormous disparity within several hill districts as well as between hill districts, but we are focusing on the hills-plain divide in this section.

[33]The Delimitation Commission had awarded nine seats to Dimapur (see Annexure to the letter of Sumit Mukherjee, Under Secretary, Delimitation Commission, dated 4 August 2005 addressed to the Commissioner of Nagaland). This is equivalent to a gain of four seats.

Table 6: Estimated number of seats and loss therein in Legislative Assembly[34]

Characteristic	Dimapur	The rest of the state
Existing seats in Legislative Assembly	5	55
Census Year 1991		
Population	177,951	1,031,595
Population share	0.15	0.85
Projected seats in Legislative Assembly	9	51
Gain of seats	4	-4
Census Year 2001		
Population	309,024	1,681,012
Population share	0.16	0.84
Projected seats in Legislative Assembly	9	51
Gain of seats	4	-4
Growth of population (1991-2001)	73.66	62.95
Census Year 2011		
Population	378,811	1,599,691
Population share	0.19	0.81
Projected seats in Legislative Assembly	11	49
Gain of seats	6	-6
Growth of population (2001-2011)	22.58	-4.84

Threatened by the possibility of loss of political representation had the past population growth trends persisted, the hill tribes overstated their numbers in the 2001 Census. Hill districts such as Mon, Wokha, and

[34]Notes: 'Existing seats in Legislative Assembly' are the number of seats in the present Legislative Assembly allotted on the basis of the 1971 Census. 'Projected seats in Legislative Assembly' for a census year is the number of seats estimated using the 'Population share' from the corresponding census. 'Loss of seats' for a census year is the difference between 'Existing seats' and 'Projected seats in Legislative Assembly' for that year. Sources: DCI (2008) for 'Existing seats in Legislative Assembly' and GoI (nd1, nd2, 2013) for 'Population'.

Tuensang were able to increase their population share (at the expense of other hill districts) that would have translated into a gain of one seat each had the delimitation been conducted as per the 2001 Census rather than the 1991 Census. The Dimapur-based tribes also inflated their population, but managed only to reduce further loss of seats to the hills vis-à-vis 1991 population shares. Non-Nagas who account for a sizeable proportion of the district's population had no incentive to overstate their headcount because 59 out of 60 seats in Nagaland are reserved for (indigenous) tribes.[35] Moreover, Dimapur's higher rates of literacy, urbanisation, relatively weaker intra-tribe solidarity, less than perfect inter-tribal coordination, and the lack of clarity about who benefits most from the assignment of additional seats to the district meant that tribes perhaps could not be mobilised as effectively as in the hills to manipulate headcounts. In the end, in 2001, the hill districts as a whole did not manage to completely avoid the potential loss of seats to Dimapur due to competitive manipulation across the state.[36]

Since the tribes were not equally successful at over-enumeration and the four seats supposed to be added to Dimapur would have benefitted only a few tribes – particularly, Sumis and Aos – that have settled in the plains in large numbers, the Census triggered conflict and litigation (for instance, Chakhesang Public Organisation & Ors. vs. Union of India & Ors., W.P. No. 67 of 2006) that concluded more than a decade later in October 2017. In 2008, an Ordinance deferred delimitation in Nagaland (and Manipur, Assam, and Arunachal Pradesh) to until after the first census after 2026, i.e. 2031 (GoI 2008). Thus, there was no immediate incentive to inflate population counts in Nagaland after 2008. Moreover, the government was alerted to the possibility of subversion of its data collection exercises. In other words, both the *incentive* and *opportunity* to overstate headcount dissipated by 2011. Unsurprisingly, the census recorded a negative growth rate of 5% in the hill districts, whereas in Dimapur growth remained positive, even if lower than the last census decade (1991-2001). In other words, in 2011, the deflation in Nagaland's (reported) population was restricted almost entirely to the hills. The over-reporting of headcount in the 2001 Census seems to have been driven by the expected loss of political representation due to the

[35]The sole unreserved seat (Dimapur-I) has also been dominated by Nagas since the late 1980s as they control the state's politics and have systematically squeezed out the 'outsiders' from the electoral space. Moreover, the political economy of Dimapur is structured in a way that non-Nagas face almost insurmountable collective action problems.

[36]If delimitation is conducted as per the 2011 Census, Dimapur will gain six (possibly, seven depending on rounding off procedure) seats at the expense of the hill districts.

impending delimitation. The deflation of population in the 2011 Census too is related to the overstatement in the preceding decade insofar as only the hills witnessed a negative growth rate.

CONCLUDING REMARKS

Modern states need information about their populations to design policies, but their official statistics are not free of errors. The Census, which is the bedrock of India's government statistics, offers a case in point. We examined a largely ignored surprise revealed by the 2011 Census: after two decades of abnormally high growth Nagaland's population supposedly declined in absolute terms during 2001–2011. Using different sources (past projections, statements of political leaders, sample surveys, and overlapping censuses), we showed that Nagaland's Census has been plagued with problems at least since 1991.

We further showed that the Census population estimates are internally inconsistent as well as inconsistent with other sources of demographic information and argued that demographic explanations alone cannot explain the dramatic changes in Nagaland's population. We also argued that political-geographic explanations based on migration driven by arbitrary colonial and post-colonial boundaries cannot explain the changes in Nagaland's population if we consider only lawful migration. Moreover, while there is no reliable data on illegal/undocumented international immigration into Nagaland, the available evidence does not support the corresponding political-geographic hypothesis.

Available evidence supports political-economic explanations of the changes in Nagaland's population, which suggest that ethno-political competition explains competitive manipulation of census statistics by sub-groups of population seeking greater political representation and, by implication, a greater share in the public pie. Tribes manipulated their headcounts in 2001 to avoid the loss of political representation to non-tribal "outsiders" in Dimapur and competing tribes in hill districts. Ultimately, inter-tribal conflict and litigation forced the deferment of delimitation in Nagaland to the first census after the year 2026 (GoI 2008). Consequently, there was no incentive in 2011 to inflate population.

The obsession with government statistics in Nagaland is a consequence of a struggle over scarce public resources in a stagnant economy,[37] where

---

[37]The state remains the biggest employer, consumer, and contractor in Naga-

people depend upon federally supported[38] government spending apportioned among communities/villages/districts according to their *reported* numbers and *measured* backwardness and they do not trust leaders and bureaucrats from other communities to pursue common good. As a result, Nagaland's development, democracy, and data deficits are bound in a structural relationship. Consequently, there are no easy solutions to the statistical woes of Nagaland as well as other geographically marginal, multi-ethnic, erstwhile special category states such as Manipur[39] and Jammu and Kashmir[40] where the society is divided into mutually antagonistic communities fighting for a fixed political-economic pie. Any attempt to mechanically fix the problem through the introduction of better data collection and processing tools will not help as the data deficit is embedded in a mutually constitutive structural relationship with democracy and development deficits.

---

land because long term constitutional-legal problems as well as extortion by insurgent factions and corruption in the state sector have impeded the growth of the private sector. This intensifies the competition over public resources.

[38]Until the implementation of the recommendations of the Fourteenth Finance Commission in 2015, Nagaland was a Special Category State that received as much as 90% of its plan assistance as grants from the central government. In 2006–07, central grants and loans and debt from RBI, etc. accounted for 86.36% of the state's receipts (GoN nd). The status of Special Category States remains unclear after the Union Government accepted the recommendation of the Fourteenth Finance Commission to raise the tax devolution to states from 32 to 42%. The Union Government has been reassuring northeastern states that their request for continuation of the existing arrangement is under consideration (*Nagaland Post* 2015, *Economic Times* 2015). More recently, the finance minister indicated that the government was considering Andhra Pradesh's demand for special category status (Swami 2016) and also seemed to suggest that the states in the North East shall continue to be treated as special category states insofar as funding for 'core of the core' schemes is considered (*Nagaland Post* 2016).

[39]Naga-dominated Senapati district of ethnically polarised Manipur recorded abnormally high growth rates ahead of the 2002 delimitation. Unlike Nagaland, the problem persists in Senapati.

[40]Guilmoto and Rajan (2013) draw attention to how religious polarisation has affected the quality of census data in Jammu and Kashmir. Elsewhere we show that unlike Kashmir Valley, where data for those below 10 years seem to have been over-reported, in Nagaland manipulation affected the data for middle age groups more than others.

ACKNOWLEDGMENTS

The authors are grateful to Azim Premji University, Bengaluru, Indian Institute of Technology Delhi, and Institute of Economic Growth, Delhi for institutional support and to participants in seminars at Azim Premji University and Institute of Economic Growth, government officials and village elders in Nagaland and Assam, R.N. Chhipa, Sanjoy Hazarika, Visakono Sakhrie, Theja Therieh, Jelle J.P. Wouters, Toshi Wungtung, and Lungsang Zeliang for helpful discussions. Usual disclaimers apply.

■ ■■ ■■

04

ENGENDERING DEMOCRACY IN NAGALAND

Moamenla Amer

INTRODUCTION

Democracy is based on the notion that all citizens have the right to participate in the managing of political affairs, and that every citizen's input is of equal importance. Participation promotes a sense of connectedness to the polity and fosters a feeling of empowerment over elected officials (Soule and Nairne 2006). A participatory public is crucial for democratic responsiveness and is seen as an intrinsic democratic good. This basic assumption emphasises the crucial role of public participation in maintaining democracies that are stable. Further, a democratic society, in principle, is a participant society in which power is shared. In actual practice, however, all democracies are plagued by systematic inequalities in participation (Lijphart 1997). Gender has been one such important factor given that women are often found to participate less than men, thus suggesting that half the world's population's interests are less well represented (Verba et al. 1994).

Gender inequalities in political participation remain an important part of 'democracy's unresolved dilemma' of unequal participation (Lijphart 1997). Understanding this participatory inequality becomes important given that gender differences in political engagement could reproduce gender inequalities in other domains as well. Thus, systematic and persistent patterns of unequal participation along existing lines of stratification, such as gender, are threats to both political equality and democratic performance (Coffe and Bolzendahl 2011). Because political participation is a central component of democracy as well as a means for achieving greater equality, gender inequalities in political participation may both reflect and further reify gender stratification throughout society (Verba et al. 1997).

POLITICAL STATUS OF WOMEN IN NAGALAND

One of the most paradoxical aspects of democratic representation in Nagaland is the absence of women in elected office. Women constitute 48.21 per cent of the population of the state (2011 Census) and in sheer numbers women constitute nearly half of the electorate in Nagaland (49 %) (Government of Nagaland 2013). However, even after over five decades of statehood, Nagaland remains the only state in India which never had a woman MLA. Therefore in the context of Nagaland, one of the most trying issues in electoral studies is the discourse of women's exclusion from electoral processes. In Nagaland there is a visible trend of men dominating the political terrain, both past and present and across the board. Consequently, the participation and, more so, the representation of women in politics remain negligible. This causes women to remain outside the centre of decision-making in terms of influence and status (Amer 2013).

Thus, it appears that despite the introduction of modern democratic systems in Nagaland and notwithstanding legal provisions of equality enshrined in the Indian Constitution, the political status of Naga women has not improved. The political status of Naga women remain by and large low-profile and unrecognised. Naga women enjoy the right to vote and to be elected to decision-making positions, but such legal provisions have meant little in terms of enhancing their political status. Without meaningful participation and representation of women in politics, vested in principles of parity, it will be impossible to build a truly democratic society.

An important measure of women development is their access to 'voice' in the decision making arena, as measured by their participation in public life. But this they have not; at all levels of the political system, from the State Legislative Assembly down to the Village Councils, women are invisible. This reinforces the perception that electoral politics in Nagaland continues to be dominated by men. A domination that should not really be, because of the almost equal proportion of the two genders in the population. If half of the state's enfranchised population is kept out of the political structures of the state, one cannot talk of democracy in any true sense. Naga women's ongoing demand to participate equally in decision-making is based on the ground that representative democracy means equal opportunities to participate in politics for all citizens regardless of their gender. Parity in terms of representation is also indicative of justice and equality of the society.

Such a situation, as it exists in Nagaland, is common to many male dominated societies, where social as well as political relations and activities are governed by patriarchal systems of socialisation and cultural practices that favour the interests of men above those of women. The quality of democracy in Nagaland would be undermined if half of the population of the state fails to participate fully in political affairs. Therefore, insights into the underlying factors contributing to this phenomenon, and what measures can be taken to mitigate this problem, makes an important area of research and concern, both for achieving gender equality in public life as well as for strengthening representative democracy in Nagaland.

WOMEN AS VOTERS

Voting is the main form of political participation in liberal democratic societies. It is a significant indicator of democratic engagement, a minimal sign of an individual's democratic participation as a citizen, and a useful indicator of the health of any democracy (Franklin 2004). Voting affects the choice of public personnel, is the main mechanism by which representatives are made accountable to the people, and is a means of determining and measuring consensus in a democratic society. However, while women across the globe can be observed in the political process through voting, and while this has a powerful equalising and mobilising effect on them, the act of voting alone is not sufficient to generate political equality (Mitra and James 1992).

High voter turnout during elections is a sign that people are willing to participate in the electoral process. According to the Report on the General Elections to Nagaland Legislative Assembly, Nagaland always recorded high turnouts in Assembly Elections held from 1964 onward (see Table 7). In eight out of the twelve Assembly Elections, women voters outnumbered male voters in terms of turnout. Thus, in almost all the Assembly Elections held in Nagaland, women voters voted at a higher rate compared to male voters.

Table: 7 Gender Difference in Voting in Nagaland Assembly Election, 1964-2013[1]

Year	Voters		Voters who Voted		Polling Percentage		Votes polled in %	Difference in votes polled by male and female
	Male	Female	Male	Female	Male	Female		
1964							76.57	
1969	93829	83102	71751	66907	76.94	80.78	78.75	4.04
1974	224166	176156	161166	136464	72.85	78.50	78.69	2.57
1977	214812	183223	176606	154795	82.24	84.48	83.27	2.27
1982	330290	266163	240272	203700	72.79	76.45	74.44	3.8
1987	319379	262574	266023	225878	83.25	85.96	84.53	2.73
1989	320611	261805	273654	225168	85.32	86.03	85.65	0.66
1993	421250	381661	387446	347489	90.64	89.70	78.95	0.93
1998							47.38	
2003	529477	485364	474181	417316	89.54	85.98	87.84	3.58
2008	666391	635875	573021	549362	85.98	86.39	85.98	0.4
2013	608299	590150	541919	538968	89.74	91.41	90.57	2.24

This shows that, in Nagaland, so to speak, male politicians are voted into power by the power of the women vote. This fact leads one to assume that, if female voters would collectively vote for female candidates, female politicians will be voted into political office. This trend of high turnout by women voters also leads to an important theoretical question, namely: 'are women exercising their basic rights of voting individually and autonomously?' It is pertinent to mention here that the principle of individual vote is a political right given to all citizens in a democracy. The exercise of this right by individual citizens is an important indicator of their response to the political rights conferred on them by the Constitution, while it also constitutes an indicator of citizens' political awareness. At the time of election, Naga women voters may vote for a particular candidate or party, but it is seldom that, as

[1]Source: General Elections to Nagaland Legislative Assembly 1964-2013, Government of Nagaland. The first (1964) and the ninth Assembly Election (1998) have been left out of the analysis due to non-availability of data by gender.

a result of patriarchal socialisation, they exercise franchise independently. There is a general perception that for many women their husband or father influences their choice of candidate or party. Further, male politicians perceive that if they can convince the male household member, the rest of his family will vote accordingly. This leads many political parties to target men rather than women during election campaigns, which reduces the importance of the female vote in the electoral process. Therefore, voting alone cannot be deemed as sufficient to bring political equality to women.

WOMEN AS CANDIDATES

Women's high participation in voting has not been accompanied by a corresponding rise in the number of women as contestants and elected representatives. Electoral success continues to elude women. While improvements in women's educational and professional status, as is the case for Naga women, may be a stimulus for women's empowerment, this is evidently not sufficient to win elected office.

Table 8: Male/Female candidates in the State Assembly Elections 1964-2003[2]

Year of Election	Total No. of Seat			Total No. of Candidate		Total	Percentage		Difference in %
	General	Reserved Tuensang	Total	Contested			Male	Female	
				Male	Fe-male				
1964	40	6	46	87	0	87	---	---	---
1969	40	12	52	142	2	144	98.61	1.39	97.22
1974	60	0	60	217	0	217	---	---	---
1977	60	0	60	203	0	203	---	---	---
1982	60	0	60	244	1	245	99.59	0.41	99.18
1987	60	0	60	211	3	214	98.60	1.40	97.20
1989	60	0	60	144	0	144	---	---	---
1993	60	0	60	177	1	178	99.44	0.56	98.88

[2]Source: Report on the General Elections to Nagaland Legislative Assembly, 1964-2013.

1998	60	0	60	80	0	80	---	---	---
2003	60	0	60	222	3	225	98.67	1.33	97.33
2008	60	0	60	214	4	218	98.17	1.83	96.33
2013	60	0	60	185	2	187	98.93	1.07	97.86
Total				2066	16	2128	97.09	0.75	96.33

The number of women candidates contesting for the State Legislature has been extremely discouraging. Table 8 gives a comparative assessment of the number of male and female candidates contesting in the Assembly Election between 1964 and 2013. In the electoral history of Nagaland, spanning a period of over five decades, only sixteen women contested out of a total of 2128 candidates. None of these sixteen turned out victorious. The difference in percentage between male and female candidates in Nagaland is abnormally high, namely 96.33%. Therefore, unlike their male counterparts, women in Nagaland have not been able to sustain their electoral participation beyond voting.

Political parties in Nagaland accord low priority to women's candidatures. Women often find their efforts to break into politics marginalised by the failure of political parties to recognise and support their viability as candidates. Though political parties have women wings, women are often not recruited to run for elective offices. Another practice of political parties, which marginalises women from politics, is that the few women aspirants that were nominated were given tickets in constituencies in which the party, in any case, had marginal chances of winning. This has been evident in the Assembly Election of 2003 when the NPF party nominated its lone woman candidate to contest against the then Chief Minister (on this particular case, see the Chapter by Kuotsu and Walling, this volume).

Parties are risk averse when it comes to distributing nominations and see women candidates as high risk. They are therefore reluctant to nominate women, especially in constituencies where political contests are tight or where they do not have a strong electoral presence. This implies that 'winnability' has a specifically gendered component – women, by virtue of their gender, are seen as less likely to win elections, and as a result they are less likely to be nominated. If women are deemed less likely to win, parties will not risk winnable seats by nominating women candidates, and in such a scenario (as happens in Nagaland) parties are inclined to nominate women only in hard-to win or unwinnable constituencies.

WOMEN AND POLITICAL PARTIES

Political parties in Nagaland are male-dominated. They have not genuinely taken up the issue of political participation by women, either inside the party through leadership posts or outside the party through candidacy on electoral lists. The gendered nature of political parties is reflected not only in the differential assignment of tasks to men and women, but also in the way men and women are positioned in the party hierarchy, in the process empowering men and women differently. This is reflected by the total absence of women in party leadership and thereby in the influence over party decisions. The exact number of party membership in the state could not be ascertained because many of the political parties do not maintain a proper record of party membership. However, if we look at membership patterns at the top level of party hierarchies the gender gap reveals itself. For instance, in the NPCC State level Working Committee, out of a total of fifty members, only five females hold the post of Secretary. In the list of the office bearers of the State level BJP, out of eighteen members only four are women; two of them were holding the post of Vice President while the other two held the rank of Secretary. Again, amongst NPF State level office bearers out of forty-eight members there was not a single woman member. In the NCP state level committee, finally, out of twenty one members, only two women were holding the post of Secretary.[3]

This data reflects the absence of women, especially at the top level of the party structure. This further indicates the marginalisation of women from the power centres of decision-making in political parties, unlike their male counterparts. The absence of women in decision-making hierarchies of political parties in Nagaland shows that the parties themselves are conservative with regard to notions of gender-equity. In Nagaland, though political parties may verbally champion the cause of women during elections, including commitments to support women in politics, this does not traverse beyond mere speeches, as even party tickets are seemingly issued only to men. This trend is not wholly exclusive to Nagaland, but part of a wider pattern. Globally, women are under-represented in leadership positions within political parties, although they usually constitute between 40 and 50 percent of party members (Balington 2012). Women hold only a limited number of leadership and decision-making positions in these political parties.

All political parties in the state have women wings. However, such

---

[3]Data obtained from different political party Central Offices between February- March, 2015.

committees exist merely for the purpose to activate potential voters. It does not help women in becoming leaders within parties. It is a relatively powerless branch of the party whose role is to mobilise women for meetings and elections. Cornwall and Goetz (2005) argue that 'women's wings' are not intended to provide women with space to emerge as leaders, but instead harness their support for the existing leadership and structures of the party.

Division of labour within the party structure is therefore on the basis of gender. Some Naga women party activists, whom I interviewed, expressed their dissatisfaction with this gendered division of labour within the party structure. The activities of women in party organisation, they opined, are mostly restricted to auxiliary and support roles. They expressed the view that, besides casting their votes, their electoral activities are confined to preparing meals for party workers or to home visitation, which in many cases are to distribute material goods to prospective voters. As such, women party members seemingly get assigned roles deemed compatible with their domestic functions.

Women committees exist just for the purported purpose of activating female voters. It does not develop women political cadres. This has led some to question the internal democracy of Nagaland political parties. Therefore, despite their entry into political parties as members, it is obvious that for Naga women, far from being elevated to positions of decision making, their conventional role of domesticity is actually remapped unto the political arena. This reveals that the spoken commitment of Nagaland political parties to advance the position of women in politics remains just a token.

BARRIERS TO WOMEN'S PARTICIPATION IN POLITICS

There are multiple reasons that explain why women in Nagaland are not able to sustain their participation in electoral activities beyond acts of voting. In assessing this problem one must examine the inter-connections between traditional socio-cultural values and practices that remain firmly entrenched in the existing systems and structures of Naga society. This is because in many cases the culture of a society determines the level of women's participation in the public sphere (Inglehart and Norris 2003).

As a tradition bound society, a plethora of cultural norms, traditions and myths successfully keep women out of the public sphere and politics. Naga culture is still characterised by male dominated structures that are patriarchal in nature and remain driven by tribal customs and traditions that are mostly unfriendly and reluctant to the involvement of women in politics. Therefore, power and authority resides in the hands of men as they were traditionally supposed to control the decision making process.

The predicament in Nagaland is that though society recognizes and advocates the desirability of giving equal opportunities to women in the political sphere, the social mindset regarding women's role in society remains traditional. Women's low participation in electoral activities is often explained by the stereotype of them being 'uninterested' in politics. While there may be a degree of disinterest among women to take part in electoral activities, the reality often overlooked is that, in Nagaland, despite major changes in gender roles in recent decades, women are usually expected to take care of the household and related responsibilities, and at the same time, for some, to handle a full-time job and a career. As a result, the basic responsibilities and patterns of their lives, with its focus on family, often make it impossible for them to sustain their electoral participation beyond voting.

Women are more likely to emerge as political candidates in states that established an early pattern of electing women to the state legislature, support women's participation in public affairs, and do not have a tradition of sex-discrimination in terms of income and gender disparities in educational achievements (Hill 1981). In fact, systematic cross-national evidence shows that egalitarian attitudes towards women as political leaders are strongly related to the proportion of women elected to public office (Norris and Ingelhart 2001). The barriers to women gaining entry into elective offices may lie not so much with the electorate, but by how society as a whole perceives women in public roles. Therefore, a more egalitarian public portrayal of women in political arenas may likely influence both whether women in Nagaland are willing to come forward as candidates for elective office and whether they can win.

The effects of a gendered socialisation should not be underestimated. It works to revitalise and reproduce gendered notions regarding the culturally appropriate place of women and men in political life. Societies in places across the world remain dominated by an ideology of 'a woman's place'. In this ideology, the place of women is situated in the private and apolitical world. Generally, gender role stereotyping is still prevalent and accepted in Naga society. Women and men are conditioned by society to play different roles. Women's main role is largely deemed to be in the household, whereas public and political leadership is conceptualised as the preserve of Naga men. They are projected as leaders with women as their followers. In fact, politics and women are seen as each other's antithesis. Therefore, the electorate as a whole perceives women as less qualified and less suited for politics compared to men and almost invariably vote for male candidates. Such prevailing attitudes towards women contribute to the lack of confidence that many voters have in women candidates, and has become a major barrier to the election of women into elective offices. Therefore, those few women who do have an interest to contest may be reluctant to do so, and those who contested, so far, failed to attract sufficient support to win.

Another reason is the historical exclusion of women from politics and political leadership in the state where women, despite constituting nearly half of the electorate, have been consistently sidelined in public life, to the extent that they never held elective offices. In Nagaland, the elective office and structures of decision-making are male centric. Even after more than five decades of statehood, there has been no woman member in the State Legislature. This indicates that the composition of the highest decision-making body in the state is markedly at odds with the gender make-up of the society. This is a domination that should not really be, because of the almost equal proportion of the two genders in the population. If the definition of democracy allows for participation of different groups in the society, then it cannot thrive by excluding women both in the context of participation as well as representation.

Men dictate, if not control, the public spaces for women and this becomes quite prominent when the subject is politics. The dominance of power in dictating who participates in political life is clearly evident by the recent and ongoing opposition to the 33% reservation of seats for women in local bodies – Municipal and Town Councils - on grounds of cultural rationales and unexamined assumptions. The ongoing opposition to the bill is only one example that illustrates the extent to which women's right to participate in politics is habitually abused, if not sterilised, by the so called 'cultural guards' of Naga society. This further indicates the existence of biases against women taking part in electoral activities. For much of Naga political history, one of the major obstacles to women's participation as candidates and officeholders has been the lack of support for female participation among the general public. The existence of public antipathy has thus operated as a significant limitation on women's political opportunities. Unlike their male counterparts, women do not receive positive reinforcement from the society at large for their participation in politics. Therefore Naga women live with an identity of being marginal, especially in politics.

Over the years electoral competition in Nagaland deteriorated in terms of ethics and values. In Nagaland, the most important factors in electoral politics are now money and muscle power. It is widely believed that elections in Nagaland are considered among the most expensive in the country. Candidates reportedly spend to the extent of Rs.10 crores in some assembly constituencies, and on an average Rs.5 crores in most constituencies (*Nagaland Post* 30-06-2009). Money power is supplemented by unbridled flagrancy in the use of arms by political thugs and party supporters in-spite of a code of conduct committing political parties to non-violence and clean elections. This is one of the reasons explaining why democratic elections in the state are held under massive military presence. Many women may not be prepared to be involved in a political environment which supports an aggressive and combative culture. These phenomena thus contribute to a situation in which women may reject, dissociate, or express reluctance to become a part of muscular style politics. Such a culture may undermine the willingness and enthusiasm, not just of women, but also of men to engage in electoral activities. This kind of electoral environment works to limit, constrain, and exclude women from participation in politics.

Considering the fact that elections over the years have become extremely expensive, female aspirants may not be in a position to muster enough funds to fight elections. Those running for elections usually receive limited financial support from their political party, and therefore must use personal funds for their campaigns, for example to develop campaign materials, travel within the constituency, and host campaigning events. Perhaps most challenging is the fact that candidates are effectively expected to 'buy' support within their constituency by doling out small amounts of money and food to supporters, as well as larger amounts of money or gifts to important people or leaders in the community. These heavy costs present a particular challenge for women, as they tend to have less access to assets than men.

Male candidates may decide to sell off their properties to finance their election bids; however, in contrast, women in Naga society do not have access to such resources. This is because properties mostly exist in the name of the husband or father (see also L. Khiamniungan, this volume). Political parties do not give equal assistance to women candidates compared to their male counterparts, and without financial assistance from the party it becomes difficult to manage an election campaign till Polling Day. Therefore, without the backing of the party machinery it becomes all the more difficult for women candidates to win an election.[4] Women must therefore achieve economic parity before they can ascend to positions of political power and authority (Oakes and Almquist 1993).

---

[4]Rakhila, Political Candidate from Tuensang Sadar II Constituency, Interviewed on 27/02/2015.

CONCLUSION

It is thus apparent that despite the introduction of modern democratic systems for more than five decades and notwithstanding legal provisions of equality enshrined in the Indian Constitution, the political status of Naga women remains by and large low-profile and unrecognised. If the definition of democracy allows for participation of different groups in the society, then it cannot thrive by excluding women. It is apparent that the challenges Naga women face in electoral politics are deep-rooted, accompanied by many inherited cultural and traditional constraints. These social circumstances and the cultural factors play a major role in deciding who play what role in democratic politics. Such constraints subordinate and exclude Naga women from participation in the democratic process. In this context a new ideology of egalitarianism and a positive attitude about women in political role could offset such cultural constraints and limitations.

Women are better represented when political elites acknowledge women's political under-representation and take steps to redress it through appointments. In this connection the political parties of the state have to play a major role because they are crucial in determining the prospects of every citizens aspiring to public office. Political parties should therefore recognise and address the gender deficit in political representation, not just within the party organisation but also in other political bodies.

Groups that have been historically excluded from the political process also have a psychological barrier to participation due to the continued dominance of the more powerful group despite legal equality. In order to overcome their marginality in politics, women themselves have to be assertive of their rights and, more importantly, they will have to overcome the psychology of subordination in politics. If they want a more responsive type of politics, they should be willing to play their part as political participants.

05

DEMOCRATIC VALUES AND TRADITIONAL PRACTICES: GENDERING ELECTORAL POLITICS IN NAGALAND

Renchumi Kikon Kuotsu & A. Wati Walling

INTRODUCTION

Modern democratic practices and values were transported from 'the West' and implanted in the land of the Nagas without preparing them for this new system (Horam 1988: 96).[1] But whereas the western system of democratic

[1] 'Nagas' here refer to the fourteen Naga tribes of Nagaland only. The meaning and origin of the term 'Naga' is sketchy as there are various versions about it. It is popularly believed that when the British encountered people settled in this part of the country, they enquired from their Burmese guides as to whom these people are. The reply of the word 'Naka', meaning 'people with earrings' in Burmese language led the British to record as 'Naga' and thus used subsequently (Nagaland State Human Report 2004: 20). This is only one amongst several explanations given about the word Naga.

governance was founded on principles of individual autonomy, self-expression, and personal freedom, with wider aims of securing both the capitalist market-economy and liberal society (Macpherson 1976:1-45), Naga society was based on traditional values steeped in communitarian ethics. This communitarian ethos of Naga society is significantly shaped around attachments and loyalties of tribes, villages, and clans, as well as by a rigid compartmentalization of gender roles, which privileges males in the public and political spheres of life. Nagas' traditional gender division culminated into the marginalization of women in the modern democratic arena and prevented them from entering the highest decision-making body, which is the Nagaland State Legislative Assembly (On this also see Chapters by Amer and L. Khiamniungan, this volume).

Although democratic institutions, elections, and electioneering processes are a reflection of modernity and rationalization, in Nagaland political leaders are elected based often on traditional practices, principles, and values (Wouters 2014). Even a cursory analysis of democracy in Nagaland shows the absence of women at the helm of decision-making. Rosemary Dzuvichu, a social activist, succinctly calls Naga democracy a 'democracy devoid of women' (cited in *Morung Express* 19-01-2017). This male exclusivity in the State Legislative Assembly is not accidental but a reflection of a society that remains deeply patriarchal. Traditional institutions[2], and their policies and practices, are male-centric, and this disposition remapped itself unto the modern democratic arena, as well as incarcerates 'Naga minds' with citizens following these traditions without questioning them. Consequently, electoral politics across Nagaland operates largely under the influence of traditional ideas and practices, shaped by unwritten laws that are male-centric in form and character. Despite the progress of Naga women in other fields such as education and employment, Naga women are yet to meaningfully engage in the field of democratic politics and gain entry into the state assembly. In recent decades, there has been a surge in theories that attempt to give voice to those sections of society that were long kept in the periphery by writers and historians. This study similarly attempts to give voice to those whose voices often go unheard; in our case these are the voices of women in the context of Nagaland democracy and elections. In what follows, we examine the apparent contradiction between modern democratic ideals and values, and the values of Naga traditional political practices. We do so through the experiences of Naga women who stood for elections in the past. But first

---

[2]Traditional institutions refer to the village pattern of administration based on kinship and clan loyalties. The institutions governing village administration and development have been christened as 'village councils' in modern times.

we situate this debate in a wider Naga context by exploring the position of women in traditional and modern Naga society.

WOMEN AND DEMOCRATIC POLITICS IN NAGALAND

Modern democracy in Nagaland was meant to start in 1952 with the notification of the Parliamentary elections issued by the newly independent Government of India. However, this election was boycotted by Nagas in response to a call given by Naga National Council (NNC) under the leadership of late A.Z. Phizo.[3] In 1957, too, elections were announced but again a boycott was put in place. In this election, three Naga politicians nevertheless filed their nominations and were elected unopposed into the Assam state assembly. The first elections in which Nagas participated was the state elections of 1964, one year after the enactment of Nagaland state. Since then, Nagaland has gone through twelve State Assembly elections, of which eleven were intensively contested and participatory.[4] In most political science literature, people's participation in elections is considered evidence of citizens' faith in democratic institutions, as well as seen as a sign of their political awakening, maturity and the acceptance of the state as an integral part of their lives (Datta 1988: 18). For India particularly, Banerjee (2011: 94) poses that Indian citizens participate enthusiastically in elections because it offers them a liminal period of egalitarianism, as each vote carries equal value, and which sharply contrasts the everyday hierarchical set-up of Indian society in terms of caste, class, and gender.

Contrary to such projections, in Nagaland, the reasons for people coming out to vote in large numbers may be rather different as they are a manifestation of local contests expressed through 'bonds of kinship, historical narratives, village and clan loyalties...monetary offers.'.. (Wouters 2015a: 130). Although Naga women have participated in elections, not a single woman has so far been elected into the state assembly (Jamir 2012; Amer 2013; Ojha 2014). Moreover, the fact that Naga women vote does

[3]A.Z. Phizo is considered as the champion of Naga tribal unification and regarded as 'Father of the Nagas' by the Nagas. Lanunungsang Ao calls him the 'legendary godfather and champion of Naga Nationalism' (Ao 2002: 20).

[4]In 1998, a boycott call of the Assembly elections was given by the Isaac-Muivah Faction of the Nationalist Socialist Council of Nagalim (NSCN IM) with an aim to enhance the working Ceasefire Agreement signed between NSCN (IM) and Government of India in 1997.

not necessarily indicate their autonomy to decide whom they cast their vote to. As we will show, Naga women are often made to follow the voting-instructions of male-dominated customary bodies or from their male family-members. The absence of Naga women in political decision-making is such that till the 12th General election, held in 2013, Naga women contested only sixteen times (out of which three women contested twice) with none of them turning victorious. In comparison, men have contested 1960 times till the last election held in 2013.[5] The ratio between male and female contests in the state assembly elections therefore amounts to 124:1. Clearly there is a marked gender divide.

The population of Nagaland, as per the 2011 census is 1,978,508, out of which women comprise 942,895, which makes for 47.65% of the state's population.[6] In the educational and professional spheres, Naga women today hold significant and senior positions. Their social progress measures rather favourable compared to many of their counterparts in places across India. Not so, however, when it comes to their political participation and status. In this realm, Nagaland sits at the very bottom. To illustrate, women in Bihar are known to suffer from low socio-economic and educational statuses, which, according to Sinha (2007: 238), is the result of myriad social ills that are of historical, economic, cultural and political nature. But even though Bihar has one of the most worrying female literacy rates in India, is has the distinction of electing a significant number of women into its assembly. This observation makes it all the more pertinent to ask what holds Naga women back from entering the political domain?

NAGA WOMEN AS 'MUTE BEINGS'

The predicament of women leadership is widely discussed among Nagas today. Not just in politics, but also among church-organisations. Akin to women's secondary ecclesiastical position in places across the globe, Naga women are regularly denied leadership in Nagaland churches. Till date, the number of Naga female pastors remains easily countable. It can be argued that, besides doctrinal beliefs and the motherhood role of women, this

[5]Source: Statistical Reports on General Elections to the Nagaland Legislative Assembly, 1969-2013.

[6]Source: www. Census 2011. Co.in/Census/State/Nagaland.html Accessed 11-12-15

exclusion traces back to Nagas' traditional practices and its exclusionary politics vis-à-vis women in the public domain.[7]

Although there is no official act or document that declares Nagaland a Christian State, given that the state has the highest percentage of Christians in the country,[8] and given that Christian discourse and rhetoric inundates the public sphere, the state is popularly known as a Christian State (Lotsuro 2000: 94). Those who advocate a more prominent role of Naga women in this Christian state invoke Biblical teachings such as Apostle Paul's exhortation on equality between the Jews and Greeks, slaves and free, and men and women through Christ (Galatians 3:28). Measured by actual participation and achievements, contributions of female members to Nagaland churches is certainly no less than men's, if not more. A Naga pastor commended thus: 'On all occasions, be it in the church programs or attendance in the church services, women outnumber men'.[9]

The Government of Nagaland, in turn, put on record, in an official document, the many contributions made to society by the women wings of churches in view of social empowerment (Nagaland State Human Report 2004: 55). The position of inequality Naga women nevertheless face in church ministries seemingly results from a fusion between the 'patriarchal domain' of Christianity (James 2010: 23) and the 'patriarchal-culture of the Nagas' (Longkumer 2010: 32). In the words of Neinu:

> Many Naga Christians and church leaders have misinterpreted Bible texts like Eph 5: 22-23... and 1 Tim 2: 11-12... and used these texts to support male dominance and women subordination (cited in *Morung Express*: 08-03-2017).[10]

Hence, while equality between men and women is part of Biblical teachings, in actual practice 'women are not given the same status and leadership in the church...' (Longkumer in Hnuni 1999: 56). Many Naga women resent the ecclesiastical arrangements that deny them roles of leadership. While some Naga women do occasionally preach from pulpits,

---

[7]An interview with Dr. Lovely Awomi James at Eastern Theological College, Jorhat on 17th Jan, 2017.

[8]90% of the Nagas are Christians.

[9]Group interaction at Urban Area A.

[10]Eph 5: 22-23, 'Wives, be subject to your husband as you are to the Lord. For the husband is the head of the wife...' 1 Tim 2: 11-12, 'Let women learn in silence with full submission. I permit no woman to teach or to have authority over men: she is to keep silent'.

one woman church leader qualified: 'The show of equality between men and women in church pulpits is only superficial'.[11] When we raised this point during our fieldwork, a young male church leader offered an alternative view, stating: 'Many a time, women themselves refuse to speak up even when they are given the platform'.[12]

It is thus alleged that Naga women themselves prefer to remain 'mute beings', or perhaps are hesitant to make their feelings known in the public arena. This became evident on numerous occasions during our fieldwork. In a group discussion involving men and women in *Yizulei* village,[13] most of the women in the meeting remained silent throughout, even though many of them were leaders of the village Women Welfare Society.[14] When we solicited their views on the absence of women in the State Assembly, and about their views regarding why so few Naga women contest elections, one of the females present replied, with considerable hesitation:

> *Maiki khan etu nakoribi, maiki khan tate najabi, maiki khan chupchap thakibi tu bishi ase. Basti laka pithor te bhi khushi bara kubule jabule nati-e le, state election tu kineka bhabhibu na'* (There is a lot of: women don't do that, women don't go there, women keep quiet. When we are not allowed to speak and go out freely even within our village, how can we think of the state election?)

To this, an elderly man replied: 'When we allow our women to go out, they become oversmart'.[15]

---

[11]An excerpt from an interview with a woman church leader on 28th Nov, 2016 at Zila town.
Note: Similar to the situation of women outside the church, 'the show of equality' here refers to the silence of women in the sense of them not openly protesting the inequality that prevails in the church set-up.

[12]All names, both of places and persons, in this article are pseudonyms. At Tajungyim village on 29-5-2016.

[13]Group discussion on 20-3- 2016 at Yizulei village.

[14]Women Welfare Societies are women associations that look into women's issues within villages. For instance, the women representatives to the Village Development Boards (VDBs) are selected by this body. They are also in-charge of the funds sanctioned for women by the VDBs with prior permission of the VC.

[15]The word 'oversmart' here denotes a negative gesture, implying that women become loose if given freedom. This expression seems in line with the universal sexual description that surrounds women narratives.

In another village,[16] the Chairman of the Village Council (VC) explained that women are not involved in decision-making within the village because they were not taught the art of administration in the *morung* of the olden days.[17] We further found that many village men believed that women's mental capabilities were lower compared to those of men, with them often quoting 'age-old' proverbs in their support. In fact, many Naga tribes have proverbs that club women and children together, implying that their mental development is the same. For example, the Aos say *'anung noza'* (women and children), a tag that seemingly communicates that women cannot be entrusted with certain responsibilities because they are 'like children'. Similarly, Lothas say *'eloe nonghori'*, also clubbing children and women together and matching their mental abilities.

The segregation of gender roles further reveal themselves in the claim that men perform heavier chores, involving physical strength, leaving the lighter chores to women. This, many Naga males opine, is practiced out of love and consideration for women's perceived 'weaker' physique. This 'benevolent act' might be appreciated at one level. At another, however, this 'benevolence' readily turns into a patronizing ideology, or is invoked to justify the exclusion of women in the public domain. From this, we may infer that 'episteme violence' is committed upon Naga women with them being considered 'domesticated beings'.[18] The questions that emerge are these: 'can we interpret Naga women's muteness as an internalised acceptance of a status quo that disadvantages them? 'Are they oppressed without them even realising this?' Or, 'are they kept "in their place" through active institutions and practices that promote male dominance?'

MALE-CENTRIC TRADITIONAL POLITIES

Nagas often claim that they practiced homespun democratic governance in villages from the time of their forefathers. Nagas' traditional political life was indeed lauded as 'egalitarian' and utterly 'democratic' by several colonial administrators and early anthropologists during the British period. Butler,

---

[16]Interaction with Chairman and Members of the Village Council at Tajungyim village on 29-5-2016.

[17]Morung is a bachelors' dormitory practiced in the olden days where young boys were taught the art of warfare and village administration.

[18]The terms 'episteme violence' and 'domesticated' are borrowed from Gayatri Chakravorty Spivak (1988).

for one, wrote about the Angami Naga, that they possess 'a form of the purest democracy' (cited in Hutton 1921: 143). For the Ao Naga, Davis, in turn, wrote: 'Each village amongst the Aos is a small republic, and each man is as good as his neighbour, indeed, it would be hard to find anywhere else more thoroughly democratic communities' (cited in Elwin 1969: 325). Regarding the Lothas, it was commented that they were 'exceedingly democratic in their village customs. Headmen have little or no power, and every man does as it seems best to him' (ibid: 352). Fürer-Haimendorf (1939: 15), in turn, had this to say: '...villages were run on a strictly democratic lines and no one could command his neighbours'.[19] Such depictions, however, rather blatantly ignored the gender-divide that existed in Naga traditional village democracies.

On one hand, patriarchal practices of Nagas was justified as an 'unprejudiced system', one that was 'neither authorised nor imposed by the patriarchal community' and one 'that allows women to maximize their skills and participate in socio-cultural and economic spheres' (Shimray 2002: 377). One the other hand, it can be seen that in traditional village set-ups, men ventured outside by keeping their women confined to the domestic sphere as a result of the socio-cultural and economic system prevalent at that time. Naga traditional practices surrounding administration, religion and rituals, feasts of merits and social prestige, as well as the past prevalence of a 'slave system' indicate notable social segregation with unequal distributions of 'power, prestige and privilege' (Ovung 2012: 23). Ovung continues: 'Social stratification in terms of age, gender, clan, religion and occupation has been in existence since time immemorial'.

As for colonial writers, their reference to an 'egalitarian' Naga society was based on the way men and women freely interacted with each other during festivals, which differed from the way they had observed the role of women in other parts of India. However, 'what happens in day to-day life is different from the festivities' (Imchen and Nienu 2012: 9). Hence, the much hyped traditional 'equality', as written about by colonial writers and reproduced by postcolonial Naga scholars, prevailed only between men as each male member was counted as equal. It, most certainly, did not prevail between the genders.

On the whole, the traditional Naga system of governance was strictly male-oriented. But few, if any, females participated in political decision-making, even as mere participants. On this, Latham writes about Naga village administration: 'His [Nagas] government is so pre-eminently patriarchal'

---

[19]Naga tribes like the Konyaks and Sumis practiced hereditary chieftainship, however.

(cited in Elwin 1969: 97). As such, Nagas' traditional democracy was vested in a male-centric democratic village polity, one that rendered women 'voiceless' in public and political life. This is the traditional undergrowth in which modern democratic institutions and practices unfolded in Nagaland.

CULTURAL PRODUCTION OF POLITICAL LEADERSHIP IN NAGALAND

While there is a clear need to study Naga women's political participation from a multi-dimensional approach, the remainder of this chapter concentrates first and foremost on the impact, or reproduction, of Naga traditional practices on post-statehood electoral politics. It explores how these practices work to relegate women's efforts in electoral politics to unsuccessful results.

The traditional Naga practice of 'representation' in village administration has always been a male-oriented system that was structured on kinship and clan loyalties. After acquiring statehood, in 1963, Nagaland was made to adopt the representative system of democratic governance as prescribed by India's Constitution. This system appreciates the British model of representative democracy based on participatory, competitive elections and universal adult franchise, thus providing the opportunity to citizens to exercise their choice in matters of governance. However, Nagas have not been able to break away from old practices generated by traditions, and have infused the modern democratic arena with primordial and partisan practices and loyalties. This form of democracy encountered in Nagaland has been christened by Wouters (2015a) as 'polythetic democracy', that is the ways Nagas have given their own culturalist meanings and interpretations to modern democratic institutions and elections. For centuries, Nagas led mostly secluded lives, except for occasional interaction with the Assamese, until their encounter with the British colonial government from 1832 onward. In their isolation, the code of conduct that developed in terms of village administration allowed only men to participate. The after-effects of this traditional system are felt in the present-day.

The Naga village system of administration is something the British did not wish to interfere with. Instead, they promulgated, at least in principle, a policy of 'non-interference'. Moreover, after India's Independence, Nagas were allowed to continue their traditional modes of administration. This was ratified, in the post-statehood era, by the Village and Area Council Act of 1978. The Village Chairperson (VC), assisted by the Village Council, was bequeathed with the authority to oversee village administration and development. The influence and power of the VC, and his council, does not end here. In terms of modern elections, he can direct villagers to behave and vote in a particular way. This often shows itself in the selection of so-called community or village consensus candidates,[20] community voting, a ban on the entry of rivalling candidates in the village, or in disallowing certain campaigns and the canvassing of supporters belonging to rival candidates within the village. These are just a few of the practices regularly imposed by Village Chairpersons and Councils during state elections.

Such tactics are considered to be tickets to success for candidates who find the favour of the Village Council. To illustrate, in the 2008 state assembly elections, the village consensus candidate from *Dangor* village received support en-masse from the village community, leading to his victory. Initially, after speculation about a rift in the family of the candidate, as his father-in-law was also keen to contest the election, the consensus candidate asserted that there was no misunderstanding in the family as he, and not anyone else, had been chosen by the village community. While such tactics are widely reported in Naga villages, what is intriguing is that when the same tactics are applied in favour of female candidates (that, too, initiated by men), the practice of collective village voting seems to falter, or certainly does not produce the same enthusiasm among village voters.

To validate this point, we will discuss, in some detail, the experiences of two women candidates, both of whom were selected by their community to stand for state assembly elections. Both candidates met the same fate: they lost the election. It may be pointed out, here, that one of the women candidates belonged to a non-Naga indigenous tribe of Nagaland. The inclusion of the experiences of a non-Naga woman candidate will also cover several other dynamics at play in Nagaland democratic politics.

DECIPHERING ELECTORAL POLITICS

An elderly Naga woman,[21] whom we shall call Susan, belonging to one of Nagaland's so-called advanced tribes,[22] twice contested the State Assembly

---

[20]The term 'consensus-candidate' refers to a candidate chosen by the village community under the leadership of the VC.

[21]Interview with Ms. Susan assisted by her daughters on 28-5-2016.

[22]The Naga tribes belonging the districts of Mon, Kiphire, Longleng, Peren, Phek, and Tuensang are considered as 'backward', and are accorded with special privileges/quotas for employment opportunities in the state government. The rest of the Naga tribes inhabiting Nagaland are considered as advanced tribes.

elections. Her personal experiences in doing so will illustrate the male-biased cultural milieu in which electoral politics operate. The first time Susan contested was in 1983. Back then, she was selected by the Village Council as the village's consensus candidate. At that time, the sitting MLA belonged to one of the constituency's smallest villages, while Susan's village was a comparatively large one. Among Nagas, the affective reality of village defines one's identity, to the extent that common courtesy requires that one first inquires to which village a person belongs when making new acquaintances. A village that produces a political leader is given special recognition and status, and, therefore, having a fellow-villager elected into the assembly is considered a matter of great pride for Naga villages.[23] Susan's village considered it below their dignity to have been defeated by a candidate from a small village during the previous election, and now wanted to ensure that electoral success would return to their homes.

Susan's own brother had stood for elections in the past. However, for reasons we don't have space to expand on, the Village Council considered that Susan would stand a better chance of winning than her brother. Susan was selected as the village consensus candidate on the grounds that, first, she had displayed an eagerness to help people, and, secondly, because her deceased husband had been a pioneering politician in the state. Susan's father, however, could not accept the fact that her daughter, rather than his son, was chosen as the village consensus-candidate, and subsequently refused to endorse or aide his daughter's election campaign. This considerably affected her chances of winning the election.

Susan's second experience with electoral politics occurred in 2003 when leaders from the most prominent regional party in Nagaland approached her to contest against one of the most powerful politicians in the state. The deeper rationale behind the party approaching her, however, was that there seemed no-one willing to contest against him, as his leadership was seen as 'undisputable'. The party, however, calculated that if he were to win uncontested, it would hurt the reputation and stature of the party. After her earlier encounter with the ills of elections (more below), Susan had become disillusioned and initially refused to stand as a candidate. In her desperation, she turned to another politician, from her own tribe, to save her from the situation. This politician, however, told her: 'Oya (elder sister),

---

[23]This is evident from the popular practice of the Nagas to publish congratulatory notes to fellow villagers for their achievements through the daily newspapers. Such notes carry contents thanking 'Mr. /Ms So and So' for enhancing the village's prestige, and bringing laurels to the village, etc.

just carry the cross'.[24]

With party leaders insisting, she eventually acquiesced and stood for elections a second time. As for her male relatives, they again discouraged her to contest, this time by saying that it will be an embarrassment to the family as she would certainly lose. Yet again, they failed to extend their support to her. Besides her family, a few women, some of whom were local leaders, also challenged her: 'Why are you going against men?' The fact she was taking on a candidate who was widely revered by the community did not go down well. Soon, she was considered an enemy of her own tribe and talked about as 'a friend of another tribe'. Despite such negative reactions, there were some women who came out in her support, however, and donated in kind and cash towards Susan's election expenses. We now analyse Susan's experiences in terms of three factors: patriarchy, tradition, and gender, even as these three factors regularly overlap and interlink rather than constituting distinct dimensions.

The Patriarchy Factor

When Susan was denied support by both her father and brother in her first election bid, it was 'family-politics', based on emotions, that jeopardised her campaign. Among Nagas, it is common practice that family-affiliations determine one's political allegiance, and members of the same family rarely support different candidates. For example, many families in *Chandenyan* village voted for a particular candidate hailing from their village for 40 years continuously, simply based on the practice of family and village-based politics and loyalties. In such circumstances, the actual political achievements and failures of a candidate becomes a non-issue. Political performance, in such cases, is clearly not the yardstick by which villagers decide whom to cast their votes for.

Had the village consensus candidate been not Susan, but her brother her father would have adopted a different strategy. He would, for instance, likely have influenced a particular cousin, known for his wealth, to extend his support. But this he refused to do for Susan. Moreover, the support of family and clansmen, which her father could have effectuated, would have strengthened her electoral base. But this, too, did not happen. This shows that Susan failed to garner enough family-support because, in large measures, of the patriarchy factor, or her father's wish to see his son, not his daughter, contesting. On being asked about the biggest challenge she faced while contesting this election, Susan said: 'the fact that my cousin-

---

[24]Interview with Ms. Susan.

brother, after first promising to help me, was dissuaded to back out'. When the Village Council selected her as the consensus-candidate, and given that she had no money of her own to spend, she had initially approached her wealthy cousin and suggested that he should contest instead of her.[25] But even though he had political ambitions, he decided against it because the sitting MLA happened to be related by marriage. Was he to contest, he thought, this would lead to ruptures within the family.

It can be argued that the selection of a consensus candidate by the Village Council goes against the grain of free and fair elections. This, however, has proven to be an effective strategy for the purpose of winning elections n Nagaland. When the selected candidate is a male, villagers seem to have no qualms about supporting this candidate with their collective votes. But this did not happen in Susan's case. While patriarchy may not have been the sole reason for Susan's failure to garner collective support, she nevertheless reflected on her experience: 'Men think that everything is theirs'.[26]

As for the family-equation after the elections, Susan's daughter reflected: 'The bad feeling continued for a long time'. This 'bad feeling' related to two things: on the part of the father-brother duo that their daughter/sister was selected, and on part of Susan that she did not receive any support from them.

The Tradition Factor

The narrative on Susan's encounter with electoral politics also demonstrates how traditional Naga values conflict with democratic values of individual choice and free and fair elections. First, the preference for male progeny in Naga families can be discerned from the way Susan's father refused to support his daughter. He resented that she was preferred by the Village Council over his son. The Village Council, certainly, had taken a leap by selecting a female candidate, as doing so went against the traditional preference for males in the political arena. Secondly, Susan's experience shows how culture makes things work differently for Naga men and women, placing women at a disadvantageous position in electoral politics. Here the traditional Naga value of attachment to one's village also comes into play, as shown by the Village Council's decision to opt for a consensus-candidate rather than allowing villagers to deliberate their votes individually and autonomously. This also

[25]As in other states in India, elections in Nagaland are costly affairs, involving huge expenses. In such a scenario, candidates without a strong financial position only have a small chance to win.

[26]Interview with Ms. Susan.

indicates the prestige and power the Village Council holds. But while Village Council decisions cannot be easily defied, the Council's subsequent failure to garner unity in the village behind Susan's candidature also shows that a Village Council cannot always control its villagers' behaviour.

Thirdly, the Naga practice of clan-alignment for electoral victory did not happen in this case, and when the wealthy and well-known cousin-brother refused to help Susan, the advantage went to a male candidate from another village. Fourthly, Susan's case highlights that right from the family, as a result of socialisation, women are not encouraged to enter into the political realm. Though the image of Naga society as egalitarian remains evocative, in actual practice socio-cultural patterns exclude women from the mainstream, so precluding them from equal participation in the political sphere. This is done by systematically denying them opportunities based on, and strengthened by, traditional values immersed in patriarchy, which allows only males to become chiefs and members in the Village Council based on patrilineal clanship (Jamir 2009: 19).

The Gender Factor

The way the political party treated Susan after persuading her to contest, just to save the image of the party, represents the way women are being treated by political parties in Nagaland, which is as 'secondary'. Recounting what had transpired between her and the party leaders, Susan commented: 'when the situation is bad, it comes to women'. Influenced by the patriarchal Naga culture, the functioning of political parties in Nagaland remains highly male-centric. On both occasions, Susan recalled that supporters of the rival candidate applied tactics of violence and instigating fear to disrupt her election campaign.

As for Susan's party, it failed to give her any importance after the election ended, even though she contributed to the success of the party in a critical way. Initially, the constituency from which Susan contested was to have only one candidate, who was the leader of the (then) ruling party. However, with her candidature, this politician was mostly confined to his constituency, making it harder for him to campaign in other constituencies to help his party's candidates there. As the face of his party, his inability to campaign across Nagaland bore negative results on the performance of his party, and thus benefitted the regional party that had put up Susan.

In a questionnaire we distributed to evaluate the attitude of political parties towards women, one question assessed whether women receive sufficient support from political parties during elections. Out of 420 respondents, 211 responded negatively, 64 respondents gave a positive answer, while the remaining 145 respondents held the view that women received support only to an extent. Further, on being asked why women were not given preference and support by political parties, out of five options provided, 251 respondents ticked: 'Naga traditions' as the main reason, followed, with 130 respondents, by the option 'attitude of political parties that women will not win'. It is believed that only when the party position is not stable in a particular constituency the party-ticket may be given to a woman (Jamir 2012; Ojha 2014).

Secondly, it is to be noted that even before electioneering starts, Susan's male relatives predicted that she would lose the election. This indicates that though there may be some Naga women with political ambitions, there remains a lack of support even from their own relatives. This is not to generalize the attitude of all male relatives, as, in our fieldwork, we also came across women candidates who narrated how their families portrayed no reservations towards their political ventures, but offered their full support.[27] Thirdly, the negative mind-set towards women in Nagaland politics was further made obvious by the remark that Susan was 'competing against men'. This notion of 'women against men' is a cliché uttered to imply that leadership and authority belongs to men alone. It is a statement oriented by culture and the particularistic socialisation of women in Naga society.

TRIBAL IDENTITY AND MASCULINE POLITICS

The experiences of another woman, whom we shall call Rachel, also offer insights into Nagas' traditional and cultural dispositions towards electoral politics.[28] Rachel belongs to one of the indigenous non-Naga tribes of Nagaland. When we met her, she narrated how the strength of her tribe, in terms of population, has reduced drastically compared to earlier times, as her tribe was the original inhabitants, and, hence, a major tribe in the area.[29] It was with the aim of regaining some of the community's past prestige and political position that tribal leaders resolved to select a consensus-candidate,

[27]Interview with women candidates; Ms. Suzie on 19-3-2016; Ms. Rosie on 22-4-2016; Ms. Jane on 28-5-2016; Ms. Leslie on 26-7-2016.

[28]Interview with Ms. Rachel on 24-4-2016.

[29]The tribe presented here belongs to an indigenous and earlier settlers of Dimapur. E.R. Grange in 1840 has recorded that 'Dhemapore' was their 'country once upon a time'. The reason for their diminishing population in present-day Dimapur is recorded as 'their innocence and simplicity of character' (Elwin 1969: 36).

and which Rachel became. She was chosen by the Council on the basis of her active involvement in the community's welfare. She was also the advisor of her community's women organisation, and therefore widely known. Moreover, she possessed the credentials of being the first women Village Council Chairperson in Nagaland.

Although Rachel accepted the decision of her community to contest as their consensus-candidate, she was acutely aware that she would not win for a number of reasons. First, she had no money, which was a fallout from the patriarchal set-up of her community which does not bestow property rights on women. Secondly, Rachel was aware of the Naga mind-set and its male-bias in politics. She had travelled across the state when her husband was a state government official. During such visits, she had interacted widely with Naga males, who had told her several times that Nagas do not allow their women to lead in public. Thirdly, there was tribalism, one of the most powerful political tools in Nagaland, and which, indeed, crept into the case of Rachel's political venture. During her campaign, Rachel was intimidated by a particular Naga National Political Group (NNPG), which was in favor of a male Naga candidate in the constituency.[30] They asked her to withdraw her candidature, which made the situation tricky for her. She recounted her ordeal thus:

> They took me to their camp twice, asking me to withdraw my candidature or to surrender my votes in favour of another candidate. When I refused to oblige to their demands, they asked from me a ransom of one lakh rupees but I refused to pay up as I was not contesting on my own volition.[31]

Although Nagas are known to be accommodative in nature and hospitable, they sometimes discriminate others as being 'different' from them. Nagas often apply terms like 'local' and 'non-local' to separate between indigenous Nagas and other peoples. This is, certainly in parts, because Nagas have gone through bitter experiences as the result of the Naga independence Movement and the counter-insurgency tactics adopted by

---

[30]Most people are familiar with the nexus that operates between the NNPGs and politicians in Nagaland. For some time now, there is a parallel government running in Nagaland with the 'NNPG's' openly flouting their presence in the day to day life of the Nagas. They also meddle in electoral politics through different tactics like intimidation, violence, booth capturing etc., where experiences have shown that those politicians having the blessings of the NNPGs are most likely to win without much hurdles.

[31]Interview with Ms. Rachel.

Indian military and paramilitary forces.[32] These experiences unite Nagas as being 'one people', despite their internal differences, and have given them the 'Naga identity', in which they take much pride.[33] According to the Naga disposition, Rachel belonged to the non-local category. On this account, the reason a Naga underground faction asked Rachel to withdraw from contesting was not solely on the ground of electoral politics. We can infer this from Rachel's own explanation: 'At times, I feel that the Nagas consider us as an enemy'.[34] She was also of the view that her electoral ambitions did not go well with many Nagas. When Rachel was the Chairperson of the Village Council, her Naga male colleagues told her bluntly: '*Ami khan tu maiki khan ke leader kuribu nati-e* (We do not allow our women to be leaders)'.

In Nagaland, generally, the practice of clan-alignment in rural villages transforms into tribe-alignment in towns. The attachment of Nagas to one's clan in matters of 'representation' in the village administration thus takes the shape of tribal affinities during elections held in multi-tribal urban settings. Hence, a community that does not preponderate numerically in a town has little or no chance of winning in an urban constituency inhabited by several tribes. Such affective clan and tribal alignments call to mind Guha and Spivak's (1988: 31) elaboration that, in patriarchal and patrilineal societies, women have no permanent clan, even though the progeny of clans comes through women. Since Naga women are not carriers of clan-lineages, the practice of clan and tribal politics in Nagaland make things more difficult for all female political aspirants. As for Rachel, she was doubly marginalised because she was a non-Naga and a woman. At the same time, the interference of the NNPGs in electoral politics further sabotaged her position.

WHERE ARE THE WOMEN IN THE NAGA DEMOCRACY POLITY?

The Nagas have succeeded in giving a cultural tone to democracy, retailoring it 'according to their own cultural values and traditional polities' (Wouters 2014: 65), but this is a cultural tone that does not promote gender equity.

---

[32]The Nagas are engaged in one of the most protracted and longest movement for an independent homeland in South East Asia.

[33]It is an open knowledge that the many Nagas do not consider themselves to be Indians even after so many years of their formal association with the Indian State since statehood in 1963.

[34]Interview with Ms. Rachel.

This phenomenon, of democracy and culture mixing, has also been theorised by Michelutti (2007: 643), in her study of the Yadavs' political participation and status in Uttar Pradesh as the 'vernacularization' of democracy. She showed how democratic politics 'have been gradually moulded by folk understandings of "the political" which in turn energize popular politics' (Michelutti 2007: 642). Transposing Micheluttti's argument to the electoral politics of Nagas, it emerges that through historically and socially embedded 'practices' derived from Naga culture, kinship structures, and values Nagas designed systems and sentiments of democratic practices that are different from other states in India. Looking at democratization processes in Nagaland through the prism of democracy's inherent 'vernacularization' helps 'to explain the dynamics of popular politics, which on many occasions develop in political and non-political spaces which are far removed from theories of liberal democracy but which are nonetheless grounded in local folk understandings and practices of democracy' (Michelutti 2007: 654). In a highly contextualised, culturally embedded study of Nagaland elections, Wouters (2014: 65) showed how 'different Naga tribes, instead of adjusting themselves to modern democratic ideals, they have adjusted democracy to themselves'. In this way, Nagas practice modern democracy while holding on to their traditional practices. One of these traditional practices that remapped itself unto the modern democratic arena is the exclusion of women from the public and political spheres.

Looking at the way elections are being conducted in Nagaland, as we have done in this chapter, shows how the whole process upturns concepts and ideals of representative democracy. In an interaction with a group of women respondents in *Tajungyim* village regarding their franchise, one respondent replied: 'How can we talk about this [voting behaviour]. This is a secret'. During interviews in public, most of the women respondents replied that that they cast votes on their own during elections. However, in the questionnaire given out to the same group, many of them responded negatively to the same question. An elderly woman respondent wrote thus: 'Elections have never been conducted freely and fairly in our village'.[35] The crux of the matter here is not so much the mode of electioneering adopted in Nagaland but a set of other questions. Firstly, why were the women considering the electioneering process in the village a 'secret'? It is apparent that what the womenfolk considered being 'secret' pertains the electioneering practices of the Nagas, which contrast liberal democratic ideals of 'secret balloting', 'free and fair elections', and the maxim of 'One Man, One Vote'. In Nagaland, some locally invented electioneering practices have become

---

[35]A comment passed by an elderly woman in Tajungyim village.

almost synonymous with the idea of an 'election'. Among these are the open declarations of village consensus candidates and the collective voting for a particular candidate, household-voting system performed by the eldest male member in the family on the pretext that it saves time, and voting according to the dictates of clan-unions (though not practiced by all tribes).[36]

These 'unique' practices are accorded acceptance in Naga political life as they have been defined and shaped by their culturalist orientations and are sanctioned by Naga customary bodies and practices. However, in all these instances, women have been rendered voiceless and are made to adhere to what is being decided by male-leaders. The comments of women in the field reflect women's awareness as well as their helplessness about the electioneering processes.

Another quandary concerns the possible reason for them saying different things in public and private. This apparent desire of women respondents to give an honest answer in a private, anonymous questionnaire after first saying something else in public needs explanation. This prompted us to examine the position and space from where our women respondents spoke. When they remained silent in the midst of men, or said something different in public from what they actually thought, it is their silence that may become their 'agency'. It is in their silence that we can find that something is not right with the publicly made claim that males and females are treated equally. Many women – both educated and uneducated – shared that they are being branded as 'feminists', 'outlaws' or 'rebels', as well as of their husbands being looked down upon as 'henpecked', whenever they speak for the need of gender justice and equality in Naga society. For such reasons, and more, it has become the 'choice' of many women to remain silent, not only in the social and political spheres but even in ecclesiastical affairs (as discussed above) of the Nagas. Such social processes and stereotyping seemingly has a conditioning effect on Naga women, and is a reason behind why they may accept the status quo of being disadvantaged. The prevalence of the notions 'good woman' / 'bad woman' in Naga society, from a cultural perspective, is not just imagination, but formulate authoritative projections that work to quell women's political ambitions and aspirations. So, then, who is a 'good woman'? According to a female respondent,[37] 'A good woman is not supposed to speak in public and is expected to bear all the brunt meted out to her in silence'.

---

[36]Read Wouters (2014).

[37]Interview with women social workers on 24-3-2016 at Wei village.

CONCLUSION

In Nagaland, when it comes to the electioneering process, several dynamics involving both cultural and modern democratic practices come together. The interplay of these factors works to disadvantage Naga women in terms of their political participation. Kikon (2002: 180) writes: 'While women are expected to be politically active as men, they have less access to the political space associated with the dynamics of power'. Naga cultural orientations have long kept women out of the public domain of decision-making (Jamir 2012: viii) due to 'the patriarchal forces and structures' (Kikon 2002: 175). Lamenting that 'most men in Naga society are yet to fully accept the idea of having women in leadership role', Ojha (2014: 50) attributes this reluctance on part of Naga males to Naga traditions. Ojha argues that this is a prime cause explaining the adverse outcome of women candidates in elections. In this way, women remain 'outsiders' in politics in Nagaland (Amer 2014: 91). Women, in this way, comprise 'the Other' in the field of democracy in Nagaland. When Nagas insist that their traditional cultural practices justify the marginal position of Naga women in politics, and do so by invoking Article 371(A)[38] of the Indian Constitution, the 'Other' is obliterated 'not only by ideological and scientific production, but also by the institution of law' (Spivak 1988: 281). The insistence on Naga traditions and culture in performing contemporary democracy places women in a complicated position, and creates a glass ceiling in terms of their political participation. This is rather startling in modern democracy where the worth of an individual is to be measured by any person's, both male and female, own abilities without any traditional or societal obstacles.

---

[38]Article 371(A) was inserted in the Indian constitution in recognition of the distinct cultures and traditions of the Nagas pertaining to civil and criminal justice and ownership of land and natural resources.

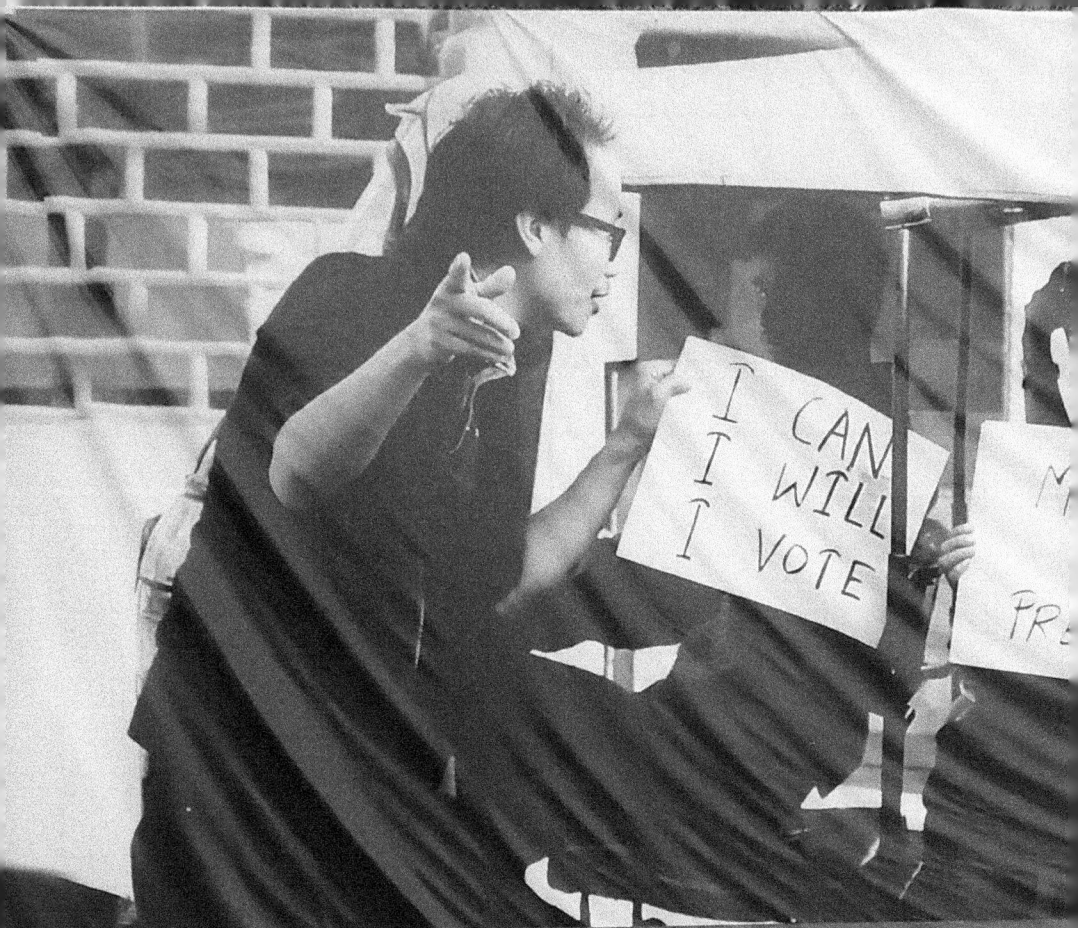

I CAN
I WILL
I VOTE

my VOTE makes

Issued by
OFFICE OF THE CHIEF ELECTORAL OFFICER, NAGALAND

06

PERFORMING DEMOCRACY IN NAGALAND: PAST POLITIES AND PRESENT POLITICS

Jelle J. P. Wouters

INTRODUCTION

Electoral politics, traditions and culture interrelate in complex ways, and this relationship is not always easy to discern; it is often elusive, but always present. Clifford Geertz (1973: 311) recognised this long ago; 'One of the things that everybody knows but no one can quite think how to demonstrate', he postulated, 'is that a country's politics reflects the design of its culture'. Geertz continued, in his distinctive prose, 'on the one hand, everything looks like a clutter of schemes and surprises; on the other, like a vast geometry of settled judgments'. He then concluded, a little dismayed, 'What joins such a chaos of incident to such a cosmos of sentiment is often extremely obscure, and how to formulate it is even more so'. In this chapter, I attempt, rather optimistically, to elucidate some of this 'extreme obscurity', even though I am not talking, like Geertz, about a country as a whole, but about a state within a country. This state is Nagaland and the setting is the 2013 state legislative assembly elections, which took place while I was conducting ethnographic research in the state.

In 1985, on the floor of the state assembly, a prominent Naga minister proposed, in vain, that Nagaland's election system be reformed, for the present election system went against 'the Naga way of life' (cited in Ao 1993: 224). This statement, while controversial then, had long been preceded by A.Z. Phizo, the erstwhile president of the Naga National Council (NNC), which struggled for Naga Independence, and who argued that 'There is no political party in Nagaland. We do not need it'. All things considered, he continued, 'Nagaland need not intimate or adopt foreign institutions [such as formal democracy] in matter of political organisation'. In Phizo's view, Nagaland was already fully democratic by traditional design, '[It is the] very spirit of our country', as he put it, hence, they would not require political parties and elections to 'become' democratic.[1] Most recently, it was Nagaland's Chief Minister who reportedly remarked that 'Election is not suited for Nagas', then elucidating that 'Selection of leader[s] would best suit Nagas' (cited in Solo 2011: 67).

This statement by the Chief Minister is not to be interpreted as an attack on modern democracy, but rather as a perceptive reading of traditional Naga polities, which, although highly diverse, share a common rejection of the principle of voting, or for that matter to raising one's hand in support or opposition, which is seen as dividing the community into 'our side' and 'their side'.[2] It is perhaps for this reason that, in the village where I was conducting field research, someone wrote in the dust that had gathered on the rear-window of a car: 'Politics is an insult to each other by vote'. Put differently, 'the idea of an elected leader was not in the scheme of life in [sic] the Nagas' (Solo 2011: 68). This does, of course, not imply that public deliberations, political divisions and conflicts were unknown within different Naga polities, far from that, but that voting or 'raising hands' was not the preferred strategy of decision-making. Yet, despite Phizo's evocative rejection of electoral politics, and later statements to his support, parties and elections not only seeped into Nagaland, but etched themselves at the very centre of Naga society.

---

[1] Clearly, Phizo's view was mirrored in his own Angami Naga background, a tribe which falls in the 'household model' of electoral politics, as discussed later, and the model which appears closest (although still significantly different) to modern principles of democracy.

[2] It is important to assert that 'Naga' is a generic term that denotes a conglomeration of tribes, and although they all identify as Naga, they simultaneously emphasise their separate tribal identities, speak divergent languages and differ, at times radically so, in their traditional social and political organisation.

However, rather than approaching the introduction of modern democracy as a radical disruption of past political practices, this is a study of continuities and connections, of linkages between past polities and present politics. Rather than accepting new democratic principles at face value, I will show that Naga tribes possess the agency and cultural creativity to appropriate, reinterpret and rework the idea of modern democracy along the lines of their own traditional polities, ideologies, and pre-statehood political cultures. That Naga tribes are both the repositories and enactors of their own particular versions of democracy, appropriations which may run counter to some of modern democracy's elevated principles, but which are, on the whole, a great deal closer to their traditional lifeworlds.

ACCEPTED WISDOM

Conventional assessments of Nagaland elections, both scholarly and commentarial, often invoke its alleged criminalisation, the interplay of money and muscles used to ensnare voters (Dev 2006; Misra 1987, Singh 1986), or on 'operation election' (Sen 1974), pointing to the large presence of armed forces in the area. While it is hard to deny that Nagaland's electoral politics routinely deviate from textbook versions of free and fair elections, as it does in many places across the globe, there is much more to Nagaland's democracy than mere manipulation, disorder, corruption and occasional violence. After all, the richest or most generous candidates do not automatically win, nor do threats and intimidations inevitably prevail. This chapter, while not downplaying 'electoral ills', departs from the popular condemnation of Nagaland's elections as a mockery, if not a slur on liberal democracy. Instead, it argues towards a more contextualised, a more culturally-embedded understanding of Nagaland's electoral processes, one which renders bare the incongruence between modern democracy and different traditional Naga polities, but also one which bestows Naga communities with the agency to remould, tailor, and adapt modern democracy to their own uses and advantages.

Prevailing descriptions about traditional Naga polities have been about chiefs and democrats (Jacobs et al. 1990), nobles and commoners (Fürer-haimendorf 1973), bodies of elders (Mills 1926), powerful chiefs (Fürer-Haimendorf 1939) and the absence of chiefs (Hutton 1921a), sovereign village states and village republics (Mills 1926; Venuh 2005; Singh 2008), extreme egalitarianism (Woodthorpe 1882), clan rivalries (Hutton 1921a), and, on the whole, represented as a continuum with hereditary autocracy, if not near dictatorship, and radical democracy at opposite ends, with (a section of) the Konyak Naga usually associated with the former and the Angami Naga as the most obvious example of the latter. While such terms are obviously simplifications of complex, multilayered Naga political systems and sentiments, I propose, and at the risk of being accused of overestimating the relationship between culture, traditional politics and contemporary electoral politics, four models – the *Angh* (king or chieftainship) model, the village consensus candidate model, the clan candidate model, and the household model – which I think help to understand how different Naga electorates elect their representatives. These four models, I argue, are best understood as extensions, or a remapping, of different traditional Naga polities, thus, building upon pre-existing political practices.

As such, I submit that Nagaland politics is not a politics of manifestos, party ideologies, competing long-term visions, public platforms and debates. Although these do play a role, they are of little help in understanding how Naga electors vote as they do.[3] Nagaland electoral politics is a politics of many things, most of them outside the scope of this chapter, but what I want to emphasise here is that it is a politics of 'primordial', partisan and affective affiliations of clan, village and tribe, and of a remapping of traditional polities unto the democratic playing field. While democratic elections are essentially a modern exercise, highly bureaucratised, rationalised and reliant on technology, this chapter shows that, in Nagaland, who gets 'voted in' largely hinges on traditional modes of decision-making and age-old loyalties.

My data are primarily 'declarations of support', as they appeared in plenty in Nagaland dailies in the months and weeks preceding the 2013 elections.[4] By relying primarily on newspaper declarations, my evidence

---

[3]This is not to argue that party differences are not marked. They occasionally are. Especially when it comes to the tension between regional and national political parties, the former insisting that only regional parties an understand the 'Naga mind' and the latter countering that only a strong national party, with strong connections to Delhi, can bring development and peace to the state. I do, however, contend that party ideologies are often not a major determinant in explaining voting behaviour in Nagaland.

[4]The 'declarations of support' cited in this chapter appeared in the *Morung Express*, *Nagaland Post*, and the *Eastern Mirror*, the three main Nagaland dailies, during the months and weeks preceding the 2013 Nagaland Assembly elections. As elections are invariably sensitive, I have omitted the names of both the supporters and candidates from the citations. I have not omitted the names of villages and clans, as it would be impossible to do so without affecting the accountability (and verifiability) of my data. My advance apologies if the inclusion of the names of certain villages or clans will incite discontentment among those who identify

is, admittedly, perhaps more anecdotal than it is methodical, although I concur with Gupta's (1995: 385) reasoning that newspaper reports must be understood as 'cultural texts' and 'socio-historical documents', and can be a great asset for 'thick description', and that it is unfortunate that they are often treated with 'benign neglect by students of contemporary life'.[5] The household model is also based on ethnography, as it was among the Chakhesang Naga, whom I include under this model, that I was conducting fieldwork during the 2013 Nagaland state assembly elections.

It must be emphasised that the four models of electoral politics proposed here are 'ideal types'. Most certainly, they are not deterministic, and, in reality, they are perhaps as often defied as adhered to. Then again, within the same Naga tribe and constituency multiple models might compete and intermingle. And while for the purpose of clarity I associate each model with one or more particular Naga tribes, this does not suggest that the model applies either exclusively to them, or that all units falling under its tribal designation practice it in exactly the same way. While my current data does not suffice to fit all Naga tribes into one of the four models, I suspect that further research would render this feasible, at least so conceptually. The above safeguards notwithstanding, I do maintain that the four models outlineed here are useful to 'think along with' as they provide certain insights into Nagaland's ostensibly so intricate electoral politics.

ANGH OR CHIEFTAINSHIP MODEL

The first model, in prominence among the Konyak Naga, and in a somewhat less pronounced manner practiced by the Sema (now Sumi) Naga, is the angh (king) or chieftainship model. The basic premise of this model is that the traditional leverages of Konyak and Sumi aristocrats have, to an extent, been remapped unto the democratic playing field with traditional rulers now influencing the voting patterns of their 'commoners'. While this does not imply that the political opinion of traditional aristocrats is necessarily definite, it suggests that their political stance tends to preponderate over the

---

themselves with it.

[5]As Gupta (1995: 385) puts it eloquently: 'treated with benign neglect by students of contemporary life, they mysteriously metamorphise into invaluable "field data" once they have yellowed around the edges and fallen apart at the creases. And yet, it is not entirely clear by what alchemy time turns the "secondary" data of the anthropologist into the "primary" data of the historian'.

majority of 'ordinary villagers'. After the introduction of democracy a few Konyak anghs joined the election fray themselves, so blurring the division between traditional leverages and post-statehood constellations of power, but most kept to their traditional area of jurisdiction, turning themselves from 'kings' into 'king-makers'.

In the past, before their enclosure into the state, Konyak anghs reigned over a village or a cluster of villages, and their powers were hereditary, autocratic, and sacrosanct.[6] In the words of the colonial administrator J.H. Hutton (1965: 23): 'the ang [sic] is a repository of fortune, virtue, or life-principle of his village'. Hutton continued: 'In some villages he is, or was, so heavily tabooed hat he must not touch the ground'. About the angh of Mon the present-day district headquarters of the Konyak area, Fürer-haimendorf (1973: 9) wrote: 'like other chiefs the ang [sic] of Mon was an autocratic ruler who had power over life and death of his subjects'. On the whole, anghs expected 'deference from the villagers as well as parts of their crops and labour: they could exercise sexual rights over the women of the commoner (*Ben*) clans' (Jacobs et al. 1990: 71). The village's *morung*, or bachelor's dormitory, in the past was a social institution common to a number of Naga tribes, and the place where unmarried males lived together, and where deliberations were held. Among the Konyak, the morung was usually an appendage of the angh's private residence (Hutton 1965: 23). About the Sumi Naga, Hutton wrote elsewhere that their traditional chieftainship was not sacred, but secular, but that like the Konyak anghs their powers were hereditary. The chieftain families, he observed, 'form an aristocracy in the literal sense of the word' (1921b: 150). A Sumi village was usually called after its founding chief, who was the 'lord of the manor'. As a general principle, the chief's house served as a meeting place, as well as dormitory for the village unmarried males. Their customary obedience to their chief, Hutton concluded, 'makes the average Sema more ready to accept discipline and orders generally than Nagas usually are'.

While the introduction of the state bureaucracy diminished the absolute authority anghs and chiefs once enjoyed, they continue to have a large say in village affairs, and, by extension, in who will be elected as the member of the legislative assembly in their constituencies. In the wake of the 2013 state assembly elections the following 'declaration of support' from a Konyak Naga village appeared in the Nagaland dailies:

---

[6]While the Konyak territory is popularly referred to as 'the land of anghs', it ought to be qualified that the ang system does not exist in the entire Konyak area, and is most prominent among the so-called Thendu section of the tribe, not so among the Thenkoh division (Mills 1922: xxxiii).

> The Zangkham Village citizens... unanimously resolve to
> support and vote for the young and capable NPF [Naga
> People's Front] aspirant candidate...

This declaration, promising collective vote from the entire village, was
signed by the chief angh, and countersigned by the local party president.
Another Konyak Naga village declared in the newspapers that:

> Angs, GBs [Gaonburas],[7] Councils and Youth of Chi,
> Leangha an Goching villages firmly resolved and selected... as
> an intending NPF candidate

This statement was endorsed by the chief angh-chum-chairperson
of Chi village, the angh-cum chairperson of Leangha village, and the
chairperson of Goching village, the last one presumably not holding the
title of angh. Similarly, the angh of Tizit village published a declaration,
countersigned by the village council chairperson, announcing that his
village had 'unanimously resolve to support..., the intending candidate'. In
yet another Konyak constituency, the angh of Nokzang village declared his
support for one candidate in the newspaper, and promised that all the 1329
voters of the two villages over which he presided would be cast in favour
the NPF. If the angh is not the principal actor, he may assume the role of
a mediator or a facilitator, as seemed to have happened in the village of
Tangnyu, from where the following 'declaration of support' was dispatched:

> The Council of Tangnyu village had called a meeting at Chief
> Ang's Palace... and decided to support and strengthen the
> Independent Candidate.

[7]The position of Gaonbura was introduced by the British who selected
a number of persons in each village, whom they thought had considerable local
influence, as intermediaries between the British administration and the village.
They were bestowed with the responsibly to collect house-tax and to submit these
to government offices, upon which they received a commission. They were also
empowered to settle local disputes, and to notify the government in the event of any
serious disturbances. Besides occasional commissions, they were also granted a red
shawl to signal their allegiance to the British, and, in some instances, a gun. After
the British departed from the Naga Hills, the position of Gaonbura was kept in
place by the postcolonial government.

In the case of the Sumi Naga, aristocratic families now tend to hold the state introduced offices of Gaonbura and village council chairperson, although representatives from non-aristocratic lineages may also hold these offices. It was under the auspices of the head Gaonbura, that Sunito village conducted a general meeting in which it was 'resolved that we will support solid franchise to the NPF candidate'. In a similar vein, it was a Gaonbura, chairperson, and the secretary of Unity village who stated in the newspaper that:

> We, the Sumi Community Council reaffirms the decision...
> to fully and sincerely support the intending NPF candidate.

On the whole, however, it appears that Konyak anghs have a comparatively larger say in contemporary electoral politics compared to the traditional aristocrats among the Sumi, although, obviously, context matters.

While the views of traditional aristocrats no longer carry the force they once did, the 'declarations of support' cited above suggest that anghs an chiefs have, in parts, been able to remap their traditional leverages, now playing a prominent role in local electoral processes. Hence, for an aspiring politician in the constituencies where this model is in vogue the essence of the matter is to win over the traditional anghs and chiefs, trying to persuade them to use their influence to his support. To be sure, this model is not deterministic. Long ago Hutton already wrote that 'a strong Ang [sic] had very considerable power, but a weak one tended to act as his fellow-clansmen advised him' (Hutton 1965: 23). The Sumi Nagas, in turn, have a long history of dissent and the break-up of villages over contests of leadership. The same dynamics apply to electoral politics today, and with their traditional powers now diminished by the state bureaucracy, anghs and chiefs perhaps more than ever depend on their own character and charisma to assert their authority.

VILLAGE CONSENSUS CANDIDATE MODEL

The village consensus candidate model, which holds that a village tends to vote en bloc for a particular candidate, figures most prominently among the Ao Naga, although it is also practiced in various villages belonging to other tribes. In this model, the unit of voting is not the individual, but the village. The village's collective vote is deliberated at the level of the village council (*putu menden*) and the village's apex body called the *senso mungdang*, which freely translates as the gathering of all male citizens, although female citizens are now increasingly part of these gatherings. A senso mungdang is only held sporadically, and if such a meeting is deemed desirable, as it often is in the wake of an election, the newspaper is used to summon all citizens residing outside the village to return home. Thus, for instance:

> Süngratsü Senso Mungdang and Village Council jointly informs to all the citizens of Süngratsü village that all male and female citizens should reach the village on or before the 18th February 2013 positively for the ensuing State Assembly Election... Any member not complying with this order will invite strict disciplinary action from the Senso Mungdang and the Village Council.

The political resolution adopted during the senso mungdang proceedings is final, and those who try to go against it risk to be condemned as 'traitors' and to be sentenced under customary law. Put differently, the political opinion of the village majority supersedes those of individual voters, who, even if they ideologically or otherwise disagree with the selected village candidate, are expected to nevertheless cast their votes for the consensus candidate.

As in the case of the traditional aristocrats, there are traditional precedents to this voting strategy adopted among the Ao Naga. The traditional Ao Naga polity has been depicted by colonial officers as the most intricate, multilayered, and complex political system among all Naga polities. It consisted, as it still does, of a number of councils, ranked hierarchically and based on age-groups, with one such age-group taking the lead for a set period of time. Unlike the Konyak and the Sumi Naga, 'there are not in the Ao tribe any hereditary chiefs' (Hutton 1965: 21). Rather, 'the control of affairs lies with a council' (Mills 1926: 177). Mills continued: 'To debate matters of importance all the councillors (*Tatar*) will meet' (ibid.: 182). The locus of authority was thus vested in the village council, which was 'composed of elders representing various clans and kindred for fixed, if fluctuating periods' (Hutton 1965: 23). They were to rule over the village, upholding the common good, with non-councillors expected to submit to their authority. This body of village councillors was assisted by a range of subsidiary bodies made up of junior age-groups, who would, in time, rise up to become councillors themselves. This age-wise ranking started with the induction of young boys into the village morung, which took place only once every three years 'with each batch undertaking on entrance certain menial duties to be performed till the entry of a fresh batch three years later, when the former took over a superior status' (ibid.: 24). Although life in the morung was abandoned on a person's marriage, he would belong, for the rest of his life, to the same grade as the cohorts of his entry in the morung, and eventually rise up to become the leading age-group in the village (Mills 1926: 177).

Among the Ao Naga, membership of the village council was the 'zenith of any ambitious village career' (Hutton 1965: 24). During this period, a man represented his kindred on the council and was entitled 'to shares of all meat killed in public feasts, as fines from village offenders, as presents to the village, or killed for entertainment of distinguished strangers' (ibid.). Unlike the position of angh or chief, whose authority could last for many years, often till their death, the position of councillor was not permanent but temporary, and after a designated period of time, 'the whole body of councillors goes out of office at once, and no one can be re-elected however influential he may be or however short a term of office he has enjoyed' (Mills 1926: 183-4). This vacating of office often went contested; at times it was even violent with the office holders reluctant to relinquish their privileges, and the new generation all too eager to assume village leadership (ibid.: 181).

Today, Ao Naga villages continue to be organised into councils, although the introduction of the state has introduced new arenas and institutions through which non-councillors can now assert power over their village, a times competing with the traditional authorities. Despite this occasional tussle between 'modern' an 'traditional' constellations of authority, the dispositions of the traditional Ao Naga polity appears to have re-constituted themselves in the sphere of electoral politics, with councillors assuming a leading role in adjudicating the collective vote of the village. Among the Ao Naga, this often results in the selection of a village consensus candidate; a village resolution which is subsequently declared in the local dailies and signed by the president and secretary of the senso mungdang. To illustrate, the Nokpu village declared:

> As resolved in its General Meeting held, the Nokpu Senso Mongdang [sic] hereby declares to support the candidature of ... in the forthcoming State General Assembly Election ... Any person found to be defying the decision made by the Nokpu Senso Mongdang [sic] shall be dealt with accordingly.

Merangkong, another Ao Naga village, declared:

> Merangkong Senso Mungdang in a general meeting... unanimously resolved to extend full support to the Independent Candidate for the forthcoming legislative assembly election... Heavy penalty and strict action will be imposed against any citizen of Merangkong who acts against the aforesaid resolution.

This village consensus candidate model can also work the opposite way around, with a village resolving not to give any vote to a particular candidate, as the following statement suggests:

> The Yaongyimsen Kosasanger Tatar passed the decision that not a single vote will be voted in favour to the Congress Candidate.

This model does not apply to the Ao Naga alone. A Chang Naga village also publicly endorsed a particular candidate and subsequently promised that 'the Village Council is fully responsible for bringing the absolute majority'. Going against such a village resolution can have dramatic consequences, as evidently happened in Yangzitong village. Here the village's apex body announced the expulsion of five of its villagers for the duration of six years for publishing a newspaper 'rejoinder' against the selected village consensus candidate. The village apex body justified its decision to expel them by stating:

> Any resolutions are issued in the interest of citizens and not to some persons or a handful of people. As such a press statement issued by few individuals has directly insulted the Suro Pumji, which is an apex body of the citizens.

In constituencies where the village consensus model is in vogue, democratic politics is less about election than it is about selection, and voting is not so much an individual exercise as it denotes collective action with each village, in a way, turning into a 'single vote', which a candidate can either win or lose in its entirety. Hence, to get elected a successful candidate must seek the support of a number of village councils (putu menden), with the backing of the village apex body, the senso mungdang. In this model, large villages assume larger powers as their collective vote can instantly put a candidate ahead in the polls. This had led at least two Ao Naga villages to join hands by combining their collective vote; the Mopungchuket and Süngratsü villages announced that they, in a joint session, had 'resolved to jointly declare their support to the Congress candidate for the forthcoming State Assembly Election'. This declaration read further: 'It is informed to all the citizens of both the villages to abide by this joint declaration'. As most villages declare their village consensus candidates months or weeks before the actual elections, the outcome of the state legislative elections among the Ao Naga is often already known before the first ballot is cast.

THE CLAN-MODEL

The third model proposed here is the clan-model of electoral politics and is perhaps most prominent among the Lotha Naga, although the rhetoric of clan unity and clan-wise electoral support is also prominent amongst various other Naga tribes. In this model, the locus of electoral politics does not reside in the traditional aristocrats or in village councillors, but in the clan leaders. As each Lotha clan, generally, has members across Lotha villages, preponderating numerically in some and constituting a minority in others, Lotha electoral politics is more of an inter-village affair compared to the first two models. The clan-model suggests that electoral politics is predominantly a tussle between competing clans with each clan uniting behind a particular candidate, subsequently trying to convince other clans to align with them. In a recent study, Ovung (2012: 122), himself a Lotha, argues that, 'every serious treatment of Lotha politics finds clan as the most important determinant in patterns of political life'. 'Clan-thinking', Ovung continues, 'dominates and the question of clan numerical strength always arises' (ibid.).

In principle, the clan model implies that each Lotha clan selects a political candidate amongst its members, or alternatively declares its collective vote to a particular candidate belonging to another clan. On the face of it, this model suggests that, compared to numerically small clans, larger clans have more opportunities to push one of its members into the assembly. While this holds true as a general principle, no single clan carries enough votes to do so alone, and clan members often live in different constituencies thus weakening their collective voting power. As a result, every clan and candidate must seek alliances with other clans in order to win the election. In this model, the most effective tactic of a political party to thwart another party's candidate is to try and set up a rival candidate in his clan, so potentially splitting the candidate's vote bank.

Why clans should be so central in Lotha electoral politics is perhaps a little more difficult to discern compared to the first two models. However, its relative importance might well relate to the Lotha's traditional landholding system, about which the colonial administrator Mills (1922: 96-8) remarked, 'compared to other Naga tribes a very large proportion of the land in the Lhota [sic] country is clan land, which is held in common by all members of that particular clan in the village'. Mills then continued: 'Every year the members of a clan in a Lhota [sic] village meet and apportion out the land which each is to cut that year... Strangely enough this delicate operation never seems to result in a quarrel' (ibid.). Seen from this angle, the primacy of clan among the Lotha is directly related to the primacy of agriculture and its clan-based landownership pattern, a traditional disposition towards a clan-based social organisation, which now appears to have been reasserted into the democratic arena.

About a month before the 2013 elections, the Ngullie Lotha clan came out with the public declaration, informing: 'a general meeting of the Ngullietsu Ekhung [All Ngullie union] was held in Yanthamo village and attended by more than 2000 Ngullies' clansmen representing all the villages'. During this meeting they resolved to select a certain veteran Ngullie politician as the 'official Candidate from the Ngullies clansmen'. The public declaration further qualified that although the Ngullietsu Ekhung did not want to 'infringe on the exercise of democratic rights by any individual', they had 'blessed and endorsed' the candidature of the veteran politician, then adding that 'no individual member is above the Ngullietsu Ekhung' and that any violation of its resolutions may compel the Ekhung 'to take measures as per customary norms and practices'.

Even if a public declaration is not done under the banner of a single clan, the clan remains the unit of measurement, as the following declaration shows:

> The... RJD [Rashtriya Janata Dal] campaign committee would like to express their gratitude and appreciation to the undermentioned supporters... for extending wholehearted support to the RJD candidate... 23 households of Patton's clan from Pangti village, 50 households of Kikon's clan from Yanshum Khel [ward] of Pangti village and Sungro, 21 houeholds of Ngullie's clan from Yanshum khel of Pangti village and Sungro, 48 households of Ngullie's clan from Yondon khel of Pangti village and Sungro.

Two other newspaper declarations coming from the Lotha area read: 'The Enny clan of Old Changsu village with 25 households declare unconditional support to the NPF candidate', and '34 households under Tsopoe's clan of Pangti village... have unanimously decided to support... in the ensuing General Assembly Election'. In certain cases, the clan-model among the Lotha gives way to a village consensus candidate model as evidently happened in Tsungiki village, where the village council came out with a statement endorsing a particular candidate as the 'official candidate of our village', further adding 'given the fact that, it is the first time we humbly appeal to all the neighbouring villages to support our village candidate'.

While clan unity during electoral politics is actively pursued, it is often more an ideal rather than an actual reality. In the period preceding the election numerous clan declarations, rejoinders and re-rejoinders emerged in the newspapers with clan representatives disputing the resolution adopted by their clan leaders, or with a clan in a certain village promising its 'collective clan vote' to a different candidate than their clans-men from a neighbouring village. To illustrate, in one village eight members of the Ezung clan questioned, using the medium of the newspaper, the declaration of support published by their village council chairperson who was a member of the Ezung clan, accusing him of spreading 'cheap propaganda'. This disjuncture between clan political rhetoric and actual practice is also shown by Ovung (2012). While emphasising that clans are the units of electoral politics, and indeed that, no serious view of Lotha politics can exclude the importance of clan, Ovung's survey about clans' internal harmony and integration shows that, compared to ceremonies (including marriages, births, and funerals), traditional festivals and community work, Lotha clans are actually united the least when it comes to elections, with only 16% of his respondents stating that elections are a period of clan-cohesion (ibid.: 76). Clearly the rhetoric of clan-wise electoral support and actual electoral practices at times refer to two different things altogether.

THE HOUSEHOLD MODEL

The fourth model, the household model, is most clearly practiced by the Angami and Chakhesang Naga tribes. Here traditional aristocrats are absent, while village councillors and clan leaders have little or no influence over the voting behaviour of 'ordinary villagers'. Instead, individual and household deliberation is more pronounced, and 'social pressure' to vote collectively, in most cases, absent. Comparatively, among the Naga people, the Angami and Chakhesang (formerly Eastern Angami) tribes appear to come closest to the elevated democratic principle of free and autonomous individual deliberation. Although it must be instantly qualified that this 'individual deliberation' often culminates into a 'household-decision' and that it is only on rare occasions that members of the same household cast their votes differently. 'Shame' is spoken of a household in which different members cast their votes for different candidates, and compared to the breakdown of the family, even divorce. Exceptions are, however, there, and I have come across a handful of families who consciously decided to divide their household votes over two candidates equally, as they happened to have close kinship relations with both. In the household model, individual voting might, on Polling Day, be substituted, by village council order, into a system of 'household voting', in which the head of the household is empowered to cast the votes of all his household members.

The Angami and Chakhesang Naga have a marked 'democratic

archaeology', a feature British officers wrote about with a sense of admiration. About the Angami Naga, Butler wrote: 'Every man follows the dictates of his own will, a form of the purest democracy which it is very difficult to conceive of as existing even for a single day and yet that it does exist here is an undeniable fact' (cited in Hutton 1921a: 143). Hutton, in turn, defined the Angami as a 'debating society' with the authority of village leaders, if they existed, being nominal: 'their orders are obeyed so far only as they accord with the wishes and convenience of the community' (ibid: 142-143). Hutton continued: 'disputes, when settled at all, were probably settled by a sort of informal council of elders, who would discuss the matter under dispute with one another, the parties, and the general public at great length, until some sort of agreement was arrived at'.

What Butler termed as the 'purest democracy' and Hutton called a 'debating society' was in actual practice more akin to the 'ideal polity' for Socrates and Aristotle, with the 'philosophically minded' and the 'virtuous' responsible for the decision-making process. Among the Angami and Chakhesang it was usually the elders, warriors and wealthy who deliberated decisions, commonly barring women, the physically feeble, and the village poor from equal participation. That said, the traditional polity of the Angami and Chakhesang was, on the whole, less hierarchical, people were less inclined to obey to authority, and this more egalitarian disposition now appears to show itself in the kind of public 'declarations of support' that filter from the Angami and Chakhesang areas. Here they are not signed by an angh or chief, by the convener or president of a village apex body, or by the president of a clan union, but by a long list of individuals, cutting across clans and villages. The Congress committee of Meluri, inhabited predominantly by the Pochury Naga (who were formerly part of the Chakhesang) declared: 'A total of 72 households hereby resign from the NPF party and joined the INC party'. This statement was undersigned by the head of the 72 households, stretching the declaration of support into an elongated column. In other instances, a single person deems it desirable to publicly declare his alliance, like a former candidate of the RJD who wrote:

> Since the party is not in a position to come to power even in
> near future, I have decided to join Indian National Congress
> (INC).

In most cases, however, it is households which are the units of measurement in the newspaper declarations. Another previous RJD party worker also resigned and publicly declared that he had done so 'along with 31 households... to support the Indian National congress Candidate'. Another declared:

> I, Mr... President Khezhakeno Unit (youth wing) and my followers resigned from my post and primary membership of the Congress and join the NPF.

In the household model, every head of the household becomes a political player in his own right, and occasionally confusion arises about a person's political alliance. When three persons from Pfutsero town found their names mentioned in the newspaper amongst those who had resigned from the Congress candidate, they instantly wrote a rejoinder, condemning the 'false declaration' made, and asserting that 'we have not resigned'.

In this model of electoral politics, 'kitchen politics' (not meant in the conventional gendered sense of household decisions, but as an electoral strategy in which candidates and party-workers visit house to house to attack voters) is the main electoral strategy. Every person, every household, needs to be convinced personally, allotted time and effort to, and while securing the support of a prominent village or clan leader might certainly benefit the candidate's local standing, it hardly suffices in securing majority support. It is this individuality, coupled by the highly personalised nature of 'kitchen politics', which renders electoral politics in the constituencies in which the household model is in vogue a very intensive and lengthy affair, often commencing many months before the scheduled date of the elections.

CONCLUSION

The above four models, although the most prominent ones, are not the only ways through which democracy in Nagaland is performed. Another variant might be called the 'range model', and holds that, in certain areas, villages located on the same hill range make collective voting decisions. This happened among a section of the Khiamniungan Naga:

> The Noklak NPF party welcomes the Thang Range Public Organisation (TRPO) consisting of five villages... The TRPO firmly decided to support the NPF candidate.

Another model might be the youth-model, as the following statement indicates:

> We, the undersigned Independent Youth declare wholeheartedly to support the candidature of...

This last declaration hails from Dimapur, which is Nagaland's most urbanised and most intermixed area, with Naga tribes and some non-Naga tribes residing there, as well as a sizeable number of immigrant settlers from other parts of the country. It is here, in this amalgam of communities, that the four models above apply the least. The five constituencies in the Dimapur plains and nearby foothills are invariably larger compared to those in the hills, the levels of intimacy between candidates and voters lower, and, in large parts because of this, party politics more pronounced than 'person-politics'. But in these constituencies, too, voting is hardly a private and individual matter. While traces of the four models are present, though less conclusively so, new collectives are formed and declare their 'unflinching', 'unconditional', and 'unwavering' support for their preferred candidates. Self-help groups, enacted to uplift the economic status of its members, are one such new collective, and in the wake of the election one self-help group declared that it had lost confidence in one particular candidate 'for showing no concern to Self-Help Groups' and 'unanimously decided to give full support' to his opponent. Also communities as a whole may promise their collective support, like the Rongmei Naga community in a particular area in Dimapur: 'The Rongmei... extends unconditional support to the NPF', or as the youth of the Kuki community did in another constituency:

> We, the undermentioned Kuki community youth have resolved to extend our full support to the Independent candidate.

If participating in elections expresses 'the symbolic affirmation of the voters' acceptance of the political system and of their role within it' (Lukes 1975: 304), Nagaland, with a voter turnout of well over 90% during the last election, which is significantly higher than the average turnout in most Indian states, seem to be among the premium Indian states in which the idea of democracy has consolidated'.[8] Yet is it also important, argues Khilnani (2009: 5) 'to explore the diverse political imaginations and arguments that sustain (or undermine) democratic politics'. Democracy as a universal set of practices and values is an ideal, and this study shows that it is just that, an ideal. While almost universal in its scope and discourse, democracy is performed differently in different places. In a way, this is obvious, American democracy is not the same as French democracy, and French democracy and

---

[8]One reason explaining his high voter turnout is because in at least three of the four models discussed above votes are cast collectively, so including those who did not intend to vote or who are enrolled on the voting list but happened to be absent in their village on Polling Day.

Indian democracy are again very different. What this chapter has asserted is that local communities, Naga tribes in our case, rather than passive absorbers of modern democratic principles, possess the agency to appropriate, reinterpret and rework the idea of democracy according to their own cultural values and traditional polities. Put differently, modern democracy has locally manifested itself as a new arena to perform 'past polities'. This is not to argue that Nagaland's electoral models may not change over time, or that the practitioners of these models are innately recalcitrant to the modern ideology of democracy. The models presented here are fluid, flexible and open to contestation, and during the 2013 Nagaland state assembly elections certain powerful local voices were raised against the selection of village and clan consensus candidates.

In the upshot, the presence of these four electoral models suggests that Naga tribes are both the repositories and enactors of their own particular versions of democracy, remoulding its institutions and principles into their own traditional polities. It shows how different Naga tribes instead of adjusting themselves to modern democratic ideals, adjusted democracy to themselves. Shah refers to this indigenous or tribal 'search for alternative, more informed models of political life' (2010: 185) as 'arcadian spaces', building upon the 'culturalist critique' of the postcolonial Indian state. These arcadian spaces, Shah insists, are not simply 'spaces of utopia', but are based on the political potential of central elements and values of, in her case, the indigenous Munda society in Jharkhand (ibid.). However, whereas Shah argues that the Munda attempt to keep modern democracy, as well as the state machinery, at arm's length, the case of the Naga shows that democracy is not so much resisted, as it is actively appropriated, reinterpreted and reworked to suit local political cultures. While ideas of balloting and elections have now firmly etched themselves at the centre of Naga society, the Naga versions of performing democracy suggest that, when seen from a local perspective, the elevated modern democratic principle of individual, impartial, and autonomous deliberation are strange ideas, indeed.

A.Z. PHIZO
FATHER OF THE NATION
HE WAS THE MAN
WHO GAVE HIS ALL
FOR HIS PEOPLE

07

SHIFTING DEMOCRATIC
EXERIENCES OF NAGAS

Riku Khutso

INTRODUCTION

This chapter locates a homegrown democratic essence in traditional Naga political systems and sentiments. This 'essence' has no written or formal constitutional base but originated from orally transmitted traditions, wisdom, and political praxes prescribed by culture and customs. In contemporary times, we witness a tension between this pre-existent Naga 'democratic essence' and modern democratic institutions, procedures, and values. However, rather than being primarily concerned with the politics of the present, this chapter adopts a historical lens and explores how Naga ideas and experiences of 'democracy' (in its indigenous, rather than liberal, sense) evolved from the pre-colonial to the statehood period.

To start with, most Naga villages had, and still have, a delegated system of representation operative at different levels of the village socio-political set-up, which may be seen as an indigenous form of political representation. This, amongst others, made the colonial officer Butler (1875: 314) characterize the Naga political ethos as the 'purest' form of democracy. More precisely, Butler's depiction of 'purest democracy' was inspired by the egalitarian functioning of Naga village republics. Early visitors such as Butler, but also Woodthorpe (who described Naga society as 'extremely egalitarian' (cf. Wouters 2014: 60), were captivated by, what I call here, the pragmatic and practical functioning of Naga indigenous democracy and society. It was pragmatic and practical in the sense that it was devoid of orthodoxies, dogmas, and established hierarchies, but proved itself flexible and adaptable to the exigencies of time.

Naga traditional political particulars deviated both from the individualism that is associated with modern, 'western' democracy (De Tocqueville 1969) and the 'pre-conditions' of secularism and capitalism out of which European and American democracies grew (Kaviraj 2011: 9-13). Naga political practices were communitarian in ethos and therefore diverged markedly from the tenets of modern, liberal democracy. For this reason alone, the term and idea of 'democracy' needs to be contextualised and individuated to the specifics of culture, beliefs, traditions, people, place, and social relations. Naga traditional democracy, as I approach it, was a culturally-inflected, deliberative process meant to reach consensus, more than that of an autonomous individual exercising his or her detached political freedom (for a discussion on Naga 'traditional' politics see also the Introduction by Wouters, this volume).

In tracing and placing the evolution of Naga ideas of democracy, this chapters discusses three historical charters that underlie present-day democratic politics in Nagaland. First, I discuss the prototypical traditional set-up and experiences of Naga homegrown democracy through a case study of *Kuzha* traditional politics. Next, I discuss the emergence of a Naga vernacular public sphere from the early 20th century onward, primarily resulting from the colonial-missionary encounter. I then zoom in on the rise and activities of pan-Naga organisations such as the Naga Club and the NNC, including the 1951 plebiscite and the creation of the NNC's *Yezhabo* (Constitution). I end with the NPC-led enactment of Nagaland state and the introduction of the Indian version of electoral democracy.

THE DEMOCRATIC ETHOS OF THE PROTOTYPICAL NAGA VILLAGE

To situate the indigenous history of democratic ideas and practices, we first require a critical appreciation of the prototypical Naga 'village republic' (Wouters 2017a). Until not so long ago, Nagas lived in individuated village polities, each with its own society, economy, and demarcated territory (Elwin 1961: 7). As such, Naga society did not have an overarching political system, but was highly fragmented. When British officers first entered the Naga

Hills, they, consequently, fought the Nagas not as a singular nation, or even as individual tribes, but as discrete villages (Butler 1875: 311, Clark 1907: 45-6, Steyn 2002: 6). This point is often stressed by Naga historians. Piketo Sema (1992: 140), for one, argues how the self-contained nature of Naga villages long remained a barrier to the realisation of a pan-Naga social and political cohesion. This preoccupation with the 'village republic' in traditional Naga politics, Wouters (2015a) shows ethnographically, remains central to understanding political competition, rivalries, and cultural proclivities in the contemporary democratic arena.

Yet, while 'the village' was historically the locus of Naga politics, this did not preclude traces of common descent, culture, history, and subtle communication networks between village societies. Therefore, an account of the essence of Naga traditional politics should include not only inter-village polarities but also embedded sensibilities. I will illustrate this by discussing the political system of the *Kuzha Netho Ketsii*, which revolved around three *Kuzha* cognate villages, namely, Leshemi, Lasumi and Zapami. In the pre-colonial era, each head of the family, known as *kriidie*,[1] would annually assemble in the oldest village, which was Leshemi, in the month of December (called *riinyekhrii*, then the first month of the local calendar) for the purpose of *teakhe-mapou* (an annual assembly of elders in which traditions and customs were reviewed) and to consume *teakhe-zu* (a special rice beer brewed for the event). In contemporary political parlance, this might be seen as analogous to a general assembly.

During this assembly, matters such as *kuzhanuokhruo* (a form of ancestral tax/religious tribute collected across the region by warriors), *ba-melhe* (a body of customary laws), *lota* (the traditional practice of agriculture), *lenyü* (religious rituals), *diemi* (an institutions of intermediaries/messengers during wars), and *rifu* (war expeditions) were discussed and deliberated. In the course of this assembly, it was also sworn that the secrets of *Kuzha Netho Ketsii* would not be divulged to anyone not belonging to these three villages. The importance of secrecy was emphasised to the extent that the *mewo* (traditional priest) pronounced an advanced curse on anyone who would violate this principle, as well as on those who would defy traditions and customs. This pronouncement was responded to by all members by saying *shai* in agreement. The resolutions adopted, agreements made, and customs confirmed during this assembly would remain in force for the following year in the three villages, and partly amongst several other villages that offered

---

[1]*Kriidie* is a term given to the family heads of sub-pedigrees within a clan in the *kuzha netho ketshii* dialect.

ancestral allegiance to the *Kuzha Netho Ketsii*.[2] After the meeting ended, the attendees would disperse to their respective villages, where their kin would instantly terminate their work to receive them with honours (Alibe 2014: 1).

The concept of *teakhe* implied a 'solemn undertaking' to follow newly adopted regulations and customs, in addition to existing traditions that were reaffirmed. This indicates that some traditions were not stable or fixed but constantly reviewed and reinvented based on present-day needs and contingencies, which exemplifies, I argue, Nagas' 'pragmatic' democratic ethos. In its form and functioning, the *teakhe mepou* was thus meant to adapt customs and traditions to the exigencies of time and so through deliberation and consensus-making. The *teakhe meopou*, moreover, was sanctified by traditional religion, as can be seen in the role of the *mewo* (priest).

From discussing the *taekhe-mepou*, I now focus more closely on the idea of political representation in Naga indigenous polities. As a general principle, traditional structures of authority revolved around family heads, clans, sub-clans, and *khels*. Political representation was not hereditary or fixed, but representatives were chosen based on their accumulated merits and virtues. Except for the social institution of priesthood, which was largely reckoned on hereditary lines,[3] for a person to become recognised as a 'representative' he had to first secure measures of social status and standing. This could be earned through bravery and by hosting lavish feasts. Each clan, generally, would delegate its most meritorious and capable person to represent the clan's interests at the village level. Thus, in the Naga communitarian system the capacities of an individual were paramount in determining political representation.

Besides bravery and wealth (and its dispensing through feasts), social and political hierarchies also revolved strongly around elders. It was often the village elderly who presided over public discussions and in whom the authority regarding village customs was vested (Hutton 1921a: 143-4). This reverence for village elders was derived out of popular respect for the

---

[2]Such ancestral allegiances to *Kuzha Netho Ketsii* were to a great extent voluntary, as was the subscription to its customs and traditions. Therefore, other villages were not included in the *tekhe-mepou* and what fell within the 'code of secrecy' remained 'closed' to them. However, given that the *Kuzha Netho Ketsii* exercised supreme spiritual authority over its descendants by virtue of being the ancestral entity, other villages regularly sought blessings and spiritual assistance to overcome different forms of calamity.

[3]The institution of *mewo* (priesthood) was not strictly hereditary, however. It was passed on to the most capable kin or clan member, or in absence occasional to an outsider. The villagers maintained a strong 'social audit' on the performance of *mewo*, who interceded with the spirits.

experience, maturity, and wisdom that was associated with the process of ageing. It must be noted here that a major critique of Nagas' indigenous ideas and practices of democracy is the blatant exclusion of women from the political domain. This is a fair critique, as various contributors to this volume discuss.

It is often assumed that in communitarian societies the individual is made wholly subservient to the community. However, the Naga communitarian experience also revealed a strong presence of 'the individual'. Wouters (2014: 64) argues how the Angami and Chakhesang Naga in particular had a marked 'democratic archaeology'. For the Angami Naga (then still including the Chakhesang Naga), Butler wrote: 'Every man follows the dictates of his own will, a form of the purest democracy which it is very difficult to conceive of as existing even for a single day and yet that it does exist here is an undeniable fact' (cited in Wouters 2014: 64). In actual practice, the Naga individual possessed a dual essence of both 'the individual' and 'the community', and it was this duality that defined the Naga democratic and social system. Added to this was the value of equality: 'Nagas are all equals', as A.Z. Phizo often emphasised (Pillai 2017).

Of course, to insist that Naga society was fundamentally egalitarian would be rather hyperbolic (consider, for one, the secondary position of women in the political domain), yet communitarian principles produced an organic form of social bonding that persisted, and was deeply meaningful, alongside the socio-economic and political hierarchies that inevitably existed. This notion of equality – with villagers following the 'dictates of their own will' – was central to Nagas' pragmatic democratic ethos. Read this way, the kernel of Naga traditional politics, despite its emphasis on community, also had something of the 'individual autonomy' that is taken as central to modern (liberal) democratic values (cf. Jayal 2001: 2).

These traditional Naga institutions and political practices, however, were to witness a radical transformation after the arrival of both colonial officers and Baptist missionaries.

THE MAKING OF NAGA VERNACULAR DEMOCRATIC SPACE: EARLY BEGINNINGS

From the beginning of the 19th century, British colonial officials and (mostly) American Baptist missionaries started flocking into the Naga Hills. They referred to its inhabitants as 'Naga', even though they were acutely aware that this denominator was not subscribed to by most Naga villages and communities themselves, who instead identified themselves primarily in terms of the clans and villages they belonged to. As late as 1875, Butler (1875: 309) recorded how the term 'Naga' was still foreign to most of the people it was supposed to refer to. Over time, however, the presence of colonial officers and missionaries gradually led to the categorization and classification of Nagas into identities that came to transcend the hitherto clan and village affiliations. Language played a prominent role in this process. A process of linguistic classification was carried out mostly by administrators, while the literalisation of selected dialects was undertaken by American missionaries. This new linguistic configuration, which started to club villages together based on linguistic affinities, worked to widen social and political horizons, and made Nagas to look, for the first time, beyond the boundaries of their villages, thus contributing to the 'making of tribes' (Wouters 2017b).

As missionaries embarked on their literary project, a process of linguistic standardisation and forms of wider social sensibilities emerged. For instance, *Tenyidie* was elevated from a village dialect, spoken in Meriema, Khonoma and Kohima villages (Shurhozelie 1992), to a standardised Angami language. Similarly, Chongli, hitherto a minority dialect spoken in a few villages, became the standard language of the Ao Naga (Khutso 2013: 13, Burling 2003). Linguistic classification so led to social classification, which then became the basis of larger socio-political conglomerates, which today are known as Naga tribes.

With colonial administrators and missionaries penetrating deeper into 'Naga lifeworlds', the traditional tenets of 'isolated' Naga village societies began to alter. This process was further augmented through the arrival of education and Christianity. In the end, it was education and successful proselytization that effectuated new social systems and nourished the emergence of a Habermasian public sphere amongst Nagas.[4] The colonial-missionary encounter ingrained new ethical and legal fundamentals among early educated Naga Christians, as literacy and Christianity infused them with new outlooks on the world (cf. Bennett et al. 2009: 3-4). While much did change in this period, this does not imply that traditional affiliations and practices became obliterated. The process, instead, was one in which Nagas began to gradually translate their hitherto independent existence and village loyalties into larger solidarities but whose allegiances were reckoned, and remained subject to, traditional affiliations.

[4]Habermasian notions of public sphere are characterised by openness of communication, and the creation of a space separate from the state in which people freely associate in organisations and bodies and can discuss and debate any issue of importance.

What I emphasise here is that these new socio-political formations, ever since the colonial-missionary encounter, were built on a pre-existent indigenous frame and networks of authority. This was translated, for instance, in terms of new authority systems such as that of gaonburas, dobashis, teachers and pastors. In a similar vein, the colonial regime built on selected indigenous practices and altered these to find consonance with colonial laws and procedures. They also codified, and in the process made rigid, traditional and customary laws. This not just constituted a rupture vis-à-vis past political practices (in which customary laws were regularly reviewed), but also saw the misappropriation of certain Naga customs, which subsequently worked to destabilise local political systems and practices.

Thus, with the codification and legal enforcement of Naga customs, the practice of reviewing and reinventing customs and traditions lost some of its previous democratic essence. This amounted to the colonial-missionary takeover of Naga indigenous institutions and values and came to somewhat strangulate the traditional essence of Nagas' 'pragmatic' politics. In its place a hegemonic space emerged in which 'western' cultural and institutional influences, Christianity, and administrative networks converged into an 'artificial' socio-political system. While this was created at the expense of significant 'cultural loss', these changes did enable a vernacular democratic space to emerge within Naga society.

THE NAGA CLUB AND THE NAGA HILLS DISTRICT TRIBAL COUNCIL

While the colonial-missionary encounter provided the antecedents for a Naga public sphere to emerge, the rise of a pan-Naga political sphere and consciousness must also account for a number of other variables. Several Naga historians trace the emergence of Naga political sphere and a pan-Naga political sociality to the mobilization of the Naga Labour Corps during the First World War, their experiences in war-trenches in France, and their subsequent return to the Naga Hills. They associate the establishment of the Naga Club, the first pan-Naga apex body, with the return of the Naga Labour Corps.

This argument is somewhat simplistic, however. The list of founding members of the Naga Club, for instance, reveals that it were mostly early educated Nagas who took the initiative, even as some France returnees were amongst them (Nuh and Lasuh 2002: 30-1). There was also a clear tribal dimension to the founding members of the Naga Club, including those who signed the 1929 memorandum submitted to the Simon Commission, which had come to British-India to study constitutional reform, and which is popularly perceived as the first expression of Naga political aspirations. This tribal dimension pertains that, bar a few, all founding members of the Naga Club and signatories of the memorandum hailed from the Kohima area (ibid.). This observation complicates the argument that it were France returnees who took the initiative because Angamis were not significantly part of the Labour Corps, which instead was largely made up from Sema, Rengma, Lotha, Ao, and Chang Nagas (Reid 1942: 162).

Another way of approaching the Naga Club would be as an 'elite club', staffed by educated and 'entrepreneurial' Nagas. Even as the Naga Club claimed to represent, and shoulder the responsibilities of, all Nagas (in the memorandum it was claimed that the signatories spoke for all Nagas), membership of the Naga Club was highly exclusive (Solo 2017). Therefore, the Naga Club as such did not signal the emergence of an inclusive democratic space. Arguing so, however, is not to deny that new socio-political formations were emerging during the first decades of the 20th century. In 1901, well before the enactment of the Naga Club, the Deputy Commissioner of Kohima took a number of Naga gaonburas to meet the Chief Commissioner of Assam in Imphal. In this meeting, these gaonburas convened to the administration that Naga villages had always been independent before the arrival of the British. Perhaps this, rather than the often cited memorandum to the Simon Commission, constitutes the first formal expression of Nagas' political consciousness.

Such and similar political expressions became more intense after the Nagas found themselves dragged into the Second World War, one of whose fiercest battles was fought in and around Kohima. Naga villagers sided with the British, and their role in pushing back the Japanese was indispensable, which the British Government acknowledged (Steyn 2002: 9-10; Yonuo 1974: 160).[5] In return for their loyalty and service, most Nagas anticipated, but not received, a 'political favour' from the British when they departed. In a wider light, Nagas' political ambition for independence coincided with the vigorous anti-colonial movement in India, and in places across the colonised world, in the wake and aftermath of the war, and these wider geo-political developments inflated the nationalist aspirations of the Nagas (Khutso 2013: 101). Therefore, the two World Wars came to further shape the rise of a Naga public sphere and gave way to new political aspirations.

[5]The commander of XIV army, Sir William Slim stated: 'the gallant Nagas, whose loyalty even in the most depressing times of the invasion never faulted. Despite floggings, torture, execution and the burning of their villages, they refused to aid the Japanese in any way or to betray our troops. Their active help was beyond value or praise'. (Cited in Steyn 2002: 9-10)

However, it was not until the formation of the Naga Hills Tribal District Council (NHDTC) in 1945 that a bolder and more representative Naga public space emerged. This Council came to offer a congenial space for Naga leaders to meet and discuss political matters (Khutso 2013: 101). The Naga Hills District Tribal Council had representatives from different tribes, and was initially enacted by the District Commissioner Pawsey. At first, the NHDTC was established to oversee the payment and implementation of reparations for the damages inflicted on Nagas during the course of the Battle of Kohima (Sema 1992: 151), and to unify the Nagas for this purpose (Steyn 2002: 69; Elwin 1961: 51; Yonuo 1974: 160-1). Interestingly, it was the official bungalow of Pawsey that became the place for political discussion of Naga representatives. Given the presence of representatives hailing from various Naga tribes, the NHDTC offered a wider public platform compared to the earlier Naga Club. The reach of this council widened further when the NHTDC took on a more political character and metamorphosed into the NNC in 1946, probably so against the will of colonial administrators.

Some scholars, such as Yonuo (1974: 154) eulogize Pawsey for the 'political renaissance' that came with the NHDTC and the NNC. Others argue that the NNC was merely a change of nomenclature from the NHDTC (Elwin 1961: 51). These perspectives however conceal the fact that whereas the NHDTC was facilitated by a colonial officer, the formation of the NNC resulted from an outburst of socio-political aspirations of Nagas themselves. It was the political anxiety that had developed for decades that ultimately led to the formation of the NNC. The NNC emerged in the context of political unrest, generated by the impending departure of the British and take-over of the Naga Hills by a soon to be independent India. This worried the Nagas as they feared 'being swamped by the Hindu and Muslim valley cultures' (Steyn 2002: 69). As such, the formation of the NNC was not simply another organisation but communicated a deliberate and conscious articulation of Naga identity and political aspirations. This is evidenced by the word 'National' within the NNC nomenclature. It was this articulation of Naga 'nationalism' that aggressively expanded the socio-political public sphere locally.

THE NNC AND THE MAKING OF A PAN-NAGA PUBLIC SPHERE

While Nagas used the NHDTC as a launch-pad for the NNC, there existed stark differences between them on the grounds of organisation, representation, and legitimacy. As far as the NHDTC was concerned, the system of representation did not thrust beyond 'tribal surfaces'. In contrast, NNC membership and networks came to include clans and villages (Nuh and Lasuh 2002: 77-91, Khutso 2013: 104-5). As opposed to the top-down functioning of the NHDTC, the NNC started to organize itself bottom-up. The NNC also took heed of previous Naga political traditions by replicating the representational system that had been in place inside villages within the NNC organisation. Thus, representatives from clans were delegated to village councils, from the village to sub-regional committees, then to the regional *Leacy* (assembly), and ultimately to the *Tatar Hoho* (Parliament) (Nuh and Lasuh 2002: 77-91). In this way, the Naga public became astutely networked within the social and political hierarchy of the NNC.

In its early days, the NNC refrained from using violence but used letters, memoranda, and discourses to negotiate a Naga political space (Khutso 2013: 106-109). This was to the extent that the NNC came to represent an epitome of critical public discourse on socio-political issues. As Naga nationalism took hold, the NNC provided a legitimate democratic space for its political expression. It was legitimate because it had representatives of large numbers of Naga tribes. In the late 1940s, as NNC leaders grappled with the political issues at hand, Mildred Archer (the wife of Bill Archer, then Sub-Divisional Officer of Mokokchung) minutely recorded the critical debates as they unfolded in NNC meetings. On the 23rd of July, 1947, the Hydari Agreement, also known as the Nine Point Agreement,[6] was debated. In the words of Archer (1947): 'though it is now ten o'clock and the hills have sunk into darkness, the Council is still sitting and no decision is yet in sight'. She also recorded how the NNC resorted to voting when no consensus could be reached, which was a radical departure from the essence of Naga traditional politics. But while the act of voting indeed constituted a rupture vis-à-vis Naga political pasts, it can also be analysed as constituting a continuum vis-à-vis the precolonial democratic system of being practical and pragmatic, including inventing new customs and traditions if the exigencies of time so demanded.

[6]As the Sub-Committee of Constitutional Assembly, led by Bardoloi and tasked to negotiate with the NNC, failed Sir Akbar Hydari, the Governor of Assam, was deputed to the Naga Hills to break the political impasse towards the end of June, 1947. After a three-day consultation i.e., 26th, 27th and 28th June, an agreement with the Nagas was signed, known as the Hydari Agreement or the Nine Point Agreement (Govt. of Nagaland: 1947, Archer 1947:13)

THE *YEHZABO* AS AN EXPRESSION OF VERNACULAR POLITICAL MODERNITY

This section builds on the previous argument but focuses on the adoption of the *Yehzabo*, or Constitution, of the NNC, and argues that in it a new vernacular political modernity was articulated. This was done not only through structuring the NNC as a political institution but also by formalizing and legalizing the political space it came to occupy.

As illustrated, Naga village polities were traditionally self-regulated by bodies of customs and traditions. Feats of this *ba-melhe* tradition (cited above), of a body of customs debated and pledged annually, became incorporated into the written Yehzabo. The written Yehzabo fostered a new tryst of conformity by recognizing the NNC as the overarching socio-political and cultural imperative. This written document bound Naga villages and identities into one.

Looking at the functional system of the NNC, as set out in the Yehzabo, several 'western' adaptations were made (Nuh and Lasuh 2002: 77-91). Nevertheless, the traditional system of a corpus of customs served as the modus operandi for the expression of 'constitutional patriotism' (cf. Calhoun 2002) the Yehzabo manifested. The written Yehzabo, as a formal expression of public discourse, was institutionalised in the form of Tatar Hoho, or a Naga parliament with hundred members and which functioned under the newly enacted Federal Government of Nagaland (Nuh & Lasuh 2002: 82-83a). Subsequently, resolutions of the Hoho garnered legal weightage as guaranteed in Article I & II of the Yehzabo (Yonuo 1974: 163-64).[7] What the Yehzabo worked to displace, however, was the traditional value of secrecy. With the gradual process of inter-village socialisation and the emergence of pan-Naga socio-political formations, the parochial nature of village polities was reduced, at least in principle. Writ large, the formation of the NNC, and the adoption of the Yehzabo, can therefore be read as an expression of socio-political selfhood, one enabled by a certain openness, not secrecy, of communication. Here the role of the English language may be emphasised, as both the Yehzabo and NNC discussions were conducted in this language.

[7] Article I states: 'the territory of Nagaland shall comprise all the territories inhabited by the indigenous Naga tribes and such other territories as Tatar Hoho may, by law, admit on such terms and conditions as it deem fit'. Article II States: 'the yehzabo shall apply to the territories as defined in Article I'.

'PRAGMATIC DEMOCRACY' IN THE 1951 PLEBISCITE

On the 14th of August, the NNC proclaimed Naga independence. However, as newly independent India would not concede to this political aspiration of the Nagas, a political tussle commenced. To add legitimacy to the Naga claim for Independence, the NNC, under the leadership of Phizo, organised a referendum on the 16th of May 1951. In this referendum, reportedly 99% of those Nagas consulted voted for Naga Independence (Steyn 2002: 85). The socio-political and historical implications of this plebiscite are beyond the scope of this paper. What I emphasise here is that the plebiscite represented the pinnacle of Naga vernacular democratic space, as forged by the NNC.

In parts, the plebiscite was a response to accusations levied by Indian political leaders that the Nagas were not unified in terms of their political aspirations (Nuh & Lasuh 2002: 116-133). To dispel such theories, Phizo, in a letter addressed to the President of India, stated that a collective verdict of the adult population of Nagaland shall be obtained through the recognised democratic method of a plebiscite (cited in Steyn 2002: 84). It was therefore to counter allegations of Naga disunity and, by extension, to convince Indian political leaders of the legitimacy of Naga political aspirations that the plebiscite was carried out. The NNC subsequently went back to the Naga public to seek their opinion and verdict. As such, the exercise of a political referendum boldly brings out the essence of the Naga democratic tradition in regards of the manner in which decisions and consensus were reached. Solo (2013) writes: 'the Naga opinion expressed in that Naga plebiscite is the only free will expression of the Naga people'. Therefore, the plebiscite bestowed ultimate political authority on the NNC as the socio-political organisation of the Nagas.

Noteworthy, here, is also the shift of Naga popular religious sensibilities from earlier 'animistic' traditions to that of Christianity. This can be discerned from the Christian discourse adopted by Naga leaders. Amongst them was Phizo, who asserted: 'We do not take Christianity as foreign religion any more than we consider the light of the sun as foreign origin from outer world'. He also said: 'I always have a feeling that God, our Heavenly Father - our creator - is with us and guiding us. What is there for us to fear?' (cited in Nuh & Lasuh 2002: 118, 128). This shift specifies that even though the vernacular democratic modernity retained strong historical continuities, the ethical and moral tenets no longer remained same. Therefore, the political soul of the new Naga vernacular democracy was overwhelmingly replaced by Christianity and its ethics.

DEMOCRATIC EXPERIENCES IN POST-COLONIAL INDIA

As political developments accelerated in the 1950s, the Naga public sphere was occupied with discourses concerning Nagas' political future. When Jawaharlal Nehru and the Burmese Prime Minister U Nu visited Kohima in March 1953, the Naga public walked out of the meeting as NNC leaders had been denied permission to meet and submit a memo to the Prime Minister by the incumbent Deputy Commissioner Barakataki (Thomas 2016: 111; Steyn: 88-89). Ramunny, who was a former Indian Administrative Officer and Advisor to Governor of Nagaland, has been quoted as saying: 'the Nagas will hear anyone but wants to be heard. His democracy, equality and classless society makes him feel equal to anyone' (cited in Steyn 2002: 89). Therefore, Nehru's denial to meet the NNC delegation did not go down well with the Naga public and resulted into collective protest. Evidently, the consequences of this political debacle would have a heavy bearing on the Indo-Naga relations as, soon after, Nehru dispatched his military and paramilitary forces into the Naga Hills to enclose the area forcefully.

The violence that engulfed the Naga Hills from the mid-fifties resulted into a perception of Naga villagers that the Indian state was inherently 'evil' (Steyn 2002: 90). Rammuny regretted this by saying: 'an opportunity was lost' (cited in Steyn 2002: 89) to engage the Nagas. To guard its identity, culture, and political aspirations, the NNC more or less successfully boycotted India's first general elections held in 1952 and 1957 (Even after statehood, Nagaland elections drew 'passive resistance' as many Nagas abstained from participation).[8]

A few years later the Naga People's Convention (NPC),[9] was organised, and met for three times between 1957 and 1959 to discuss a way out of the conflict (Nuh & Lasuh 2002: 191-198; Yonuo 1974: 221-242). These three conventions involved a large section of the Naga public and culminated into a sixteenth point agreement that, in turn, led to the enactment of Nagaland state, as part of the Indian Union, in 1963. Set aside the differences between the NNC and the NPC, going by the mass involvement of the Naga public in

---

[8]There are people known to the author who neither take part in elections nor take up government jobs as they see these as 'impositions'.

[9]It might be qualified here, however, that a former Intelligence Bureau official revealed in his book that the NPCs were engineered by the Intelligence Bureau in order to delegitimizee the popular mandate garnered during the plebiscite of 1951 (Mullik 1972; Thomas 2016: 5).

NPC meetings, even the formation of Nagaland statehood was mediated in Naga democratic style.

My analysis ends here, but on a final note: the authoritative entrance of modern Indian democratic institutions and competitive elections after the formation of Nagaland statehood radically changed Nagas' democratic experiences and expressions. The 'imposition' of Indian democracy and elections interfered with the remains of the Naga pragmatic practice of consensus-making (a disjuncture somewhat mitigated today by the selection of consensus-candidates, as is regularly reported across Nagaland constituencies). Whereas earlier, Nagas were able to be 'practical' in adapting themselves to changing political circumstances, a similar resilience did not emerge in relation to post-statehood democratic institutions and electoral politics, which many agree have been corrosive of the Naga communitarian ethos. This has not only caused a political disjuncture between the Central Government and the Nagas, but over time worked to alter Naga homegrown democratic and public sphere in radical ways. This set the stage for the disorderly and confused political practices contemporary Naga society is evidently immersed in.

■ ■■ ■■

08

MAKING SENSE OF CORRUPTION IN NAGALAND: A CULTURALIST INTERPRETATION

Venüsa Tinyi and Chothazo Nienu

Nagas were once celebrated as honest, simple, and hard-working. Narratives on how outsiders, particularly colonial administrators and writers, were impressed with the honesty of Naga villagers abound. However, if social behaviour and issues in contemporary times are any indication, characterizing present-day Naga society as honest seems to be an overstatement, if not preposterous. Naga society witnesses corruption, nepotism, and misappropriation of development funds, and the number of such cases remain on the rise. This makes one wonder how a society earlier labeled as 'honest', and amongst whom the value of honesty itself was highly regarded, became caught up in an apparent 'culture of corruption'. This chapter attempts to understand contemporary corruption in Nagaland. Arguing against the grain of conventional interpretations of corrupt behaviour and practices, we argue that corruption in Nagaland is not simply the failure of moral values but is intricately and significantly connected to the traditional ethos of Naga social and political life. To make this point, we situate contemporary corruption in the larger narrative of Naga culture, but with particular focus on the Chakhesang Nagas.

A glimpse into recent happenings may help us to get a sense of the issues we are trying to address here. Corruption has risen to prominence in public space and discourse in Nagaland: rallies, relentless discussions on social media, write-ups and rejoinders in local dailies, speeches in public gatherings and conferences, sermons in churches and evangelical camps, and so on. These discourses have been accusatory, not even sparing Nagaland churches and Naga national groups from accusations of corruption. Talk about corruption has been so pervasive that it connotes some sort of epidemic outbreak. As a case in point: when the committee Against Corruption And Unabated Taxation (ACAUT), an organisation formed primarily to fight corruption in the state, organised an anti-corruption rally in August 2017, its leaders estimated that a massive sixty-five thousand people attended the rally (*Nagaland Post* 27-08-2017).

That epidemic forms of corruption have crept into Nagaland government is also commented upon by voices beyond Nagaland. Patricia Mukhim, a leading journalist, lamented how certain members of the Nagaland Legislative Assembly broke traffic rules in Shillong (Meghalaya). Though this traffic violation of Naga legislators has hardly any connection with the dismal road conditions in Nagaland, she grabbed the opportunity to highlight the pitiable roads back in Nagaland. Her Facebook post went viral, resulting in Naga legislators receiving widespread condemnation on social media with commentators linking Nagaland's bad roads with rampant corruption within the state machinery. On the other hand; while Nagaland politicians are habitually accused of corruption, they also habitually speak out against it: 'It [corruption] is a major factor hindering development' said T. R. Zeliang, the Chief Minister of Nagaland in his speech during the Vigilance Week in 2017 (cited in *Eastern Mirror* 29-10-2017. He added:

> Very unfortunately, people do not look down on corruption because they have accepted it as a way of life. Honesty is treated as outdated and not in tune with the times. We need to make honesty as a new fashion for the scenario to change

Interesting to note here is that the previous culture of Naga honesty is directly pitted against the contemporary culture of corruption. While things are not that simple and straightforward, Zeliang's basic intuition appears valid, and is shared by many of those who cherish the ways of our forefathers. In what follows, this chapter brings these two perspectives – traditional honesty and contemporary corruption – together by discussing the intricate relations that seemingly exist between corrupt practices today and the ethos and values characteristic of Naga village polities in the past. More deeply, we address the often asked question: 'Why is it that corrupt Naga leaders are voted into power again and again, even though Naga electors know that they are corrupt?'

The next section first discusses conventional views on corruption. This section sets the tone for the subsequent section in which we outline different explanatory accounts of corruption in Nagaland. Next, we discuss the past communitarian ethos of Naga society. This is done with the view to understand the social structures and relationships that existed within traditional Naga communities, and to highlight that this type of social relationships not just persist in contemporary Naga society but continue to determine behaviour and actions. Against this background, the fourth section analyses some notable features that define the local relation between morality and leadership. Section five presents an analysis of contemporary democratic practices with special reference to electoral politics. In the final section, we bring all these arguments together and offer our perspective on the contemporary 'culture of corruption' in Nagaland.

WHAT IS CORRUPTION?

The problem of corruption is hardly a recent or modern development, but perhaps as old as civilization itself. Aristotle (1976), for instance, discusses corruption in relation to various forms of governments, with some forms of government being more susceptible to corruption compared to others. In India, corruption was intriguingly discussed by Kautilya (1915: 94):

> Just as fish moving under water cannot possibly be found out either as drinking or not drinking water, so governments servants employed in the government work cannot be found out (while) taking money (for themselves).

Corruption is here linked with public work and administration, which requires the exercise of power. History suggests that it is extremely difficult to exercise power without misusing it. The words of Lord Acton on the relation between power and corruption have turned proverbial: 'Power tends to corrupt and absolute power corrupts absolutely'. Corruption, however, is not 'context-free' or a problem that appears and disappears in thin air. Power is its biggest and inseparable alley. As such, any understanding of corruption must also look at how power is contextualised, institutionalised, and shared and expressed in a given socio-political context. As Pierce (2016: 5, 8) puts it succinctly:

> Corruption's meanings are multifaceted and polyvalent... [it]
> refers to a variety of phenomena. Its meaning is contextually
> dependent, but more importantly its social utility stems in
> part from its protean qualities.

According to Transparency International (2017), corruption is 'the misuse of *entrusted* power for private gain'. This could be 'grand, petty, and political, depending on the amounts of money lost and the sector where it occurs'. It is 'grand' if it is committed at a high level of government, enabling senior officials to benefit at the expense of the public good. It is 'petty' if it is indulged in by middle and lower level officials in their immediate dealings with the public, and it is 'political' if it consists of the manipulation of policies, institutions, and procedures in the allocation of state resources. From a different angle, as Piliavsky (2014) shows in the context of Rajasthan, corruption can be associated with the failure of those in power to cater to the personal expectations and needs of those who elected them. Hence, a politician's inability to feed and care for his people can be perceived as corruption by the people, even if in legal terms there have been no acts of corruption. Thus, accusations of corruption do not necessarily revolve around the illegal acquisition of wealth alone but also depend on societal perceptions, expectations, and judgments.

Meanings and understandings of what corruption is, and what it is not, also change over time. Drawing an analogy with biological degradation, Pierce (2016: 10-11) analyses corruption as social degradation in which a society falls from an earlier 'higher' position. Corruption can also serve as a conceptual critique; for instance, the term corruption was used in the past to denote a so-called civilised society being polluted by influences from a supposedly less civilised nation. When officials of British India sought to 'buy' influence at home, their critics saw these practices as indicating the corruption of a civilised nation, i.e. Britain being corrupted by British India (ibid.). Conversely, the so-called civilised nations were also thought to corrupt the societies they colonised, especially through various policies and measures that advanced imperial interests (Angeles and Neanidis 2010). From yet another angle, corruption is seen as an inevitable social and historical phase through which every country needs to pass in its development trajectory (Pierce 2016: 10-13). That said, corruption is hardly exclusive to developing countries but also prevails in developed countries, even though often through more subtle networks that are difficult to detect.

Pierce (2016: 12-3) further argues that in the 1960s and 1970s three different understandings of corruption emerged, namely: economic, political, and ethnographic. In terms of economy, corruption was understood as rent-seeking behaviour by which benefits are gained without returning benefits equally.[1] In political understandings, the focus was on relations and the distinction between private and public spheres. It became argued that while people could be honest in the private sphere, they could become 'amoral' while operating in the public sphere. Then there was the issue of patronage, often dispensed along ethnic lines, with politicians competing not over ideology but for privileged access to state resources. Ethnographic studies on corruption, in turn, focused on actual actors engaged in corrupt behaviour, exploring their motivations, perspectives, and concerns. Thus, not only has corruption been understood differently at different points of history, it can also be analysed from a number of vantages. In this chapter, and in the context of Naga society, we aim to locate 'corruption' in the confluence of modern political institutions and Naga cultural values and practices.

POSSIBLE EXPLANATIONS OF CORRUPTION IN NAGALAND

In this chapter's introduction, we highlighted the pressing problem of corruption in contemporary Naga society. This section discusses some possible explanations for this prevalence of corruption.

First, corruption among Nagas is not age-old, but arrived with the imposition of Nagaland state on Nagas in 1963.[2] As such, it is a modern occurrence. The formation of Nagaland state was not seen, by most Nagas, as a solution to the Naga struggle for a sovereign state of their own. Rather, it was perceived as an imposition, one that defied the wishes of many Nagas, and who subsequently found it impossible to strongly identify themselves with the new Nagaland state. Prior to the enactment of Nagaland state, this resistance to Indian state structures can be read in the 1952 and 1957 election boycotts as well as in the opposition against the introduction of Indian administrative and police services in the Naga Hills. There were indeed cases of Naga individuals who refused government jobs offered to them because of their commitment to Naga independence (even today it is not uncommon to witness tirades by Naga nationalists against those public

---

[1]In Economics, a transaction takes place only when two parties agree that the good(s) or service(s) they exchange are of equal value(s). An economics understanding of corruption, usually understood as 'rent seeking', consist of exchange where equal values are not exchanged.

[2]Here we understand corruption primarily in terms of the misuse of public office, public work and public money.

figures who serve in the central government, who they accuse as 'Agents of the Indian Government'). In the early days of statehood, because of the gap between Naga society and the Nagaland government, it was easy for those in power to run the government the way they liked, and so without being questioned by the Naga public. While doing so, they offered jobs and state contracts to those who supported them, or who were related to them by bonds of family, clan, village, and tribe. The consequences of these initial manifestations of corruption can still be discerned today as the majority of government employees continue to belong to those tribes whose leaders first adjudicated over Nagaland state institutions.

Secondly, modern institutions of state have seemingly not been properly understood by most Nagas. Ever since their entrance into Nagaland, these institutions functioned as 'externalities' and did not take into consideration the general will and interests of the Naga people. Taking advantage of the people's ignorance about their rights and privileges, those in power misused and abused their offices to serve their own personal interests. On the other hand, as though to complement the behaviour of corrupt officials, many Naga villagers thought (and continue to think) that the state government is first and foremost a job-giving and money-giving agency, not something they also have duties towards. This is because the government is perceived by them as foreign in nature, and further because the Central Government bears nearly all the costs of administration and development in Nagaland. Most Nagas reasoning would be something like this:

> It is not a shame but a loss if we don't take as much as possible from the government since state resources and benefits are a form of charity; they are meant to be taken and profited from.

Thirdly, in contemporary times a strong linkage between elections and corruption is articulated by Naga civil society organisations, including churches. They deduce that corruption is the consequence of the 'buying' and 'selling' of votes in election seasons. Khekiye Sema (2017), a leading activist for clean elections, details the logic of this argument:

> You have no right to complain [about corruption] because you sold your vote, you sold your right. The moment the MLA or the candidate purchased your vote, what he does with the power that he get from that vote that you sold is his business, not yours.

The analysis here is that during elections candidates spend so much money to procure votes that after elections, instead of utilizing funds for development purposes, legislators divert these to their own pockets. They must do so, first, to reimburse themselves for past election expenditures and, secondly, to prepare themselves financially for future election expenses. Allegations of percentages being deducted from contractors by politicians has now became household talk across Nagaland, needing no further elaboration.

Echoing a similar logic and concern, the Nagaland Baptist Church Council (NBCC) embarked on a Clean Election Campaign. In anticipation of the 13th state elections, Nagaland churches have been organizing workshops and seminars that promote clean elections, anticipating that achieving this will near mechanically put a stop to corruption. To that end, the NBCC entered into an eighteen point agreement with political parties. It was agreed that, amongst others, political parties and politicians would not:

1. Buy votes with money;
2. Insist/force clan, khel, village, and family to declare support for a particular candidate;
3. Distribute alcohol, drugs, or other intoxicants to voters;
4. Provide feasts, picnics, or organize processions;
5. Use force, intimidation and undue influence to the voter.

Other explanations can be forwarded to explain Nagaland's 'culture of corruption'. However, for our purposes here we limit ourselves to the above three. While these three explanations provide us with reflections on the conundrums of corruption in Nagaland, we are persuaded that these reasons by themselves remain inadequate to tackle some of the most urgent questions of corruption. For instance, while acknowledging that the way in which Nagaland state was 'imposed' against the wishes of most Nagas, and the perception of the government as a foreign institution, can explain the local absence of belonging to the Nagaland government, this explanation fails to explain why most Nagas take part in elections to decide who should be in control of the state they feel so little commitment towards. Election feasts, rallies, campaigns, pamphlets, and manifestos, and a host of other political activities have carved out space in Naga society. In fact, some are willing to fight, even die, for their candidate during elections. These are hard questions to address within the explanatory schemes introduced above.

Questions can also be raised against the third perspective, i.e. that clean elections will end corruption in the state. The real question here is: 'will the clean election campaign, even if successful, solve the issue of corruption and mal-governance in the state?' Put differently, 'will those people not receiving money during elections bring about a corrupt-free state?', or 'will it result in the disappearance of scams, backdoor appointments, and nepotism?' Putting the question the other way around: 'will Naga electors stop seeking the help of their politicians once they stop receiving money during elections?' In our opinion, such a scenario appears out of tune with reality. For one, gifts and monies that change hands during elections (or for that matter election feasts) cannot be understood only in the transactional terms of selling and buying votes. Gifts are offered and received to cement existing social relationships or to initiate new ones. These gifts come with obligations; 'givers' and 'recipient' do not necessarily understand such exchanges as a transaction but perceive of these as part of a traditional practice to maintain, strengthen, or celebrate social relationships. This can also be discerned from the way in which candidates help out families with only few votes disproportionally to some larger families. If 'gifts' were purely transactional larger families should ipso facto receive larger gifts and monies compared to smaller families, but this is not necessarily the case.

Yet another observation is that many people habitually seek help from their political representative, even for relatively small issues. This culture will not simply disappear since the expectation to be 'helped' is part of existing relationships, and the expectations that come with it. There are cases in which villagers spend days, even weeks, in the residence of their MLA, and to assume that these practices would instantly disappear once people strop receiving money from the candidate during elections remains doubtful.

The first two explanations – Nagas lacking affinity with the state and having misunderstood state institutions – are no doubt important from a historical and political perspective, but it is the third view – that corruption is linked to elections – that seems most widely argued today. However, our doubts concerning the validity of these explanations lead us to an alternative explanation. But before we come to that, the next section first sketches the structure and functioning of Naga 'traditional' politics, which we deem imperative because our interpretation of corruption is directly related to this.

THE NORMATIVE ETHOS OF THE NAGA COMMUNITARIAN SOCIETY

In what follows, we take the theme of identity as our vantage into the traditional structure and ethos of Naga society. Across Naga society, what an individual does, or becomes, was long secondary to the group or community he or she belonged to. Traditionally, a person located his or her identity primarily in, first, his clan and, secondly, his village. Even today, clan-identities remain more fundamental compared to village identities, even though the latter is also indispensable as there is no Naga who either does not belong to an (ancestral) village or has forgotten about it. This dual identity of a person (clan and village) is so fundamental that to be disowned from the clan or ex-communicated from the village is equated with the loss of identity. Ex-communication in the context of most Naga communities is therefore the worst possible punishment that can be awarded to any wrong-doer.

These traditional affinities did not significantly change after the arrival of modernity and Christianity as clan and village identities remain particularly strong (Wouters 2017a). In the words of H. Sema (1986: 10), among Nagas 'the collective life took precedence over the individual'. Any Naga would acquire his identity through a network of socio-biological relationships. In this relational structure, a person's activities and societal roles were regulated by a set of expectations and customs. Clan members, for instance, were responsible for the poorer and aged segments of their clan; the elder son in a family was required to act and behave in a certain way; any village elder was expected to correct erring acts of village youth; a rich person was expected to perform the 'feast of merit'. Regarding the latter, it was not unusual for clan members to advise, or urge, wealthy clan-members to throw these feasts. In a different context, they may encourage a strongly built youth to participate in a village wrestling contest, the winning of which bestowed pride and standing not just on the individual but on the clan entirely. In fact, when a clan-member would participate in a wrestling competition, all clan members were expected to support him financially or otherwise.

The communitarian structures of the Nagas were thus predominantly defined by duties and responsibilities of an individual to his family and clan. Assistance was given and received in ways that was not transactional. By virtue of one's relational status in the society, a person was expected to give, and could expect to receive, help. A person may provide help continually throughout his life to some persons, and likewise another person may receive help throughout his or her life, but always so without any expectations, that is except to respect the values that determine the social relations that structure these modalities and moralities of 'giving' and 'receiving'. Notions of rights, equality and justice, too, were defined in the context of social relationships, rather than measured in an abstract, individual sense. The same is true when it comes to the evaluation of an action as being right or wrong, honourable or shameful, just or unjust. For instance, it was considered right, just and honourable to take revenge against someone who had harmed or insulted a clan or family member.[3]

---

[3]This point is explored in greater details in Tinyi's 'Head-hunting Culture of

The social standing of a person or a clan was often evaluated by considering the manner in which members of a clan or village supported each other. In Tinyi's (2017: 59) words:

> They [community members] take care of the members in times of sickness and troubles. When a person is in need but without family to support her, the clan or neighbours or the entire village would come forward to help. The need may be one of building a house or cultivation or providing health care in times of sickness. And when a person dies, there are elaborate ways to honour the dead. If the relatives and clan of the dead do well to pay their due respect to dead, the dignity of both the dead and the relatives are safeguarded; such an act can also earn dignified honour to the dead and to the relatives and clan as well. In other word, it is mainly in a relationship that a person finds her identity and dignity; in it she finds her self-worth and meaning of existence.

Failure to look after the needs of clan members in times of exigency was looked down upon by members of other clans as a sign of disunity within the clan, and would be talked about in the village. The clan members were thus under the obligation to look after one another, the failure of which would result into gossip and disapproval.

In a similar fashion, the idea of justice was guided by this relational ethos. Justice was intricately related to ideas of shame and honour. Projections of shame and honour were never individualistic but shared by all members of a family or clan or village, depending on the context. Thus, if someone from another clan insulted any member of a clan, such an act was not seen as an isolated, personal matter. To the contrary, members of his clan were expected to defend the honour of their insulted member by exerting revenge. Failure to take revenge would imply shame, not only of the individual that was directly insulted but of his clan as a whole. In another context, if a member of a clan would do something considered wrong, punishment would be given by the village not just to the erring person but to the clan as a whole. As such, justice was meted out not individually but collectively, and therefore was, in a way, impersonal in nature (Tinyi 2017).

Having noted the above, we now explore the concept of honesty within the Naga traditional context. Anyone familiar with narratives about Naga pasts knows that even the practice of locking doors was long unheard of. Locks were unknown not because houses lacked valuables but because of a culture of honesty that prevailed. To steal was to invite curses, while laziness – taking from others without working for it – had no place in the society. Certain rituals were in fact conducted against liars and thieves. For instance, among the Chakhesang Nagas a ritual was performed annually to curse those who engaged in thievery. In this ritual, a cat would be pierced by spokes or spears by villagers. It was believed that non-confession by thieves would result in them suffering the same pain and agony as had the cat, and that they would make cat-like noises at the time of their dead. The performance of this annual ritual impacted the psychology of the village youth and worked to deter them from developing any stealing habits.

In Naga villages, private property was highly respected, which continues to be the case today. For instance, it is common for a villager to come and tell the owner if while hunting or fishing in the jungle he had stopped by in a hut that is not his own to cook a meal, and for its purpose used firewood. To cite another case; a person carrying a bundle or a piece of wood from the jungle would, if too heavy to carry, simply and safely put it on the wayside and place a small stone on top to indicate that the bundle has an owner. In this case, no-one would think of snatching the bundle away. Remnants of such practices still exist in rural Nagaland. Take, for instance, the different road-side markets where there are no shopkeepers but only items left on the roadside for travellers to buy. Price tags will be given against each item and a customer would leave the amount either at the same place or in a small box positioned there. The trust that the owners have on the honesty of travellers reflects the deeper culture of honesty that long characterised Naga society.

LEADERSHIP IN TRADITIONAL SOCIETY

Before we move on to discuss issues of democracy and elections in contemporary Naga society, we, in this section, first briefly examine the roles and virtues of leaders in Naga traditional society. Notions and expectations of leadership were largely a continuation of the communitarian ethos of assisting one another, as prescribed by social relationships. As a general principle, everyone was expected to support each other in times of need. However, the expectation of a leader to provide help was significantly and substantially higher compared to what was expected of an ordinary villager. In fact, the idea of a leader refusing to help his people was counter-intuitive to the concept of leadership itself. It must be noted here that leadership here entailed not helping everyone possible but that help had to be extended to the particular social group to which the leader belonged, usually his clan and village. This implies that leadership was a closed concept, bounded by membership to a particular social group.

This practice of helping can be understood in terms of providing solutions in times of conflict or crisis, or by defending the honour of members in relation to other social groups, or by providing material support to the poor. The relationship was akin to a family with leaders fulfilling a parental role of providing care and protection. The actions and activities of leaders and 'ordinary people' were therefore not merely transactional since there was no question of choice. Rather, it was morally and culturally incumbent for a leader to help members of his social group. At the same time, a member of one social group could not claim help from a leader of another social group. When a leader did help a person belonging to another social group, acts of giving and receiving were not bound by a prior sense of duty or right. In sum, an act of helping one another was first and foremost defined by social relationships.

Seen from another angle; the function of a leader may be correlated to, and evaluated by, how he defended and promoted the dignity and honour of his social group. Generally, the dignity and honour of a person or group was safeguarded fiercely in traditional Naga society. These values were treated almost as 'sacred' or 'taboo'; they were not subject to questioning. In a sense, they constituted the heart and soul of one's quest for a meaningful existence and identity. No group, no matter how strong or arrogant, would treat any other group as lesser human beings. Though taboos regarding performance and non-performance of ritualised actions, and the consumption or non-consumption of certain foods, may be uniquely associated with certain social groups or clans, they were never seen as standard norms for the division of society into a caste-like social structure. In other words, everyone was regulated by the same set of norms and values. Questions of honour and dignity were associated with moral integrity on one hand and with competitive cultural practices, including the ability to take revenge, on the other. As such, they can be linked to ideas of shame and disgrace. Leaders and elders were crucial to ensure that the dignity and honour of their social group was not compromised.

Since honour was sacred, it could never be compromised or suspended, not even in times of conflict. Thus, even if two parties were in conflict, they were bound to honour and respect each other. Opponents were considered worthy and every word used against opponents, especially in public space, would be carefully weighted so as to not insult each other's honour. Conflicting parties would address each other in highly dignified terms. Even in personal or informal contexts, if words insulted the dignity of an opponent the reaction would surely be intense and invite '*rünü mote*' (words of displeasure).[4] In such a case, justice or revenge would be sought, and which was seen as justified. In the meantime, members of a group would be advised not to talk about the shameful things of the group to other people.

Now, what is the purpose of our elaborating on this? It is the following. Within Naga culture, any talk that might embarrass or shame other persons was shunned or discouraged. This included allegations and rumours. 'Character assassination', in contemporary parlance, was seriously viewed in traditional Naga culture. We argue in the next section that this practice of 'holding back one's tongue' created a fertile ground for corruption.

CONTEMPORARY LEADERSHIP AND CORRUPTION

Keeping the above discussion on the traditional ethos at the back of our minds, let us now analyse the issues facing contemporary Naga society. A system of governance founded on a modern liberal ethos has been introduced in Nagaland. Though it is supposed (actually Constitutionally guaranteed) that Nagas' traditional values and practices are safeguarded, it can be discerned that the Nagaland government is increasingly abandoning or replacing Naga traditional values and practices with modern constitutional and liberal values. Without here going into the details of modern values and their various theorizations, it suffices to highlight here that modern liberal values privilege the individual over the community. In a 'liberal culture', the subject matter of ethical evaluation is action; an action is judged to be right or wrong without giving much importance to agency or the community-background of the actors, unless it involves juveniles or those who are mentally challenged. Generally a person's status or identity is not considered in the passing of value judgments on a particular act.

To an extent, modernity, as a project, is an attempt to eliminate all traditional identities, to eliminate the notion of 'the other' and replace it by a set of individual rights. To offer a loose and one-sided characterization of the modern state, one might argue that the state exists first and foremost to protect the rights of individuals and related values such as equality, freedom, and dignity. It is committed to protecting these values and ideals against institutions (including those that are part of the state itself) and social groups

---

[4]This is an expression in *Chokri* language. It may be pointed out that though the issues discussed in this section basically capture the sensibility of the *Tenyimia* culture, this seems more or less true of Naga culture in general.

that may undermine those values. As Naga society is now officially governed by such modern systems and values, one cannot help but experience a gap, or indeed a conflict, between these two systems of norms and values – the traditional and the modern and liberal. Perhaps a 'tug of war' is a proper ideology to explain the current tension that exists between them.

It remains unimaginable to deny our socio-cultural identity, grounded, as it is, in relational structures with associated sets of values and norms. Yet, it might be suicidal to turn our backs against the promises of modernity. Amidst this tension, the question we pose is: 'what is the role of Naga leaders, especially elected representatives, in contemporary Naga society?' We will now try to locate and analyse the problems and challenges of corruption by way of responding to this question.

Elections are viewed, as illustrated above, as a fundamental cause of corruption in Nagaland. Our main attempt here is to understand the factors that come into play during elections. Derivatively, we will show how the factors that decide the fate of leaders in elections continue to influence the decisions and actions of elected leaders even after elections are over. It is common knowledge across Nagaland that without money winning a constituency is virtually impossible. But it is also the case that money alone does not guarantee electoral success as the richest or most generous candidate does not automatically win an election. Besides money, the politics of identity is also a prime factor. This identity politics exerts itself variously at the levels of clan, village, region, language, and tribe.[5] By identity politics, we primarily mean a kind of politics that defines the relation between 'the self' and 'the other'. The identification of a potential candidate begins either within his identity group, or with the 'money power' an individual possesses. If someone possesses both, he is deemed to stand a good chance of winning. But even if a person is very wealthy, it is unimaginable for such a person to be able to discard his identity and still win.

Why, then, is group identity so crucial in Naga electoral politics? It is because of the concept of 'help' we discussed above. A leader is expected to help his people as much as possible. And since the government is perceived by many as an external institution that freely doles out development monies and employment, an elected representative is expected to secure the maximum of state benefits and resources to his particular social group. In this way, the government becomes somewhat like a hunting ground and social groups see their candidates as hunters. Each chooses their respective candidates by assessing his potential as a hunter – that is, who will bring

[5]In the more multi-cultural and cosmopolitan places such as Dimapur, tribal politics dominates while in the rural areas, clan and village politics dominates.

more food and is able to safeguard the honour of the people. To exploit this analogy further, a leader is praised if he successfully brings more benefits to his group and looked down upon in the event of his inability to bring any such benefits. Note that in hunting, neither is there any specific rule nor can one be blamed for hunting successfully.

As crude or bizarre as this analogy may appear, we hold that it points towards a significant truth of Naga cultural behaviour. Corruption in one form or the other has existed since the inception of Nagaland statehood, but these practices were hardly raised as an issue of concern until quite recently. Partially we believe that this silence relates to the traditional perception of a leader and his responsibilities. If the MLA of a constituency hails from a particular village, and succeeds in helping his villagers by 'misusing' his position, his act is unlikely to be questioned as a form of corruption. Rather, people in his constituency would reason along the following lines: 'they [that village] are fortunate to have such a capable leader'. This is because they read the MLA's actions from the relational structure of community. For them, the MLA is only fulfilling his duty to his people. Moreover, most Nagas are still not in the habit of publicly accusing 'others' of indulging in corrupt behaviour since they remain influenced by a traditional system which shunned talking negatively of others (as discussed above).

However, when an MLA would, out of respect for clean governance, fail to privilege his clan, village, and his constituents more generally, he is unlikely to be re-elected again. In fact, his leadership qualities will be questioned and his inability to help soon construed as his weakness, making people talk about him as a 'good-for-nothing MLA'. Soon, his electors will develop grudges against him. This is a serious challenge every politician in Nagaland faces. A Naga politician is expected to help individuals either by providing monetary help, government employment, or other state benefits; next, he is also expected to help the people he represents by bringing general development such as roads, schools, and hospitals. At the same time, he is expected to perform his duties and responsibilities as per the law of the state. These three expectations – personal help, community help, and following the law – are inconsistent with each other. Being true to his office and to the law would mean the privileging of the common good over personally helping his kin and electors. In fact, if a politician chooses to legally and honestly perform his duties, he will be left with no resources to help his social group, or to accumulate the personal riches he requires to contest the next election. It would also mean that he has to initiate appropriate actions against those government employees who are not performing their duties satisfactorily. However, his doing so would also mean that he has to compromise on the obligation to help and protect 'his people'.

In this way, each Naga politician is bound to face what we call a trilemma – the responsibility to be true to his office, to help members of his clan, village, and tribe individually, and to bring forth development for his constituency as a whole. This conundrum is not only experienced by an elected member but may also occur in the lower echelons of state, though not necessarily in the form of a trilemma. Wouters (2017a), for instance, showed how the introduction of Communitisation, an act meant to improve the management of public services and utilities through the involvement of the community in the state, failed because the nourishing of social relationships and the fulfilling of kinship obligations take precedence over the kind of rational-legal, detached governance envisaged by the Communitisation Act.

CRITIQUE OF CONTEMPORARY LEADERS FROM A TRADITIONALIST PERSPECTIVE

Our attempt to problematize the culture of corruption from the perspective of Naga traditions may be interpreted by some as an attempt to absolve or explain away corruption. The problem of trilemma faced by elected leaders may even give the impression that Naga politicians are the innocent victims of an authoritative Naga communitarian ethos. But this, to be sure, is not our objective. We are as troubled as most Nagas with the culture of corruption currently prevailing. Our intention, rather, is to locate the problem of corruption in the gap between modern and traditional political practices and principles, and to argue that without understanding this it is impossible to deal with the problem of corruption.

At the same time, we want to argue that it is also possible to problematize corruption from a Naga culturalist and traditionalist perspective. To do so, we need to revisit some core values and virtues associated with Naga traditional conceptions of leadership. A traditional Naga leader was assessed not solely on the basis of the help and protection he could offer, but also by some other qualities, such as honesty, moral integrity, and simplicity. A leader's role was thus not limited to his ability to protect and promote the honour of his clan, *khel*, or village. Traditional Naga society being governed by notions of shame and honour, only those leaders with an impeccable integrity were recognised as leaders. Without possessing such qualities, a person aspiring to be a leader at the clan or village level would immediately be questioned or rejected by his kith and kin as he would surely bestow shame and disgrace on them. Leadership was primarily sacrificial in nature and hardly anyone would try to use the position of leadership for selfish material gains. Leadership was traditionally also something that was recognised by others on the basis of

Figure 6. *Nagaland Post*. Reproduced with permission..

one's qualities and virtues, not claimed by oneself.

The question of material gains in connection with leadership positions also throws some light on the Naga philosophy of wealth or possession. Here we explain this relationship with special reference to the Chakhesang Nagas. Wealth, among them, was not accumulated for its own sake. There was no philosophy that celebrated the accumulation of wealth as an end in itself. Rather, the celebration concerned the sharing of wealth with the community. Wealthy people were given respect only if they performed 'feasts of merit' (feast provided to the whole village in return for social status). Feast-givers earned the right to wear a certain type of shawl and to decorate their houses with certain designs, both of which communicated their social ascendancy. Monoliths would also be pulled and erected in their honour. For the Chakhesang, to become a feast-giver and to be recognised as meritorious was the dream of every villager. It was considered shameful not to perform a feast if one was wealthy. In fact, the main drive for a villager to become wealthy, mostly through his exploits in agriculture, was to perform this feast. Wealth in itself could become the object of scorn and derision unless this wealth would benefit the community in one way or the other. Among relatives and clan members, no strong ownership of wealth could be claimed individually; instead the language of ownership would sound somewhat like this: 'our house', 'our cattle', 'our field', and even 'our children'. It must also be highlighted here that in this context there was no short-cut to becoming rich as it could only be achieved through hard work (or inheritance).

In this light, let us now look at present-day Naga politicians. How many of them are respected by the people for their integrity and honesty? This is for anyone to speculate. What we see is that even 'ordinary people' in the remote villages usually do not think highly of politicians. To the contrary, politicians are generally viewed as dishonest and untrustworthy. They are not seen as sacrificial and selfless leaders, but increasingly as selfish individuals whose philosophies of leadership and wealth are inconsistent with traditional Naga values and practices. Though their language of politics is often in line with the traditional language of common ownership and belongingness – they may say 'our people' or 'our future' – they will hardly use this type of language to refer to their personal wealth. Instead, wealth has been privatised by them. Their wealth has become opaque and, what is worse (from the viewpoint of traditional Naga politics), inaccessible to the community. In the hand of the political leaders, the past purpose of wealth to serve and benefit the community has been redefined. They have corrupted the traditional concept of leadership and built their personal kingdoms. As such, hardly anyone sees them as selfless and upright leaders. No traditional ethos can explain and justify the palatial houses they built for themselves when public schools and roads, for instance, are in ruins.

CONCLUDING OBSERVATIONS

Very rarely do we come across people, including politicians, who confidently talk about the 'blessedness' of modern politics in Nagaland. The general view of democratic politics is that is 'dirty' and corrosive of Naga traditional values. The irony, however, is this: people are willingly fighting tooth and nail during elections instead of staying away from what they call 'dirty politics'. Undeniably, and sadly, the politics that is loved so much today by Nagas is electoral politics. Perhaps the reason is related, consciously or unconsciously, to the traditional practice of pursuing status and honour. Looking back, we know our history, among others, to be a history of rivalries, fights, and competition at every level of social classification, from inter-family to inter-clan, to inter-village to inter-tribal contests. In this socio-historical setting, the victory or achievement of one and the feelings associated with it were shared by everyone associated with that person. Conversely, if a member of a family or clan did something wrong, the entire family or clan faced the shame.

The interesting fact of this type of social behaviour is that people were more motivated by the idea of winning compared to them being unmotivated by the fear of losing. The whole clan or village would generally contribute to support if someone was to represent the clan or village in a game or competition. Games and sports were not treated simply as entertainment but were significantly linked to the honour of the family or clan or village. Among the Chakhesang, for instance and as noted, it was a common practice for the kith and kin to support and raise a wrestler. Election has seemingly come to replace or substitute this traditional culture of competition.

Having now been largely influenced by modern democratic systems and its liberal projections, educated youth, as well as Nagaland churches, have begun to accuse Naga politicians of being corrupt. They, however, often do so by overlooking the traditional values and practices that shape the tenets of leadership in Naga society. At the same time, it is not uncommon to see these protestors approaching their elected representatives for 'help' to their clan, village, or tribe, not realising perhaps that seeking favours based on social relations is what is termed 'corruption' in modern democratic parlance. This also partially explains how a politician widely known to be corrupt is nevertheless elected again and again. We have argued that social relationships are prior to, and consequent upon, the action of an individual or group in Naga society. As such, the problem of corruption goes deeper than electoral politics. Ensuring a clean election will not ensure good governance. We have to look at our social norms and values carefully in order to tackle the problem of corruption.

We end on the suggestive note that it is possible to provide a critique of Naga leadership cum corruption from within our own culture. Consequently, it may be more useful, as an intellectual exercise, to first learn to critique our own culture from within rather than to critique it only from the lens of modern or 'external' cultural influences.

■ ■■ ■■

09

PATRIARCHY AS STRUCTURAL VIOLENCE: RESISTANCE AGAINST WOMEN RESERVATION IN NAGALAND

T. Longkoi Khiamniungan

INTRODUCTION

In its set-up and values, Naga society is deeply patriarchal, as can be seen in manifold and deeply entrenched patriarchal structures that produce and reproduce gender inequalities. In this chapter, I approach the subordinate position of Naga women, particularly in the fields of politics and 'the political', as a manifestation of 'structural violence'. In Johan Galtung's (1969: 168) widely cited definition, structural violence exists:

> When human beings are influenced so that their actual somatic and mental realisations are below their potential realisations... Violence is here defined as the cause of the difference between the potential and the actual, between what could have been and what is.

Galtung illustrates this distinction between the *potential* and the *actual* with a range of examples, among them:

> If a person died from tuberculosis in the eighteenth century it would be hard to conceive of this as violence since it might have been quite unavoidable, but if he dies from it today, despite all the medical resources in the world, then violence is present... If people are starving, when this is objectively avoidable, then violence is committed (ibid: 171).

Working with Galtung's approach, Paul Farmer (2004: 307) reiterates that structural violence invokes '"sinful" social structures characterised by poverty and steep grades of social inequality, including racism and gender inequality. Structural violence is exerted systematically – that is, indirectly – by everyone who belongs to a certain social order'. In what follows, I use the framework of structural violence to discuss and debate the resistance against women reservation of electoral seats in Nagaland by, most vocally, male-dominated tribal apex bodies. More broadly, I will illustrate how a range of traditional, patriarchal societal structures prevent Naga women from equal participation in politics, and argue that this created an institutionalised gap between their 'potential' and 'actual' realisations, making the contemporary role and status of Naga women within the political domain an instance of 'structural violence'.

DEBATE ON WOMEN RESERVATION IN NAGALAND

The issue of women reservation of electoral seats in Urban Local Bodies (ULBs) is intensively debated in Nagaland (see also Chapter 13 by Hausing, this volume). Legally, the reservation of 33% of seats in urban local bodies is ingrained in the amended Nagaland Municipal Act (2006), which itself was a much delayed response to the 74th Amendment to the Indian Constitution that came into force in 1992 to streamline the form and functioning of urban local bodies across the country, including the inclusion of women reservation.

Proponents of women reservation in Nagaland insist that reserving seats for women is not just about empowerment but concerns giving equal recognition to Naga women. They argue that several socio-economic, political, and cultural structures continue to prevent Naga women from contesting and winning elections, as is evidenced from the observation that, after fifty years of statehood, not a single women has been elected into the Nagaland state legislative assembly.[1] Protestors against this Act, however, cite that women reservation infringes on Naga customary laws and traditions, as safeguarded by Article 371(A) of the Indian Constitution. They call both women reservation and taxes of land (needed to finance Urban Local Bodies and part of the same Municipal Act) as 'alien' to the Naga 'way of life', and therefore violating Naga culture, traditions and customs.

For long, the Nagaland Government was seemingly on the side of the opponents of women reservation, and variously sought to circumvent women reservation. When this failed, the government simply delayed the holding of fresh elections for urban local bodies. This, however, changed in 2016 when the Nagaland Legislative Assembly finally went ahead and allocated 33% of the electoral seats to women. This was immediately protested by Naga tribal Hohos, and a host of other civil society organisations. When the government refused to give in, Nagaland plunged into chaos and violence. The state government sought to impress upon the protestors that women reservation did not infringe upon Naga customary laws and traditions, arguing along the lines that towns and municipalities are modern manifestations in Nagaland and therefore exist outside the realm of Naga traditions and customary laws.[2] They also reiterated that women reservation was solely meant for municipal elections and did not apply to the wider state assembly elections. Rosemary Dzuvichu, an influential member of the pro-reservation Naga Mothers' Association (NMA) remarked thus:

> The question of reservation for women in Nagaland's municipal council is for the Municipal First Amendment Act to be implemented and not a movement for reservation in the state assembly constituencies (cited in *Eastern Mirror* 15-01-2016).

[1]Crenshaw (1991: 1244) termed this interaction between multiple levels of discrimination as 'intersectionality'. She maintains that 'race and gender intersect in shaping structural, political, and representational aspects of violence against women...' (see also Wouters, 2017c: 21). It is therefore not a single form of discrimination that prevents women from equal political participation.

[2]In a recent development, however, the Nagaland Government altered its earlier stance and now argues that Article 243(T) to the Indian Constitution (which directs women reservation in ULB elections) contradicts Article 371(A). The government sought to qualify that their stance did not mean that women's rights will be denied, but that there could be special laws enacted to facilitate the role of women in politics (*Nagaland* Post 16-12-2017).

For over a decade, the NMA had been pursuing women reservations in various courts. They questioned, among others, how the Nagaland Government could have allowed ULB elections to take place in the past without women reservation, as this clearly contravened the Indian Constitution. They also questioned how the Nagaland Government could thereafter have postponed these elections for successive years. Women reservation, they insisted, was not optional on part of either the Nagaland government or society, but a constitutional provision meant to empower women across the country. This was also explained, several years ago, by Nagaland's then Chief Minister:

> There is a commonly held view amongst some Nagas that traditionally women do not have any role in public governance in Naga society... it is also gratifying to note that many enlightened people in the State no longer subscribe to this view. In modern times, societies which do not accord an equitable and honourable status to their women and are considered to be backward, undeveloped or even primitive... as long as we want to have municipal bodies in our towns and cities in accordance with the relevant Act, reservation for women cannot be done away with. It needs to be clearly understood that ULBs and reservation for women come in one package, and cannot be separated now in view of the constitutional provisions already mentioned before (Neiphiu Rio 2010).[3]

The Chief Minister's stance, however, failed to garner the support of most Nagaland civil society bodies. Sano Vamuzo, former chairman of the Nagaland Women Commission, opined that women reservation in Urban Local Bodies creates the fear among Naga men 'that Naga women will come to state assembly politics'. With Naga civil societies resisting women reservation, and the Nagaland government initially obstructing and delaying its implementation the NMA filed a writ petition to the High Court. It read:

> Since 1992, the Indian Constitution has included requirements for Municipal Councils in urban areas of the various states. These requirements include reservations for Scheduled Castes

[3]This key note address has been taken as proof that the Nagaland government at first gave its support for implementing women reservation in ULBs election. (Filed by NMA in the Guwahati High Court, No. W.P. (C) No. 147 (K) 2011).

and Scheduled Tribes, as well as women. While Nagaland is exempted from the Constitution's Panchayat system, it is bound by the Municipal Council system, including the 1/3 reservation requirement for women...Minister of Urban Development stated: 'No customary practice [against reservations for women], which by the evolution of time has attained the force of law, has been furnished. Therefore, the Act as amended is valid law'. But the government continues to resist implementing the law.[4]

Interestingly, women reservation in Nagaland Village Development Boards had long been in force in Nagaland, and had been introduced without notable resistance. Dzuvichu explains:

More than 1200 Naga villages follow the VDB Model rules of 25% reservation of seats for women and surprisingly since the beginning of this concept in 1980, no village council has objected to this reservation of seats or the 25% reserved funds (cited in *Eastern Mirror* 15-01-2016).

or as the NMA stated:

At the village level where customary law and social practice is deeply entrenched by respective village councils, reservation for women in village development management committees have been implemented smoothly without any resistance or reference to violation of customary law or social practice or even Article 371(A) till date by either village councils, tribal Hohos or Naga Hoho (NMA memorandum submitted to Nagaland governor).

That said, a distinction must be made, in the context of VDBs, between formal 'representation' and actual 'participation' as there often exists a gap between these. Most women, for instance, are nominated into the Village Development Board by male village leaders (rather than elected by the village community), and instead of them actively participating in decision-making, their roles are regularly reduced to serving tea and cooking meals during VDB meetings. In an interview, Meru, President of the NMA, remarked

[4](Filed by NMA in the Guwahati High Court, No. W.P. (C) No. 147 (K) 2011).

thus: 'In most of the villages, women members in the VDB are kept for making tea or simply to fulfil the attendance requirements'. She discussed the following case:

> In one of the Angami villages, women members protested and demanded that the audit, which had been pending for several years, be carried out and completed. The male members of the Village Development Board immediately issued a complaint to the Deputy Commissioner seeking the removal of the female members from the Village Development Board. Their complaint was, however, crushed as women representation was mandatory in Village Development Boards.

In an interview, a Sumi VDB member articulated a similar grievance: 'Women are usually there to fulfil the quota. We are consulted by male members now and then, but in the end they never accommodate our opinions'. While women reservation for Urban Elected Bodies in Nagaland is imperative in the process of elevating Naga women to a level of political equality, this gap between 'representation' and 'participation' in Village Development Boards simultaneously reminds us that reservation for women is not an end in itself, but must also involve equal participation in decision-making processes.

INDIAN LAWS VERSUS NAGA CUSTOMS

Central to the debate over women reservation is the status and interpretation of Article 371(A) to the Indian Constitution, which decrees:

> Notwithstanding anything in this Constitution, no act of parliament in respect of – (i) religious or social practices of the Nagas, (ii) Naga customary law and procedure, (iii) administration of civil and criminal justice involving decisions according to Naga customary law, (iv) ownership and transfer of land and its resources, shall apply to the State of Nagaland unless the Legislative Assembly of Nagaland by a resolution so decides.

This clause, which privileges Naga customary law over Indian statutory laws, was added to the Indian Constitution as early as in 1963, yet, as

Wouters (2017c: 20) writes:

> more than five decades later, the legal implications of this amendment continue to be debated with some insisting that, to the letter, Article 371(A) almost makes Nagaland a 'foreign country within the Indian Union', as no laws or polices designed in Delhi apply to Nagaland unless Nagas – here represented by the state legislature – adjudge it as appropriate to Naga traditions, customs and cultural proclivities.

But what if these Naga traditions and customs, which Article 371(A) elevates and safeguards, are, deep down, patriarchal structures that hold back Naga women? What if Article 371(A) itself has turned into a structure that prevents women from achieving political equality? What if Article 371(A) is not liberating Naga society, as it was meant to, but has become part and parcel of the 'structural violence' exerted against Naga women? Theoretically, Williams (2011: 1) invokes a general dilemma that exists between customary law and equal citizenship:

> Customary legal systems in many countries pose a serious threat to women's equality rights by legitimizing and enforcing gender discriminatory rules with respect to marriage, divorce, property, and a host of other issues. But freedom to practice one's culture and religion is also a fundamental human right. It is possible, then, for a state to both respect and make space for the customary legal systems of its various populations, and at the same time, protect the equality rights of its women citizens? Simply choose between these projects, necessarily sacrificing one to another?

Transposed to the Naga context, it is this tension between the 'freedom to practice one's culture' and the need to protect 'equality rights' of women that needs to be mitigated. As it stands, I argue, Article 371(A) serves as a pretext for the male appropriation of modern institutions and procedures across Nagaland.[5] As societies evolve, traditional cultural practices must be adapted to new values and changing circumstances. A body of customary law, after all, represents the standards and morals of a community, which are hardly static over time (See Khutso, this volume, on how, in the past,

---

[5]Article 371(A) is also a matter of 'bargaining power' (Bina Aggarwal, 1997: 5) between the Indian State and Nagaland Government, and by extension between Indian law and Naga customary law.

Naga traditions and customs were, in fact, adapted to the exigencies of time). In the end, Naga society possesses the agency to define and exercise the kind of customary law and procedures it deems suitable to the times. However, rather than adapting customary laws and procedures, Naga males – as represented through tribal apex bodies – have seemingly appropriated the definition and practice of customary law, making it rigid and hostile to the aspirations of Naga women. This has culminated into a predicament in which Article 371(A) has transformed from 'protecting' Naga culture, traditions, and autonomy to an Act that participates in the 'suppression' of Naga women. Put differently, Article 371(A) has become yet another 'structure of patriarchy' that holds Naga women back from reaching their full potential.

Naga tribal apex bodies now habitually invoke Article 371(A) to explain and justify its resistance against women reservation. Vekhosayi Nyekha, co-convener of the Joint Coordination Committee against reservation, stated thus:

> This article 371(A) was not something gifted to us, we have earned it and we will not let it get diluted. We respect our mothers and sisters, but as per our customs, we don't allow them to have political powers. Traditionally, women in the Naga society have not enjoyed any right over land. They haven't had much voice in the village councils, the core of Naga society where men have been the ones to exercise control and take decisions' (cited in *Hindustan Times* 08-02-2017).

This interpretation is objected to by the NMA, and other women rights activists. Others offer a more multifaceted reading and insist that Article 371A refers only to selected areas of Naga social life, and that modern democratic institutions and ULBs elections are not amongst these (the point initially also adopted by then Chief Minister Rio, as discussed above). Kakheto Sema, an advocate, argues:

> In the context of Nagaland, whether or not women's reservation in ULBs violates Naga customary practices and laws is itself a debatable issue. However, with the incorporation of 243T in the Constitution of India, the said debate has been effectively removed from the purview of Article 371(A). This would mean that those who protest against women's reservation as violative of Article 371(A) of the Constitution of India, are actually protesting a non -issue (cited in *Morung express* 15-01-2017).

Perhaps aware that confronting women reservation head-on would not draw them much sympathy in both national and international arenas, Naga tribal bodies resorted to the issue of 'taxes of land' to oppose the Nagaland Municipal Act, pointing out that such taxes are antithetical to Naga traditions and that therefore the entire Act must be opposed. This argument, however, I pose, operates as a 'mask' or 'semantic cover' to protest what they deeply resent: women reservation. To illustrate; a Sema village chairperson, whom I interviewed, had this to say:

> Women cannot rule us and we will not tolerate women in decision making body, since forefathers time, women were kept out of bound from decision making and meant only for household chores.

A Lotha village chairperson similarly articulated:

> We will not allow women to rule us. If need be, we men settle a dispute with traditional weapons and may even kill each other. Do you think women can do that?

Such and similar remarks indicate how Naga customs and traditions are readily invoked by local leaders and tribal apex bodies to justify the existing non-participation of Naga women in political decision-making, and which holds back (to return to Galtung (1969) definition of structural violence) their true political potential. That such customs and views are nevertheless – directly or indirectly – protected by Article 371(A) to the Indian Constitution implies that this Article itself has become a powerful structure that reproduces and reinforces the 'structural violence' of patriarchy exerted against Naga women.

VOICES OF NAGA WOMEN

On the politics of representation, Anna Philips (2000: 11) writes:

> No one can better express the distinctive perspectives of a group (women) than someone who is a group member and that no one else is likely to be a better judge of group interests. By their presence in the decision-making chamber...

they also make it more likely that members of dominant groups will recognise and speak to their concerns. I find it plausible enough to think of a well-informed agricultural expert as representing the interests of farmers, but much less plausible to think of a well-informed (male) expert on gender as representing the perspectives of women no one else is likely to be a better judge of group interests.

Following Philips' lead, this section gives further voice to the views, experiences, perceptions, and concerns Naga women articulate about the resistance against women reservation, as well as regarding their wider status in the society. Echoing, in a way, the words of Philips (2000), Meru, President of the NMA, stated:

> We Naga women do not desire to undermine Naga men, but male leaders don't know the particular problems and concerns of Naga women. So unless Naga women are part of decision-making bodies, their problems will not be addressed.

At the same time, we must be careful not to essentialise Naga women as a homogenous category. For one, there exist palpable status and class differences among Naga women, and while carrying out research I found that not all Naga women agreed on the need for women reservation (In the same way, to be fair, do not all Naga males oppose women reservation). I found that some highly educated Naga women bureaucrats, and several of those part of the affluent layer of the Naga community, were either reluctant to comment on women reservation or reasoned against it. On this Meru commented:

> Some of the women bureaucrats are against women reservation. Their claim is that women don't need reservation as women can enter politics on their own merit, without the need for quotas.

In arguing so, they do not oppose women empowerment, but insist that a quota system is not the best way to achieve this. Their concern follows the lines of Kishwar (1996: 2872-3) that 'reservation will ensure that women will enter the electoral only against other women and never get an opportunity to contest against men, a sure way to perpetually ghettoize women's politics'. There are also Naga women who are seemingly content with the status-quo. An Ao Naga respondent, for instance, told me:

> Even if women are not allowed to participate in meetings, our husbands seek advice from us. What we tell them in the

> morning and evening will be reflected in their meetings. So,
> even if we don't have a platform for our voice, our husbands
> represent our ideas and that's sufficient for us.

Another respondent went even further, telling me: 'women should not become leaders, as we don't know how to draw unbiased judgments'. The question to ask here, however, is whether these views are the result of their individual agency or resulting from their internalisation of the patriarchal structures and sentiments they were socialised into. These views, however, represent a minority as most Naga women I spoke to argue in favour of women reservation. A Naga female church leader opined:

> Some years ago Naga women were perhaps not educated
> enough to participate in the political domain, but this has
> changed. We are not less educated than men. However, since
> the existence of patriarchy prevents us from participating
> equally, women reservation is required. It is time we deal with
> our own issues.

Another reason reservation is required, Meru explains, is the nature of democratic politics in Nagaland itself:

> Elections are determined by money, arms and ammunition.
> Given that women don't generally possess these, they stand
> no chance of winning elections against male candidates who
> resort to such methods.

Politics in Nagaland is indeed known as a grim and murky game, one not exempted from physical violence, and this indeed further disadvantage the political position of Naga women. This section gave voice to some of the many Naga respondents I interviewed in places across the state. It is my impression that most Naga women are of the opinion that things need to change, and that women reservation can be an important step leading to this change. At the same time, I showed that it would be analytically (and politically) mistaken to approach 'Naga women' as a singular category.

STRUCTURES OF PATRIARCHY

This section discusses and illustrates how structures of patriarchy systematically produce and reproduce gender inequality in Naga society. The domain of the Naga family is the first site in which patriarchy is created and sustained. The family, Lerner (1986: 127) writes, 'plays an important role in creating a hierarchical system as it not only mirrors the order in the state and educates its children but also creates and constantly reinforces that order'. Then there are the spheres of education, religions, and politics, which, too, reinforce structures of patriarchy. While such structures are many and varied, I will here mainly concentrate on the following: division of labour, crimes against women, marriage, property, language, and gender stereotyping.

I start with a widely circulated video-clip taken at a protest rally against women reservation. In it, a tribal leader is seen and heard addressing the crowd as follows:

> Thank you for coming forward to protest against this 33% women reservation. We will continue this protest until it will be overcome. We will have a daylong protest tomorrow, and I request all male members to come with a lunch boxes, whose contents should be prepared by your wife, sister, mother, or daughter.

This statement reveals the position of Naga women within the conventional Naga family structure, and, among others, reinforces their prescribed place in it, which is in the private rather than the public domain. Paradoxically, or perhaps purposefully, this tribal leader selected a site of protest against women reservation to reinforce this societal prescription. This distinction between the female 'private domain' and the male 'public domain' also pervades the division of labour in Naga society. An 'emancipated male', for instance, helping his wife in household chores is readily ridiculed as 'weak' by the society, while a female engaging in 'male activities' is similarly rebuked (more below). Nyekha thus asserted:

> Naga women work at home and in the fields. Men go to war. Men make the decisions. That's Naga culture for centuries and we won't allow anyone to destroy our culture (cited in *The Sydney Morning Herald* 19-02-2017).

This division of labour, amongst many other things, leads to 'hierarchies and inequalities because men and women labour are not valued or rewarded equally' (Bhasin 2003: 35).

Then there is the issue of crime against Naga women, and particularly the way these are often concealed from official statistics. *The Hindu*, basing itself on a report from the National Crime Records Bureau, declared Nagaland state as the safest state for women in India:

with an estimated female population of over 11 lakhs (in 2014), the rate per lakh population comes to six. In fact, it is the only State in our country to have rates of crime against women in a single digit (*The Hindu* cited in Wouters 2017c: 22).

Statistics, however, often do not tell the whole story. What must be qualified here is that 'cases of crime against women, when they occur, are regularly dealt with by customary bodies, and are therefore not always officially reported' (Wouters 2017c: 23). Put differently, both the definition of 'crime against women' and punishment for its perpetuators often end up in the hands of male-dominated village and tribal bodies. In terms of sexual and physical assaults by a husband to his wife, these customary bodies, for instance, expect the issue to be resolved within the confines of the family, but which, in actual practice, often constraints – given the patriarchal set-up of the Naga family – the Naga female victim from obtaining justice.

Let me illustrate this. As I carried out research, I came across a case in which a man, in a bout of rage, manhandled his pregnant wife and kicked her out of the house. Her expected delivery was just a week away. She subsequently got herself a rented accommodation. However, the family of the husband intervened and brought her back, insisting that no woman can stay alone, even though she herself no longer wanted to stay with her abusive husband. This male appropriation of both what constitutes a crime against women and how it should be resolved also revealed itself in the widely reported Dimapur mob lynching of an alleged rapist in 2015 (*Times of India*: 06-03-2015). The rape-accused, in this instance, was a non-Naga, which enraged those Naga males involved in the lynching. They were stirred by a patriarchal 'possessiveness' and resented an outsider 'doing it to our girls'. Crucially here is that this crime made local headlines because it was committed by an 'outsider'. Had the perpetuator be a Naga, the crime would have likely been buried or settled by a customary body without resorting to legal proceedings, leave alone violent retribution.

I now turn to the domain of marriage. A female relative once told me: 'A woman needs only one identity, which is the identity of her husband. So, she just needs to get married'. I was struck by her comment because she was a senior bureaucrat, while her husband held a comparatively lowly-paid job. Despite her professional success, she derived her identity not from her achievements but linked it to her husband. This instance can be interpreted along the lines of Lerner's (1986: 217) argument that 'the system of patriarchy can function only with the cooperation of women'. Consciously or unconsciously, Naga women may thus end up strengthening the existing patriarchal systems and sentiments. To illustrate this further, a female friend once advised me: 'Since you have several brothers you can buy a plot of land'.

I immediately interjected: 'what do you mean by brothers. If I want land I will buy it in my own name'. When, I however actually bought land I found, to my astonishment, that the document was made in my younger brother's name. This was done consciously by the landowner given that Naga women are not expected to privately own land.

Such sentiments remain deeply ingrained in Naga society and may, in the case of landownership, be a reflection of customary property arrangements as inheritance is structured exclusively through the male-line, while patrilineal descent and patrilocal residence further strengthen this male-dominated material base of Naga society. A popular saying among the Khiamniungan tells: 'women are like the wind, they go wherever the wind blows', thus indicating that women have no fixed property or place of belonging, as opposed to males. Associated with this is a societal preference for male progeny. In a report of the North-East Network in Kiphire District, a Naga female said: 'My husband fed me with the meat of bigger animals when I gave birth to a boy, but when I delivered a girl, I was treated to a smaller-sized animal'. Another respondent said: 'My husband was the only son in his family. So when I gave birth to a girl, he was so upset and that is when I felt the pressure [to give birth to a boy]' (cited in *The Wire* 24-11-2017).

On the position of Naga women, Hokiye Sema, President of the Central Naga Tribal Council stated:

> In Naga society, a woman is not equal to a man. We give women all respect but they cannot make decisions. Even in our village councils, women speak only if they are invited to give their opinion to the men. Providing 33 % reservation to women amounts to giving her the same status as men and it gives men an inferiority complex. Giving women equality will destabilise our society and our ancient customs... In India, men are considered to be superior to women as per customs and that has to be taken very seriously (cited in *Firstpost 05-01-2017*)

This statement shows, among others, that Naga women are seen both as 'secondary' and 'a-political' (Kyung Ae- Park 1999, Khiamniungan 2013). Take the example of voting. While Naga women vote in elections, in actual practice their voting behaviour remains male-oriented with them, more often than not, casting their votes based on the instruction of their male kin. This explains that while the percentage of Naga women voters is consistently high, not a single Naga woman has so far been elected into the Nagaland Assembly (on this dilemma see also Amer, this volume).

Naga languages, moreover, also tend to be highly gendered, and are so another mechanism through which structures of patriarchy are kept in place. In the Khiamniungan language, when someone asks a male if he is married he will ask: *shao joa nye nou?* (who have you taken?). A Khiamniungan woman however is asked this question differently: *shao phe ki ho juno?* (With whom are you living?). Similarly, in reference to a married woman it is said: *nungphi ki ho juno* (she lives with that man). This difference between 'taking' and 'living with' implies a social hierarchy. It illustrates Bhasin's (2002: 18) contention that 'language is patriarchal' and therefore 'carries and reflects gender biases and inequalities'. While growing up, in spite of being a responsible child doing all the household chores, I was regularly reprimanded with the words *meniu haito meniu haile thejumo* (you are a girl, behave like a girl). As I refused to be bound to the private domain, relatives would also now and then rebuke me, saying: *melo mongsai* (you have a man's hormones). Women being outspoken in social gatherings are often ridiculed by males, who may say: *meniu hai to nye sui kei ho* (women are not to speak or draw judgment on a sensitive issues. This is how decision making happens).

But it is not just language through which Naga women are made to 'conform' to societal expectations. The right to speak itself is highly gendered. During my fieldwork I often found that my female respondents were reluctant to comment on political or sensitive issues. One respondent told me: 'I don't understand these questions. I cannot give you any answers. You'd better ask my husband'. She said so despite my questions concerning a women issue.

In sum, the above examples are part of a network of patriarchal structures that work to reproduce gender roles and stereotypes that seek to prevent Naga females from participating in the domain of 'the political'.

CONCLUSIONS

Structural violence operates through inequality and injustice. This chapter variously illustrated how Naga society is rife with patriarchal structures, values, and male-dominated institutions that work to hold back Naga women from achieving their full political potential. Given that any structural and systematic discrepancy between 'the actual' and 'the potential', in Galtung's (1969) definition, constitutes structural violence, the ongoing resistance against women reservation by (mostly) male-dominated tribal bodies can be interpreted as an act of violence against Naga women. If, in resisting women reservation, Naga tribal bodies invoke Article 371(A), this Act itself, I argued, becomes a mechanism that works to continue and justify the present patriarchal set-up of Naga society. While women reservation may not offer an immediate solution to the subsidiary status of Naga women in the fields of politics and 'the political' – the example of Village Development Boards, for one, shows a gap between 'representation' and 'participation' of Naga women – it may well be a crucial first step towards countering, and ultimately dissolving, the manifold patriarchal structures and sentiments that continue to hold back Naga women.

ACKNOWLEDGMENTS

I thank Archana for her consistent support while writing this chapter, as well as Jelle J P Wouters for his tireless efforts in making this chapter better.

▪ ▪▪ ▪▪

10

EXPLORING CIVIL SOCIETY IN NAGALAND

Zhoto Tunyi

This chapter explores the emergence and role of Naga civil society organisations. I contend that civil society organisations in Nagaland have a historical and cultural set-up of their own and that, consequently, the workings of Naga civil society organisations and the political positions they take must not be framed in terms of universalistic, or 'western', concepts of civil society, but ought to be situated in a local historical context, one blemished by protracted political conflict. Naga civil society organisations, to begin with, did not emerge in times of peace and societal harmony, but in an atmosphere of political uncertainty and armed conflict. Consequently, most Naga civil society organisations function in relation to the Indo-Naga conflict. What further sets them apart is that, in their functioning, they are shaped by Naga traditions and sentiments of tribal belonging. As such, most, though not all, Naga civil societies bodies are 'closed' rather than 'open' organisations. This, for one, seemingly contravenes liberal political projections of the public sphere as an inclusive and open space.

Modern democracy was introduced in Nagaland comparatively late as the first participatory elections were held in 1964, a year after the enactment of Nagaland state. Ever since, however, democratic institutions and elections have co-existed with the Naga Movement for Naga sovereignty, whose organisations and leaders formally reject the legitimacy of Nagaland state and 'Indian elections'. As such, democracy in Nagaland is a site of contestation. Chasie (2000: 47) argues that Nagas' experience with democracy has been difficult because of the 'unresolved Naga Political Issue with simultaneous "insurgency" operating during the entire period'. In a later writing, Chasie (2005: 258) adopts an even more pessimistic view:

> The destruction of democratic values and institutions, and a general atmosphere of intolerance, means the required bases and building blocks for a democratic society are missing. As a workable settlement of the Naga Political Issue has not been found, the spiral of sustained conflict and violence only makes things worse.

While the Naga Movement first began as a struggle for Naga independence, it has since degenerated into a cycle of inter-factional feuds as a multiplicity of Naga nationalist groups struggle over hegemony and power. As a result of this, the conflict came to permeate all spheres of life. It is against this backdrop that civil society organisations in Nagaland became more prominent and outspoken in recent years, both in terms of fostering peace and in positioning themselves politically.

CIVIL SOCIETY IN NAGALAND

The exact contours of civil society are hard to define in the abstract because it has divergent historical trajectories and contemporary manifestations in different places. For my purposes here, I follow Harris' (2010: 39) definition of civil society as:

> Referring to a field of social activity, bound by the rule of law, where people come together on terms of equality as right-bearing citizens, freely associating with each other, able to form organisations on a voluntary basis, and to deliberate about matters of common, public concerns.

Or, as Chandhoke (2003: 30) describes it: 'a plural space where people in association with each other can debate and contest their version of the political, and hold state, institutions, and official accountable'. A conceptual problem regarding the idea and workings of civil society – or the 'third sphere' of political activity, separate from both the state and market (Cohen and Arato 1992) – is that its theoretical underpinnings trace back to 'western' political philosophy and historical experiences. That said, the idea of civil society has long been internalised in places across the globe, including India. Most theorists now agree that a thriving and autonomous civil society promotes democratization and good governance.

Among Nagas, this 'plural space' of associational life is organised along the lines of tribal public organisations (Hohos), church councils, student associations, women organisations, in addition to range of 'ad-hoc', issue-based, civil society organisations such as the Joint Action Committee (JAC) for women reservation that was formed out of the controversy related to the 2017 municipal elections (see Chapters by L. Khiamniungan and Hausing, this volume). Akin to places across South Asia, the most influential Naga civil society organisations, which are tribal hohos, were built along pre-existent, pre-modern identities (cf. Gellner 2010). At the same time, as Varshney (2002: 4) poses, such 'ethnic form of association building need not be equal to traditionalism if they meet the functional or purposive criteria'. Put differently, while tribe-wise Hohos built on traditional identities, they are simultaneously modern in the objectives they pursue. As each Naga tribe has a Hoho of its own, the landscape of Naga civil societies is fragmented along tribal lines, and this, it can be argued, impedes notions of pan-Naga citizenship and belonging, even though 'over and above' these tribe-wise apex bodies exists the Naga Hoho, which claims to represent all Naga tribes. Recent history shows that tribal apex bodies variously associate and disassociate from this pan-Naga Hoho, however.

Civil societies, in their contemporary sense, are a relatively recent development in Nagaland. These include the Naga People's Movement for Human Rights (NPMHR) in the late 1970s, Naga Mothers Association in the early 1980s and the Naga Hoho in the early 1990s. What binds these together, in a way, is that they were born out of conflict and felt the need to mediate towards a political solution of the Indo-Naga conflict. Prior to the establishment of these civil societies, the Naga public sphere was dominated by the Church, whose pastors and leaders now and then operated as a mediating force between the Centre and Naga underground groups. These civil societies often found themselves restricted in their functioning because they were regularly 'tagged as front/mouthpieces of armed opposition groups' (Kikon, this volume) by the Indian state and therefore viewed with misgiving and their freedoms impeached. Even after the 1997 ceasefire, such sentiments continue to inform the military apparatus. 'In the early years of the ceasefire', Manchanda and Bose (2011: 51) write:

> General K V Kulkarni, convener of the Ceasefire Monitoring
> Mechanism... label(ed) organisations like the Naga Hoho,
> the United Naga Council (UNC), Naga Mothers, NSF, Naga
> Women's Union Manipur (NWUM, Naga People's Movement
> for Human Rights (NPMHR) as 'proxies' of the underground
> groups.

Over the past decades, the Government of India has blacklisted several
Naga civil society organisations at different points of time on the accusation
of them backing pro-militant groups. As such it can hardly be said that
Nagaland civil societies have operated in a 'free space'. At the same time,
there is no doubt that Naga civil societies have been pre-occupied with the
Indo-Naga conflict. This could hardly have been otherwise as this has been
the most pressing issue in Naga society for long decades. Abraham Lotha
(2016:286) surmises:

> The NSF, NPMHR, Naga Hoho and Naga Mothers Association
> (NMA) have been like a family - the Naga Hoho as the father,
> NMA the mother, NSF and NPMHR as the two children -
> each a separate entity and yet unanimous in their stand on
> Naga political issues. Individually and in collaboration, these
> civil society organisations have been active in articulating and
> promoting the political cause of the Nagas.

A recent trend that can be discerned is that the Naga Hoho, NPMHR,
and NSF (Naga Students Federation) increasingly articulate Naga political
aspirations and identity through a framework of universal human rights and
indigeneity. In this way, they have also been offered solidarity by a host of
international organisations that seek to promote the rights of indigenous
peoples.

A NAGA PUBLIC SPHERE AND CIVIL SOCIETY IN THE NAGA HILLS: REVISITING THE PAST

Having briefly characterised the landscape of civil societies in Nagaland,
this section takes a step back to situate the historical emergence of Naga
civil society organisations and the public sphere more widely. Among Nagas,
the emergence of civil societies can be traced to the colonial period which
saw the pacification of the Naga uplands, the introduction of uniform
administration, and the entrance of Christianity and education. These
forces led to the expansion of the social and political horizons of hitherto

Naga village based polities. While, as Khutso shows (this volume), a limited form of public space traditionally existed between cognate Naga villages; as a general principle the public space was long confined to the village boundaries. Yonuo (1974: 154) observed that these Naga villages often lived in a state of war, one against another, which prevented bonds of unity or projections of common interests to emerge. It was only after British colonialism that a public space emerged that cut across distinct Naga villages. I will now briefly discuss some Naga organisations that occupied the early Naga public sphere.

The Naga Club

The first socio-political organisation of Nagas that transcended village polities was the Naga club, which was established in 1918 in the aftermath of the First World War. According to Piketo Sema (1992: 141), this class of intellectuals consisted mostly of Gaonburas, Dobashis, Teachers, government servants, pastors and educated people, in addition to a number of France returnees (after serving there as part of the Naga Labour Corps). The primary objective of this Club, Piketo Sema continues, was to look after the welfare of the Nagas by developing feelings of fraternity and unity among them. In this way, the purpose of this club was social rather than political in character. Or at least so initially as over time, the Naga Club took on a more political character. Horam (1988: 37) writes:

> They were preparing themselves politically in the event of India gaining her independence from the British – a happening they then visualized as being imminent. Thus their chief concern was the political future of their homeland after the exit of the British. The Naga Club was still in its infancy then, but the pattern of the future had already been installed in their minds.

Thus, over time, the Naga Club became a discussion platform on Naga political affairs (Sema 1992: 142). Some scholars see the Naga Club as the prototype political organisation of the Nagas. As a civil society organisation – a term then not yet used – the Naga Club was indeed monumental because it for the first time presented a pan-Naga political voice. This emerged from the text of the Memorandum it submitted to the Simon Commission, which reads: 'We the undersigned Nagas of the Naga Club at Kohima, who are the only persons at present who can voice for our people...' (see Khutso, this volume, for a critique of the Pan-Naga pretensions of the Naga Club).

Naga National Council (NNC)

After World War II, Pawsey, then District Commissioner of the Naga Hills, facilitated the formation of the Naga Hills District Tribal Council (NHDTC) in April 1945. The envisaged objective of this organisation was to unite Naga tribes to effectuate post-war reconstruction. Less than a year later, however, this organisation re-established itself as the Naga National Council (NNC) and turned into a platform to deliberate Nagas' political future.

The NNC started as a federal body with twenty nine members representing different tribes on the principle of proportional representation (Nuh and Lasuh 2001; Yonuo 1972). The NNC pursued the political unification of the Nagas, and every Naga was made a de facto member. It engaged in public discourse to work out the idea of the Naga nation. In so doing, Naga communities were drawn into a dialogue over issues of common interests, including their political future. But while in its early years the NNC functioned somewhat akin to a civil society, it soon transformed itself into the prospective government of the Nagas. The *Yehzabo,* the NNC's Constitution, states that the national government of Nagaland shall be the 'Federal Government of Nagaland'. This government was to be constituted along the lines of a federation of tribes:

> Each area or territory inhabited by the communities of a tribe shall be constituted into a federated unit to be called a Region and each of the Regions shall be given autonomy to the extent of management of local affairs and administration (NNC Constitution).

After the outbreak of violence in the mid-1950s, the NNC was forced underground, and took up guerrilla warfare to fight for an independent Nagaland. As such, the NNC shifted from a civil society to a government to an underground outfit.

Apex Tribal Organisations

Besides the emergence of pan-Naga bodies such as the Naga Club and the Naga National Council, the late colonial era witnessed the emergence of tribe-wise Naga bodies. In 1923, the Lotha formed their tribal council, while the Ao tribal council was established in 1928. Other tribes soon followed suit. Each tribal council formulated as its prime objective to represent the interests and needs of the tribe, as well as to represent the tribe in the wider political and public sphere. In the present-day, these tribal apex bodies are often found competing over access to the state, including the allocation of development funds and government employment. This tribal character of

Naga civil societies has its repercussions on the functioning of the state. At the same time, these tribal apex bodies position themselves politically in relation to the Indo-Naga conflict, often taking sides with one or another Naga faction. The Chakhesang Public Organisation has gone on record, for instance, stating that 'the CPO believes in the principles of the NNC which is a movement and an institution. The CPO expects all to recognize the NNC and considers it as the legitimate ground where all Nagas must meet and unite again for a better future' (Krocha and Dukru 2013: 10). The Angami Public Organisation (APO) in turn reaffirmed their political stance in relation to the Naga Plebiscite of 1951, as well as rejected the Shillong Accord of 1975 (Chasie 2000: 65). The Ao Senden, the Ao Naga apex body, however stated that:

> The Ao have already given their mandate (to the NSCN-IM) during the consultative meeting held at Camp Hebron in 2004. The mandate was given by the Ao people to uphold the Naga political issue, to negotiate with the Government of India at the highest level without preconditions and in a third country (*Morung Express* 28-06-2010).

In this way, different Naga tribes, as represented through their apex bodies, have variously associated themselves with dynamics within the Indo-Naga conflict.

NAGA CIVIL SOCIETIES AGAINST THE INDIAN STATE?

A distinguishing feature about the historical emergence and contemporary manifestation of most, though not all, Naga civil societies is that they regularly position themselves in opposition to the state, its institutions, procedures, and laws. The 'state' here, it must be qualified, refers primarily to the Indian state, or the Centre, rather than Nagaland state explicitly, even as the latter is of course part of the former. The Naga Club, as discussed above, commenced this process of 'state resistance' by submitting a memorandum resisting Nagas' possible inclusion within the Indian fold. The NNC, in turn, resorted to public discourse, a plebiscite, and civil disobedience to oppose Nagas enclosure into India (see Khutso, this volume). But not only do the Naga Club and the NNC have a history of resisting the Indian state, several contemporary civil societies in Nagaland also regularly adopt political positions that oppose or contravene the Indian state. While doing so, they resort to Article 371(A) of the Indian Constitution which was inserted – as a political compromise to the Naga demand for independence – to safeguard

Naga culture, customs, and traditions. In a way, what the Naga Movement, in its various forms, tried to achieve by going 'underground', several Naga civil societies tried to achieve 'overground'. A senior member of the Naga Hoho, who I interviewed, narrated thus:

> Naga undergrounds took to the jungle to oppose Nagas' inclusions into India. But all of us Nagas cannot join the underground. So, some of our elders started this forum [Naga Hoho] to back the National Movement in a different way. Several other Naga civil societies were established with this objective in mind. As a civil society, we can do and say things that Naga armed groups simply cannot do without immediate repercussions, especially before the 1997 ceasefire. When, for instance, we write a memorandum or meet the Indian Government for a political issue that concerns Nagas, we can approach them as a lawful civil society organisation, not as a militant outfit, even as our ultimate objectives do not differ significantly from the Naga Movement.

In the remainder of this section I will invoke three examples in which Nagaland civil societies have positioned themselves against the Indian state in recent years with the dual aim of fostering a settlement to the lingering Indo-Naga conflict and to protect Naga culture, tradition, and identity. I begin with the 1998 election boycott. Nagaland's 9th State Legislative Assembly elections were held on the 23rd February 1998. This election, however, was never an ordinary one but was preceded by a boycott call issued jointly by the National Socialist Council of Nagalim (NSCN-IM), and Naga civil society organisations led by the Naga Hoho. A year prior to the election, the NSCN-IM had entered into a ceasefire with the Centre, and in this context it was postulated that Nagas needed no fresh elections but a political solution. To this end, the Naga Hoho submitted a petition to the Centre asking for the deferral of the election. Crucial here is that this request did not come from the Naga Movement directly – in which case it could have been interpreted by the Centre as 'unlawful' – but by a lawful (that is, operative within Indian laws) Naga civil society organisation. When the Centre nevertheless refused to heed to this request, a number of protest rallies were held across Nagaland as well as in Delhi, including the staging of a hunger strike by the Naga Students Federation (NSF).

With the Centre rejecting the demand, the Naga Hoho, in conjunction with the NSCN-IM, took matters into their own hands and on the 20th of January 1998 declared that any politician filing his nomination would be considered 'anti-Naga' and face consequences. The Naga Hoho also asked sitting MPs and MLAs to resign on or before the 7th of February 1998 as a gesture of support to the peace-process. Regional parties in Nagaland, after a thorough debate amongst themselves, arrived at the decision not to participate in the election and supported the boycott call. Some MLAs did resign, namely those belonging to the Naga People's Council and the Naga Democratic Movement (Naga Hoho 1998:8).

The reason why the Naga civil societies did not want fresh elections in Nagaland can be considered from a number of angles. The Naga Hoho (1998: 4-5) articulated the following apprehensions:

> a) That, various groups/factions will get involved in booth capturing, muscle exercise and recourse to all forms of extreme manipulations.
> b) That, polling booths will become a battle ground for the candidates to win over each other as the Nagas had experienced in the past.
> c) That, whichever political party came to power it will sabotage the peace process because power and money was their ultimate goal.
> d) That, the post-election scenario will witness bloodshed, sharp division among people, and deceit, which will be detrimental to the ongoing peace process.
> e) That, it wanted in to show to the outside world and that the Nagas was a distinct race having the rights for self-determination.

The Nagaland Baptist Church Council (NBCC) also announced its support for the boycott call, and urged Naga citizens to express their opposition by displaying 'a white flag or garment on Sunday, 22 February, as a symbolic declaration of support for a just peace' (Nuh 2006: 34). It further instructed Naga congregations to set aside that day, a Sunday, 'for prayer for the process of building peace, understanding and reconciliation' (Nuh 2006: 34).

But while all regional parties heeded to the boycott call, the Congress Party refused to do so. Its election manifesto read:

> The Congress party's ultimate political goal is to help achieve a final and lasting solution to the Naga political problem. It has been our avowed policy that we are prepared to lay down our offices as and when permanent solution of the Naga problem between government of India and Naga underground is arrived at. For this no sacrifices would be considered too great by the party and its government (Congress Party Manifesto 1998).

While the Congress Party thus promised that it would willingly vacate its offices was a political solution to arrive, they refused to boycott the election. Congress candidates (as well as several independent candidates) thus defied the boycott call and filed their nominations. Those who boycotted the election accused the Congress Party and independent candidates of betrayal. The Naga Hoho, on its part, refused to recognise the Congress government that was formed after the elections.

In addition to the election boycott, Nagaland civil society organisations have also variously positioned themselves in opposition to pan-Indian policies, procedures, and laws. Prime among these is the recent opposition against the *Nagaland Municipal and Town Council Act* (2006). I will not discuss the background and intricacies of this opposition here (for this, see Chapters by Hausing and L. Khiamniungan, this volume), but highlight that Nagaland civil society organisations, most vocally tribal apex bodies and the Naga Hoho, resisted women reservation and land tax (as ingrained in the Act) as this would constitute, they argued, an infringement on Naga traditions and culture. They insist that by virtue of Article 371(A) Naga culture and customs are safeguarded from 'Indian laws', and that if Nagas wish to remain politically and culturally different and distinctive, the protection of Article 371(A) is crucial. Chuba Ozukum, President of the Naga Hoho surmised this view by arguing that the Municipal Act is 'quite detrimental to the sanctity of traditional land holding system and customary laws'. In a statement, the Naga Hoho qualified further:

> The contention of the Naga CSOs is that the amount of autonomy and authority that they have exercised over the last 5 decades of statehood which can be taken as internal self-determination will be disturbed and break the status which will allow rooms for other constitutional laws to creep in future, thereby opening a floodgate of other laws which they are able to stopped so far. Knowing fully well that Nagas are distinct in all aspects be it in appearance or landholding system or tradition and religion, etc., the Government of India has inserted the provision of Article 371(A) with a view of its historical and philosophical perspectives... What we need to remember is that as of now this provision is the only bond of relationship between Nagas and Indians and nothing more (cited in *Eastern Mirror* 13-09-2016).

Particularly noteworthy here is the Naga Hoho's asserting that Article 371(A) should work to prevent the 'floodgate' of Indian laws from entering into Nagaland. This further indicates that Nagaland civil society organisations work to keep (parts of) the Indian state at bay. A final case I wish to highlight is the recent opposition to the implementation of Aadhaar Card compulsions and regulations in Nagaland. The Naga Students Federation identified the Aadhaar Card as a 'big threat to Naga customary law and identity'. It argued:

> It is nothing but a direct challenge of privacy threatening even the idea of Nagas' right to self-determination. Imposing of such drastic nationalizing policy upon the Nagas pending the final Indo-Naga solution is inimical to the process of the Indo-Naga peace dialogue.

Then turning to Naga customary law and Article 371(A), the NSF added:

> Free enjoyment of social benefits within the fabric of collective social identity is sacred to the Nagas and any denial thereof in the name of identity numerisation is inimical to the social and religious practice of the Nagas (cited in *Morung Express* 1-11-2017).

Here the opposition of a Naga civil society organisation against a pan-Indian policy, that is Aadhaar Card regulations, is two-pronged: it is opposed because of its 'nationalizing' tendencies and and because, amongst Nagas, social security and welfare is traditionally arranged within the community, not through detached 'identity numerisation'.

What the above three examples – election boycott, protest against women reservation and land tax, and opposition to the Aadhaar Card – bind is that they show how Nagaland civil society organisations position themselves against Nagas' complete enclosure within Indian institutions, policies, and laws. In doing so, Nagaland civil society organisations 'covertly' align themselves with the rationale of the Naga Movement, which is to keep the Indian state at bay. As such several Naga civil society organisations have a marked history of 'opposing the Indian state'.

CONCLUSION

This chapter traced, in an abridged form, the historical emergence and contemporary role of Nagaland civil society organisations. A few general points emerge.

First, the emergence of Nagaland civil societies trace back to the colonial era which witnessed the widening of the Naga public sphere and saw the enactment of the first more or less pan-Naga organisations such as the Naga Club and later the Naga National Council. But while the emergence of a critical public sphere was no doubt shaped by the experience of British rule and as such a reactive process rather than an indigenous expression, it did set the stage for the articulation of Naga identity and political aspirations after British withdrawal from the Naga Hills.

Secondly, a double movement can be discerned in the constitution and functioning of Naga civil societies. On the one hand, the emergence of the Naga Club, the Naga National Council, and, much later, the Naga Hoho promoted the idea of pan-Naga fraternity and citizenship by seeking to represent the interests and needs of all Nagas. This movement, however, has been counter-posed by the emergence of tribe-wise apex bodies which seek to represent the needs and interests of individual tribes. The objectives of these tribe-wise apex bodies now and then conflict with pan-Naga configurations.

Thirdly, the landscape of Naga civil societies by and large emerged in reaction and response to, first, Nagas' enclosure into the Indian fold, and, secondly, to the protracted Indo-Naga conflict. It was thus amidst political uncertainty and conflict that civil society organisations first emerged and began to function. This had both repercussions on the ways the Centre viewed Naga civil society organisations and on the primary engagement of many civil society organisations, which is both to facilitate the peace-process and to safeguard Naga culture and identity.

Fourthly and finally, Naga civil society organisations, in their contemporary manifestations, regularly position themselves in opposition to the Indian state and its policies and laws. As is evident from the statement of the Naga Hoho member (cited above), Naga civil society organisations operate, if not as a direct extension or 'mouthpiece' of the Naga Movement, then certainly in conjunction with the rationale of Naga cultural integrity and self-determination. This objective can also be read in the 1998 election boycott, opposition to the Municipal Act, and resistance against the implementation of the Aadhaar Card. As such, a distinguishing feature of Nagaland civil society organisations may well be that they aim to keep Nagas 'free' from 'nationalizing' institutions, policies, and regulations.

■ ■■ ■■

11

EXPLORING THE PHOM NAGA EXPERIENCE WITH MODERN ELECTORAL DEMOCRACY

B. Henshet Phom

INTRODUCTION

The Phom Nagas are one of the major Naga tribes inhabiting Longleng district in eastern Nagaland. The population of the district, according to the 2011 census, tallies 50,484 individuals spread across 50 recognised villages and six townships. Like most Naga tribes, the exact origins and recognised migratory routes of the Phom Naga remain obscure, but legend has it that the Phoms were birthed by *Meihongnyiü* (seen as the mother of human beings) in a place somewhere to the east. They subsequently travelled through Pongngaihong, Apaihong and Chenchongliho to their present territory, also passing through 'Yingnyiüshang' and 'Longterok'. Therefore, the Phom apply the term *Ying-hi-Long* as the basis of their socio-cultural and political traditions (Phom 2005: 1-2).

For traditional Nagas, the village was the centre of socio-cultural and political activities. Each village, in a way, was an independent sovereign and democratic republic, including boundary demarcations (Ao 1997: 81). In this, the Phom were no exception. Each Phom village polity had a well-structured political system that included a village council. While all important village matters were discussed in a village assembly, the resolutions adopted were executed by this council. Traditionally, membership of a village council entailed manifold responsibilities, and was often more of a burden than a privilege. Representatives were selected clan-wise to ensure that all village clans (usually between five to ten) would have their views represented at the level of the village council. For the Phom Naga, an aspirant village council member had to possess at the minimum the following qualifications: he had to be a bona fide citizen of the village, not be an 'illegitimate son', and not known for immoral behaviour. There was no retirement or fixed tenure prescribed for members of the village council and members could discharge their responsibilities for as long as they remained physically and mentally fit (Phom 2015: 11-2). Much, however, changed in terms of traditional Phom governance after the arrival of modern democratic institutions and elections.

THE ARRIVAL OF MODERN DEMOCRATIC ELECTIONS IN TUENSANG

The winds of change can be traced to the inauguration of Nagaland state in 1963, after which formal democratic institutions and competitive elections started to impact Phom village polities in various ways. It must be qualified here, however, that compared to western Nagaland, where the first post-statehood elections were held in 1964, eastern Naga tribes, including the Phom Naga, were given a temporary respite from elections because, historically, their territory lay outside the direct ambit of colonial administration. Consequently, the first elections among the Phom were conducted only in 1974.

During the colonial era, Tuensang region was declared an 'Excluded Area' and was still largely unadministrated by the time of British withdrawal in 1947. It was only after India's independence that a separate Tuensang administrative circle was established, at first as an outpost of the Mokokchung sub-division with headquarters at Tuensang Town, built on land donated by Tuensang village. In 1951, this administrative circle became elevated into a sub-division with an Assistant Political Officer in charge. In 1952, Tuensang area became part of the North-Eastern Frontier Agency (NEFA) and was governed directly by the Assam Governor at the behest of the Central Government. NEFA's headquarter was established in Shillong and the Phom, and other eastern Naga tribes, administered from there. However, in 1957, the Tuensang Frontier Division was transferred from NEFA and merged with the Naga Hills District of Assam to form an administrative unit called the Naga Hills Tuensang Area (NHTA), consisting of three districts:

Kohima, Mokokchung, and Tuensang. In 1963, this territory became a full-fledged state. Over time, Tuensang District was sub-divided into districts, Mon (created in 1973) and Kiphire and Longleng (created in 2004).

The inauguration of Nagaland state came with special provisions for Tuensang District because of its historical exclusion from colonial administration and its relative backwardness. Instead of the introduction of an electoral system, a Regional Council was created to govern the district for a period of ten years. Regional Council Members were selected based on tribe and region and through local-level consensus-making (one may note here that the selection of members to the Regional Council by consensus was relatively uncomplicated back then as there were very few educated persons in the area). The Regional Council was empowered to nominate (again, not elect) its representatives to the Nagaland Legislative Assembly. This 'selection mechanism' remained in place for ten years, after which the Regional Council ceased to function and the people of the district were made to participate in competitive elections to elect their political representatives to the Nagaland Legislative Assembly. Today, the four districts that make up Eastern Nagaland are represented by 20 elected members.

ELECTORAL TRENDS IN LONGLENG DISTRICT

When the first state elections were held in Nagaland in 1964, forty seats were filled through polling by the inhabitants of Kohima and Mokokchung Districts. In addition, six members were chosen, through consensus-making, from Tuensang District by the Regional Council. Of these six, none belonged to the Phom community. In 1969, too, forty seats were contested in Kohima and Mokokchung, but this time the number of seats allocated to the Tuensang Regional Council was increased to twelve. Of these twelve, two were Phom and both joined the Naga Nationalist Organisation (NNO), which made the ruling government. It was therefore only in 1969 that the first Phom Nagas entered the Nagaland Legislative Assembly (Rahman 2008: 163).

In 1974, Phom Nagas, and Eastern Nagas more widely, cast their votes for the first time. The Delimitation Act (1972) had fixed the total number of Nagaland constituencies at sixty, of which two covered the Phom area, namely 49 Tamlu Constituency and 50 Longleng Constituency. Over the past decades, several Phom MLAs from both Tamlu and Longleng constituencies held ministerial berths as well as important portfolios. Moreover, Chenlom Phom was appointed as, first, Deputy Speaker and thereafter as the Speaker of the Nagaland Legislative Assembly in 1987 (Murry 2007: 163-166).

A noteworthy feature of electoral politics among the Phom is that electors attach more significance to candidates than to the parties they represent. Defection and party-hopping have frequently occurred and Phom politicians seemingly portray no qualms about switching their political allegiance from one party to another. Such fluctuating political allegiances by Phom politicians are done for a variety of reasons, ranging from safeguarding the interests of the Phom community, increasing one's position in the state-wide power-hierarchy, to sheer personal and selfish gains. Consequently, no political party has succeeded in consolidating a permanent foothold among the Phom Naga (Rahman 2008: 165). Put differently, Phom legislators do not generally uphold party principles, but are led by other motives. Noteworthy, too, among the Phom, is that successful MLAs tend to hail from a limited number of villages. In the Tamlu Constituency, MLAs have hailed interchangeably from five villages, while from Longleng constituency MLAs have so far emerged from only three villages.

When state assembly elections approach, a festive atmosphere is witnessed among the Phom. Villagers organise themselves into competing groups in support of rival candidates. Each group enjoy the feasts hosted by their candidate, and spend their time canvassing in his support. Supporters congregate in political camps, where they are entertained and offered meals and drinks for several days (Rahman 2008: 166-67). This is done first and foremost to maintain unity and to ensure that none of the party-members switch their political loyalty. What is also witnessed is that most prospective voters demand monies, food, and drink in return for their political support. Levying such demands is actually not part of Phom traditions, but signifies a modern trend that can be traced to the onset of competitive elections.

In the run up to elections, village councils usually call for a consultative meeting with all villagers to study the political situation. Often, during such a meeting, the village council decides whom their village should support or, alternatively, resolves to divide the 'village vote' among rival candidates. In such instances, 'autonomous' and 'individual' balloting is substituted by 'village voting.' Likewise, when a Phom politician decides to contest an election, it is to the Village Council of his natal village that he first turns to request support. This is the first step in a wider political campaign aimed at acquiring electoral support.

Village council decisions to allocate the village's 'collective vote' are considered final, and those individuals who defy such a decision risk punishment under customary law. There are indeed cases of villagers having been banished from the village for disobeying the Village Council (On this see also Chapter 6 by Wouters, this volume). On the eve of an election itself, village gates are usually fortified with sharp bamboos and village youth instructed to keep vigil to prevent persons from rival parties from sneaking into the village and potentially upsetting the decision made by the village council. Those villages that have one of 'their own' contesting usually do not even allow candidates from other villages and parties to enter the village precincts. While village councils are associated with 'traditional governance' and politicians and elections with 'modern politics', these examples show that both interconnect and cannot be seen in isolation from one another.

The significance of Phom village councils in modern elections can be seen as a reflection of the role of 'the village' within Phom notions of identity and belonging. This also shows in that most Phom villages insist on having a candidate of their own, even if they know that their candidate stands little chance of winning the constituency. For them, it has become a status symbol to have a politician in their midst, and winning the election appears secondary to the kudos of having such a candidate. In some villages there have been multiple candidates contesting the same election. This usually prevents the village council from having a 'consensus-candidate' and leads households in the village to divide their votes among the contestants. They do so in order to not displease any of the village candidates. Others are more cunning in their motivations, however, and share their family votes so that some of their family members will, in any event, be with a winning candidate.[1]

I end with highlighting one final electoral trend in the Phom area. While, during state elections, Phom villagers let themselves be guided, as noted, by the politician rather than the party he represents, this logic is found operative in its reverse during elections. During the latter, villagers tend to support the candidate of the party that is in power in the state. This indicates that, during state elections, villagers want their particular candidate to win by any means, regardless of the party he represents, but that during Parliamentary elections they tend to support the government in power, hoping that, by doing so, they may avail more facilities and other state benefits.

The electoral trends discussed in this section may not be exclusive to the Phom tribe and Longleng district, and similar trends can be observed across Nagaland. Yet, they offer a window into the ways democracy and elections are perceived and engaged with by the Phom Naga, and highlight the confluence between traditional village councils and present-day politicians and their electoral politics.

[1]Bauting, Chingjei and Himei in an interview with the writer at Longleng on November 06, 2017.

PHOM NAGA EXPRIENCES WITH ELECTORAL DEMOCRACY

It is widely observed and argued that the present system of politics that has grown in post-statehood Nagaland is doing more harm than good to Naga society, as it degrades traditional Naga political practices and values. Modern democracy, if anything, has come to divide Naga villages, and not just during election seasons but also afterwards as elected politicians tend to allocate government jobs and state benefits mostly to those who rallied in their support, thus excluding those in the opposition. This taking of 'political revenge' happens to the extent that villagers 'from the opposition' are regularly denied even that which is rightfully theirs. Almost everything - call it 'political privilege' - goes through the party line (Phom 2003: 3).

After the inauguration of Nagaland state, Nagas initially felt ambivalent towards the electoral system and shouted such slogans as 'elections go away from Nagaland.' However, of late, there is also a realisation that instead of following the rules and procedures laid down by the Election Commission, many Nagas (politicians and villagers alike) are manipulating and misusing the electoral system for selfish ends. Thus, democratic ideals are being marred by the villagers themselves. For example, the system of 'one person, one vote' has been misused by village councils and turned into a village 'collective vote', which, in fact, is antithetical to democratic ideals.

In what follows, I will discuss some of the experiences Phom villagers have had regarding the modern democratic system, including competitive elections. I do so through a number of questions posed to respondents from the Phom tribe. I present the answers to these questions in a number of tables.

Table 9: Do you think that the present system of election is suitable for the Phom people?

	No. of respondents	Percentage of Respondents
Yes	12	20%
No.	48	80%
Can't say	00	00%

The table above shows that 80% of the respondents indicated that the present system of election is not suitable for Phom Nagas. Several of them qualified that democracy and elections are in themselves good systems but that Nagas have subverted them by permitting 'money' and 'muscle-power' to enter the democratic system. One respondent opined that while an election was good for the individual, as he would receive some personal benefits from politicians, it was bad for Naga society as a whole. Other respondents cited booth-capturing, money politics, and agitated rivalries between parties and politicians as further demerits of the modern democratic system. The use of 'money' during elections, according to one respondent, prevented 'upright' persons from winning, as they cannot compete in terms of resources with 'less upright' but wealthier candidates.

While democracy and elections are thus evaluated mostly in negative terms, as well as blamed for various social ills, a silver lining can perhaps be discerned in the increased realisation of the importance of 'clean elections'. This is largely the result of successive Clean Election Campaigns spearheaded by the Nagaland Baptist Church Council (NBCC). Churches in Long District subscribe to this need, and so have several other Phom civil society organisations.

Table 10: Can a voter easily meet their elected representative after the election is over?

	No. of respondents	Percentage of Respondents
Yes	12	20%
No.	48	80%
Can't say	00	00%

Table two shows that most Phom villagers find it difficult to meet their MLA outside of 'election times.' As many as 80% of my respondents stated that once elections are over, it becomes challenging to meet their elected representative. Many respondents found this paradoxical as, during elections ,politicians would be easily accessible, even 'begging' for their votes. Once elected, however, their disposition seems to change. Quite suddenly, they distance themselves from the public that elected them, by using bodygaurds to keep the public away, and insisting that people need to seek formal permission to meet him.

Table 11 returns to the intimate relationship Phoms have with their natal villages, and explores perceptions of inter-village inequalities and power hierarchies that are produced or reproduced by modern democratic politics.

Table 11: It is observed that under the present election system it is difficult for small Phom villages to have an MLA. Do you agree?

	No. of respondent	Percentage of Respondent
Yes	39	65%
No	21	35%
Can't say	00	00%

This table reveals that 65% of the respondents agree that it is difficult for a small Phom village to ever see one of their own to ascend into the Nagaland Legislative Assembly. Votes, respondents explained, tend to be adjudicated by village councils, whose members decide whom villagers should vote for, and that therefore larger villages (with more votes to allocate), or those Phom villages who agree to form an inter-village coalition, stand a better chance of seeing one of 'their own' elected.

Ultimately, elected politicians are prone to using their privileged access to the state and its resources to benefit their own villagers and followers. Consequently, not only are Phom politicians who hail from comparatively large villages better placed to win elections, larger Phom villages experience higher levels of development and material welfare. Put differently, small Phom villages experience a double-disadvantage: their smaller numbers of votes prevent them from seeing one of their own elected into the assembly and because of that they have lesser access to state benefits. In this way, the modern electoral system in Nagaland has widened the gap between bigger and smaller Naga villages, or between those villages having a legislator and those having none.

THE WAY FORWARD

It is observed that the present electoral system is not suitable for the Nagas as a whole. Nagas long claimed to possess an 'indigenous' democratic form of government, but when judged today, the true ideals of democracy are missing. Democracy stands for equality, liberty, and fraternity, which implies that all citizens are equal and free. But these ideals are not found in the present democratic system in Nagaland. We must, therefore, try to find a system that promotes a just society; a system that works for equal development of every quarter of our land.

Democratic institutions, particularly elections, have proven to be utterly divisive amongst the Phom, and Nagas more widely. During elections villages become sharply divided, resulting in the corrosion of community cohesion. 'Money' politics causes disparity within the village, while, more broadly, the way democracy is performed in Nagaland causes regional inequalities. Such negative experiences and evaluations suggest that change is needed. However, changing the electoral system may not be easy, as this would undermine India's Constitution. What could be changed, however, is a stricter adherence to the rules and regulations of India's Election Commission and, relatedly, greater adherence to the tenets of clean elections as spelled out by the Nagaland Baptist Church Council.

In the longer run, however, an attempt can be made to adapt the current election system to suit it better to both traditional ways of Naga governance and present needs of Naga society. The idea of Area and Regional councils, which existed in the 1980s but lies defunct now, may be revisited. In this system, based on the devolution of power, each village had its representative. This system enabled each village to have their own village representative in an area council, whose members in turn elected Regional Council members. In this way, each village would get an opportunity to send a representative to speak for their needs, concerns, and interests. Such a system could potentially mitigate the divisions and inequalities created by the current electoral system.

■ ■■ ■■

12

CITIZENSHIP FROM BELOW: ESTABLISHING CONTINUITIES OF BELONGING IN NAGALAND

Michael Heneise

far from solely imaginative, individual and collective senses of belonging are shaped by and hinged upon both the material and symbolic manifestations of place.

Kelly Baker (2012:24)

Only the contingent future, which is the eventual, occurrent topos, can teach us about our past and about our present.

Reiner Schürmann (2003: 556).

INTRODUCTION

The ambiguities of citizenship and belonging amid protracted political conflict are familiar tropes in Nagaland's fraught history, and poignantly expressed in personal biographies of loss and displacement. Democratic citizenship, though often articulated as an '"outer frame" of duties such as voting, paying taxes, and obeying laws' (Burns and Burns 1991: 462), also entails the ongoing struggle for greater inclusiveness and equal rights. Citizen rights, we must acknowledge, are not automatically guaranteed by the state, but are indeed 'created far more by those who actively shape them and live them in the thick of personal and social struggles' (ibid: 13). This chapter examines the interiorities of 'citizenship from below', and specifically looks at the ways in which conflict-related dislocation aggravates temporal continuities in experiences of belonging, thus contributing to estrangement from prevailing moral-political systems. Where legitimised relations are fleeting, outsiders, including other-than-humans and the divine, can provide new avenues for refashioning continuities of emplaced belonging, including citizenship.

A majority Christian state, believers often articulate grievances associated with unscrupulous political leadership, and bankrupt governance, while the church invites them to relocate their aspirations for authentic governance elsewhere – in the eschatological hope of an unfolding heavenly kingdom. Yet, the hankering for direct democracy characteristic of clan institutions invariably resurfaces. But this urge stems from deeply rooted experiences of kinship and familial belonging shared by clan and non-clan members, citizens and non-citizens alike. Theologies of divine governance are now part of Naga national discourse, but also inextricably fused with earthly aspirations for maintaining ethnic congruity. Sometimes this gives the impression that clan patriarchy – the dominant moral-political system – relieves itself of the responsibility of turning outwardly toward the broader citizenry – including families and communities that live alongside, but are not members of Naga clan lineages. It also raises questions about the extent to which church and clan may sometimes collectively eschew responsibility for the broader social present. Though provisional (i.e. non-lineage based) forms of belonging may not be disabling for everyone, for many it means that the kinds of kinship rootedness upon which belonging and affiliation – to family, clan, tribe, nation, and indeed 'Christian nation' – ultimately rest, or make fundamental sense, are ephemeral or perpetually out of reach. Certainly, traces are found in the routines of domestic work, in the gathering of ingredients and preparation of old family recipes, in the sharing of images in photo albums, and in personal biographies narrated during meals. Many non-Naga communities settled in Kohima, some for as many as five generations, including many Nepali, Bengali, and Tibetan families that entered during British times and after, are especially conscious that the full dynamism of nurtured kinship relatedness is only possible while embedded within the congruities and enduring patterns of genealogical systems - systems they lack in their fullness. Among the ethnic Nagas, this relationship has served to maintain a surety of belonging, and spans a lifetime for lineage members, and those (women) able to graft themselves back into genealogical lines through marriage. Patrilineality, however, neither envisions an open society, nor is typically accommodating of concerns for members that cannot, or do not follow clan norms, despite the great strength and normativity of Christianity throughout the state.

Drawing on ethnographic research in Nagaland, and recent studies linking kinship and relatedness to memory (e.g. Carsten 2010), and place (e.g. Baker 2012), this chapter briefly examines the role that Christianity, omens, and domestic work play in constructions of belonging among displaced families now settled on the fringes of close-knit clan communities in Kohima, the administrative capital of Nagaland. Here, in other and other-than-real sites, visitors, including ancestors, have agency to help in establishing kinship continuities, and can offer new pathways and insights about the future. Whereas everyday life is characterised by unpredictability, belonging can be achieved in the company of 'others'.

SPATIAL CONFIGURAIONS OF REMEMBRANCE AND FORGETTING

As already noted, notions of belonging and social legitimacy often rest on temporal and material continuities, and in Kohima village, like so many villages in Nagaland, patterns belonging through privileging lineage, but also via intentionally congruous clan spaces that are rarely cut off or fragmented from the larger clan wards. Lines delineating ward and village boundaries, for example, although often quite invisible to the visitor, still hold their significance in terms of what lies within and without clan jurisdiction. What lies beyond the village line is traditionally the domain of the ambiguous 'other'. While this 'other-scape' encompasses the full visible horizon, it is necessarily parsed into clan-owned forests and cultivated fields that one visits by day. It is also, however, traditionally a terrain where unknown dangers are wildly imagined. Presently, this ambiguous terrain is dominated by an urban populace, with shops, colleges and student hostels, shopping malls, wealthy residential areas, overcrowded slums, and various building complexes with government offices. Kohima's diverse population of roughly 250,000 virtually envelops the much smaller (albeit the state's largest) 'village' of 15000, but the distinction between those who belong, and those who don't among the village's four main wards is clearly, and regularly, communicated – whether in everyday casual conversation and transaction, or through official edicts circulated by clan youth organisations. Such diktats are largely directed to clan members, and pertain to business within the village periphery. They often contain threats – fines, and ultimately violence – if the demands are not met. Such demands usually include the prohibition of rental and labour contracts among non-clan members, and the hiring of Muslims as day-labourers on village construction sites. However, the dominance of the village in local and state politics is also not lost on the broader Kohima populace, and village attitudes towards 'outsiders' is sometimes strongly felt by the town's inhabitants, especially as village leaders also control the sale of village land where much of the town sits, control the extraction of rent, and own most of the town's largest business establishments.

In many respects, though the village settlement itself is closed to non-members, its 30-odd exogamous clans maintain a strong sense of belonging and affiliation to place. And this has served well in times of war, as even a temporary abandonment of village homes – such as in the Japanese occupation of the village in 1944, or displacement of many clan communities by the Indian Army in 1956 – does little to alter the centuries old spatialised genealogically-governed material configuration.

However, another way of maintaining congruity is through processes of forgetting – or indeed removing cues that might incite unsanctioned or unwanted processes of re-experience (Connerton 2009). There is a sense in which spatial configurations, and the objects placed within them in the village, constitute the limits of sanctioned social memory. In other words, social memory or re-experience is often reflective of what is already acceptably externalised and materialised in clan spaces. Paramount here, is a clan's ancestral claim to traditionally settled spaces within the larger clan wards, and this is conspicuously expressed in the myriad – sometimes quite large – graves of ancestors, placed within often cramped house-plots. What is not acceptable, however, is any open challenge to these configurations, or any kind of knowledge that may potentially threaten village congruity. This becomes particularly poignant considering the severity of divisions, often among close kin, following efforts by Indian security forces to extract information, including names of fellow clansmen, associated with the Naga nationalists in the early years of the Indo-Naga conflict. Based on these activities – of compliance and non-compliance – imprisonment, torture, and disappearances were a regular occurrence, and the systematic burning and destruction of select homes and clan areas in the village meant that sections of the community were forcibly removed or displaced, often fleeing to neighbouring villages. Certainly, there are deep wounds and a great deal of resentment associated with these events, and they continue to affect the way older generations presently living in the village interact with their neighbours. However, the near total silence among elders on these grievances, and the absence of any significant mnemonic devices such as memorials, or published histories of these events, significantly curtails processes of re-experience or remembrance among younger generations.

Collective forgetting, though deeply painful for many, is thus necessary for the sake of long-term community congruity.

The anthropological literature on memory over the past twenty or so years (spurred by Connerton 1989 and Halbwachs 1992) has opened new avenues of research around the ways in which communities and societies manage memory, particularly in relation to disruptive events. This is done through a manipulation of spaces and materialisations or 'collective mnemonic mediums' such as physical objects or ritual practices (Empson 200, see also Antze and Lambek 1996; Argenti and Schramm 2010; Said 2000; Humphrey 2003). In contexts of political violence, memory can be 'a source of negotiation and conflict in society, perpetually open to revision and effectively rendering past and present consubstantial' (Argenti and Schramm 2010: 7). Here, rather than conceiving 'memory' as a storehouse of major events, and historical content for retrieval in constructions of identity, it is conceived as a process of re-experience; necessarily intersubjective, relational, and often conditioned by material continuities. For example, scholars concentrated at the subjective level, on the role of politics of everyday life, in constructions of the person, and generally on knowledge production and trans-generational transmission (e.g. Empson 2007; Hoskins 1998; Kuchler 1987; Radley 1997 [1990], and Strathern 2005), find that processes of remembrance are conditioned in that they are 'constrained by what constitutes a compelling narrative and the available materials for reconstruction' (Cole 2005: 4). Particularly potent are discussions related to processes whereby individuals and communities absorb, negotiate and transform loss or separation, and how these fragments become the ingredients of 'creative refashionings, in and through everyday processes of relatedness' (Carsten 2010: 24). Equally important, different generations often converge and diverge in terms of their own constructions of identity in relation to familial, political, religious or national affiliations, and how they may 'embody different temporal dispositions' (ibid: 24). The Naga context sees these processes occurring at multiple levels. If villages themselves have not consciously limited materialities that invoke processes of re-experience, centrally-controlled political censorship has ensured that any collective processes of remembrance are quieted (with few exceptions).[1] This can often

---

[1]Khonoma village - the birthplace of the Naga nationalist leader Phizo, and in some sense the heart of Naga nationalist movement - and several other villages that constitute historic landmarks in the early Naga nationalist movement, often display overt challenges to Indian official history. An example is Khonoma's multiple public memorials to villagers killed in combat with Indian forces, and the twenty-foot memorial to Khrisanisa Seyie, the first President of the Federal Government of Nagaland on the Kohima-Khonoma road, stating: 'Nagas are not Indians; their

be forcefully done, as these more subjective dispositions to the family and community histories are largely at odds with India's official histories. In the absence of due diligence in reporting, in publically accessible sociological and historical research, and public remembrance rituals on par, for instance, with the programmes of the Kohima War Cemetery, ethnographic work, and attention to personal biography, and traces that typically endure in the domestic sphere, can play a role in maintaining continuities necessary for establishing notions of belonging.

This study maintains that belonging may be a nexus or linkage between the ostensibly distinct domains of remembrance or re-experience, and kinship. Here, broad and formulaic notions of forms and functions of mnemonic mediums employed in the processes of re-experience of major political events, are linked in important ways in constructions of self and identity. Kinship scholarship has focused on important symbolic and pragmatic facets of local practice – gender, personhood, procreation, feeding, naming, the house – to the detriment of their cumulative, wider political significance (Carsten 2010). A merger of the two necessarily reshuffles the deck toward subjective, often intimate, individual circumstances that 'point to the myriad articulations - of temporality, memory, personal biography, family connection, and political processes – that are manifested in subjective dispositions to the past, and in the imagination of possible futures' (Carsten 2010: 1). Here, what is suggested is a continuum where subjective particularities in terms of memory recall are most marked in contexts where notions of the self are less situated. In other words, more decisive separation and/or alienation from kinship relations correlates with more fragmented notions of temporality and space in memory recall. Carsten's ethnographic work among adoptees seeking to reunite with their birth kin illustrates this continuum most aptly, albeit in a Western context (ibid: 83-104):

> Different kinds of kinship combine with particular historical and politico-economic circumstances to produce dispositions towards certain kinds of temporal elaboration, and particular kinds of memory (and forgetting) work. The chains of continuity that are elaborated and highlighted between kin can take many different forms, and these have a wider political resonance. Thus, the funnelling down of kinship, together with a concentrated gaze on the self, that are characteristic of European and North American societies is constitutive

---

territory is not part of the Indian Union. We shall uphold and defend this unique truth at all costs and always'. Attempts to silence such overt displays would likely be provocative in an already politically tenuous ceasefire, and thus are left alone.

of, and reflects, an ideologically based, political separation between the world of family and intimate relations, and the world of overtly economic and political exchanges (ibid.: 90).

Here, rootedness and continuity in kinship relations is seen to directly affect the condition of the self. In this context, however, political and economic imperatives that come to bear on families and on individuals are often eclipsed by their symptoms, and the growth of psychoanalysis as well as the mass proliferation of self-help media, are two ways of gauging, in the largest sense, the extent to which a society recognizes its own complicity in kinship alienation (ibid.: 90). It is perhaps in this very notion of recognition that loss and suffering can be most generously used to source restorative reconfigurations in day-to-day relatedness. The ability for people to develop new relationships are here predicated on the ability to consciously acknowledge loss. Carsten writes: 'In this sense, we might say that a work of memory is the necessary counterpoint to kinship relations in their broadest sense' (ibid: xx). Memory work that, due to present circumstances, is rendered difficult or indeed not possible at all, constrains these abilities to relate in new ways, and indeed to articulate notions of belonging such as citizenship. For families living on the fringes of Kohima village, establishing continuities is an everyday struggle, and the following section explores the ways in which one family, an elderly couple, works through these difficulties in creative ways.

MATERIALISING KIN RELATIONS IN THE ABSENCE OF BELONGING

Atsa and her husband Apfutsa, both octogenarians, reside just outside of the village boundary, and below one of the four main wards in Kohima village. Atsa's home sits on the north-western slope of the village, about twenty metres below one of the many roads crisscrossing the hill. The small structure which she and her husband rent is sunken about 12 inches on the downslope side, and looks as though it could plummet down the steep fifty-foot cliff with the next heavy rainfall. The detached outhouse is a patchwork of tin roofing scraps wired to a wooden frame, and straddles an open ditch that joins a larger canal taking the sewage down towards the national highway. Atsa and Apfutsa's neighbourhood is on clan land near the old American Baptist missionary compound. The large hillside plot was donated in the Indo-Naga peace effort in the early 1970s, becoming the Transit Peace Camp following the Shillong Accord signed between leaders of the Naga National Council and Indian government in 1975. Bounded on all sides by a high fence, the Peace Camp resembles a cloister - a community of Naga Army veterans waiting patiently for India to fulfil its half of the deal. The north-western slope of Kohima village, and surrounding Atsa and Apfutsa's rented home, is a settlement made up largely of Khonoma villagers, a village higher in the hills 15 miles away. Khonoma is the home of members of A.Z. Phizo's [the first NNC President] Merhema clan. Having fled when the Indian Army laid siege to Khonoma village in 1956, the repeated targeting of Phizo's clan members throughout the war dissuaded them from returning to Khonoma.

Atsa, aged 27 at the time of the 1956 siege, was separated from her family in the chaos that ensued, and fled southward towards Manipur. She, along with a few clan members, lived in the forests on the southern side of the Dzükou valley for several months, receiving food and help from members of a Zeme Naga village just over the Nagaland border in Manipur. This Zeme village had a long history of aiding refugees from Khonoma, most notably following the infamous 'Battle of Khonoma' in which British-led forces attacked, burned, and dispersed the village in 1880. Atsa was eventually taken in by a Kuki village in the Senapati district of Manipur where she stayed for several years. She then returned to Kohima in search of her family, and found them and many of her fellow clan members clustered on the edges of Kohima village where they presently reside.

I first visited Atsa in early 2013, just at the start of the heavy winds. She was troubled by a dream she had a few nights before and shared her dream as she prepared tea. Having rented a small room in their house during fieldwork, I had come to mend a window that had shattered in the high winds a few nights before. In Atsa's dream, all seemed fine at first:

> I could walk like I always have from the house to the kitchen; up and down from Vonuo's kitchen down the hill. But in an instant, it felt like everything had changed in my dream. I suddenly could not support my own weight. My knees began to buckle. Apfutsa called me and I couldn't come. I was dragging myself along the floor. When I woke up I found the broken window and that is a very bad sign.

The following morning, Atsa's niece, having heard about the broken window, asked her: 'who do you think will die now?' In his eighties, Apfutsa struggled with a lung infection over the winter, and everyone was aware that it might just be his time. Apfutsa was originally from a Rongmei Naga community in Imphal, the capital of Manipur state, and was a former footballer who learned to play from American soldiers stationed in Manipur during the Second World War. He loved the game and played professionally as a left-fielder for the 'Manipur Eleven', one of the few professional teams from greater Assam in the '50s and '60s. He recalls with great joy the various tours throughout the Northeastern states, finally reaching the championships in Calcutta. This old athlete seemed to weather this most recent storm, and though he had a rough winter, he regained his strength. The sense at that point among Atsa's family and neighbours was that the sign of the broken window - plainly visible to anyone entering the living room - told of something that had not yet taken place. But what could it be? 'What then', some of the family members were asking, 'will befall Atsa?'

The omen had overshadowed a potentially important message in the dream. Atsa's niece Agu mentioned to me that the dream seemed to be about Atsa herself, and probably related to her increasing incapacity to care for Apfutsa, given their age and frailty. Agu's expression was shared by several other family members, a feeling of the inevitability of Apfutsa's approaching death. His death was, in many respects, not the tragedy itself – though it certainly was lamentable even though he was now quite elderly. It was because Atsa had lost so many family members in such a short period of time.

Atsa's knees began to swell a few weeks after her dream, and she now used a walking stick to get around. But her knee problem seemed to be more than an ailment, and indeed there were moments when, having just heard news of someone falling ill, or a death in one of the neighbouring clans, she would say something to the effect of 'oh, I felt it in my leg, I knew that someone in that neighbourhood was not good'. In one of our earliest conversations she told the story of her meeting her mother's ghost after she died. Her house had been locked, and she and her two sisters had gone to bed. Her mother appeared in the early morning hours. Atsa heard a sound that woke her, and she saw her mother at the foot of her bed. The ghost reached out and touched her leg, which she felt, and then left the house through the front door. When they all got up the next morning, her sister found that the latch on the front door had been opened during the night. I had difficulty understanding whether she connected the memory of her mother's ghost touching her leg, with her present knee condition. Local healers such as the Ao healer she consulted for massaging her leg shared the common experience of being visited by a spirit in the context of a dream, while in their teenage years. In the dream, they are invited to receive a gift, and if they agree they are tutored in spirit-mediated human healing (cf. Joshi 2012). Indeed, Atsa's regular comments regarding her capacity to 'feel' invisible forces - though materialised in pain - perhaps the flow of spirits now coming to entice living human spirit kin to come with them, the logic accompanying shamanic 'calling' seemed to be at play as well.

Though I encouraged her to consult a doctor, she showed little interest. In a series of side comments, she indicated that she distrusted the new medical facilities in town, the treatments, and the confusing pharmaceuticals. She critiqued what she saw as opportunism, as these facilities seemed to pop up out of nowhere in recent years, and were expensive. Consulting a physician invariably led to a string of additional expenses, and consultations seemed rushed, and at times she felt they were too eager to write chemical prescriptions for any mild discomfort, and often without a physical examination. For almost a decade her daughter Roko had complained of severe migraines and there seemed to be no agreement among the various medical practitioners of what exactly afflicted her. However, they were unanimous in prescribing strong painkillers which, in the end, severely injured her kidneys. At forty-seven years of age, and caring for five children, Roko was bedridden and could no longer work. The daily dialysis treatment she needed was not available locally, so a makeshift bedside system was devised in her home, and her ten-year-old daughter learned to use a syringe and administer the medicine.

As with her neighbours clustered around her, Atsa was acutely aware of her contingency. Roko's father (Roko means 'abundant with luck') was a Nepali officer temporarily stationed in Kohima, who later transferred to Shillong, never to return to them. When Roko was a teenager, Atsa married Apfutsa who was a close neighbour and then accountant in the new Nagaland State bureaucracy. Following his career in football, he earned a decent wage as a government servant, and was able to save while also supporting his seven sons from his first marriage. Since Atsa did not marry into a local Angami clan, she had no land of her own to cultivate. She also believed it was foolish to place her hopes in finding employment in the offices of the government administration, to which many other immigrant families in Kohima were drawn. After all, her husband, having served for nearly four decades in government offices, received a monthly pension of 20,000 rupees (about £240.00), covering their basic needs, but little more. This seemed evidence enough of the moral bankruptcy that Atsa felt characterised government institutions, institutions that she remembered at one time as being more honest and fair.

Atsa's sense of belonging centred on her relationship with local vegetable, meat, and milk vendors which she continuously nurtured. Her relationship to her father's clan, for example, was violently interrupted. She left the protection of her clan not as a clan woman typically does through marriage to a neighbouring clan. She left running as her home burned in the midst of war. There had scarcely been an opportunity to materialise continuities in, for example, the way that clan lineage members were able to. Her relationships, with a Nepali officer, and with a Manipuri Rongmei footballer-turned-accountant, were not mediated by her father's clan, and in fact were not officiated by the church. She thus forged her own way, following a logic of survival and non-dependence on the clan. Atsa's son-in-law once said 'girls are only free during the first two years of their lives', reflecting on the reality of girls and women as the main producers and providers; a reality and expectation that accompanies them throughout their lives. The activities of cooking, of preparing *akhuni* (a traditional condiment of fermented soya), were not only about generating side income, and were more than the social value of their exchange (as in Mauss' 1924 seminal study of *hau* in 'The Gift'). The preparation of *akhuni* allowed Atsa to generate, to create, to bring into being an aspect of her past, possibly a trace of her mother, that was there for her, just that it was something she could make visible and tactile through her techniques. For example, Atsa was often caught unawares talking aloud to an invisible companion. She would sometimes get quite irritated if interrupted, but the conversations revealed them to be conversations with her mother. Her regular preparations of *akhuni* were 'processes of materialisation' of kin relations, which are 'attempts to arrest the ambivalent movement between presence and absence' of that which the *akhuni* itself embodied (Harries 2010: 403). In other words, she was seeking to be 'haunted by the thing itself, which is both insufficient to, yet in excess of, these materialisations' (ibid: 403). Regarding these kinds of absences, Fowles (2010: 27) suggests:

> When absences become object-like, when they seem to exist not merely as an afterthought of perception but rather as self-standing presences out there in the world, they begin to acquire powers and potentialities similar to things. Object-like absences (or what Fuery (1995: 2) refers to as quasi-presences), in this sense, become full participants in the social characterized by their own particular politics and, at times, their own particular emotional and semiotic charge.

As discussed above, the patrilocality of clan homes and their kitchens forecloses the possibility of female home or land ownership. Only in the rarest of circumstances will ownership pass to a daughter, or be sold out of the clan to an external buyer. When a woman marries she leaves her father's home and moves into a newly constructed house, typically in the sub-clan area of her husband. If the husband is the only son, or the youngest son, he and the bride will reside in the husband's father's home, though the bride will cook in a separate kitchen. In every case, marriage entails a new 'hearth', and this domestic setting accompanies the bride all her life, and often until death. In Kohima, men rarely outlive their wives, so the hearth is finally extinguished when the bride dies in old age.

If one were to identify a space or setting where dreams were told the most, a space par excellence for dream narration, the hearth, according to Hibo (2012: 4) is 'where the whole family was allowed to sit together along with friends, visitors from neighbourhood or even visitors from other villages. Taboos were often interpreted, shared and warned from these kitchen talks.' In many ways, the domestic sphere is removed from clan meeting spaces (which are exclusively for clan men), and this division entails a broader bi-sedimentation of everyday community life. It is in the domestic sphere that dreams, omens, and stories of ancestors are most often shared. In many ways, the activities of the 'hearth' are situated but unsettled, gendered but non-exclusive, non-public but nodal and 'plugged in' to a broad informal network that includes other married women in the clan, but extends to vegetable, meat, and milk vendors, among others, often from other communities, and sometimes from beyond district and state borders. This domestic 'economy' is decidedly egalitarian, and mixes bargaining and buying with socialising. The 'hidden transcript' (Scott 1990) of Atsa's hearth and the broader domestic economy is not entirely 'opposition' (or indeed 'rage', as suggested by Scott) against the clan, but constitutes a carefully performed set of techniques that reflect a general ambivalence towards patriarchal power. These might emerge as methods of contestation in some instances, and of complicity in others (ibid.). Put differently, a community of non-inheritors, married clan women constitute a 'horizontal' collective (Thomas & Humphrey 2007) but this 'collective' is not always clearly in opposition to the pervasive vertical structures of power within the clan. This paradox is only a contradiction if viewed outside of the *longue durée* of genealogical temporality. Domestic practices are situated in in-between-ness, engaging in both sustaining vestiges of traditional conservatism through old recipes and food preparation, but also creatively incorporating new ways of making relations through ongoing interaction with a larger domestic economy.

The impossibility of clan membership is met with alternative processes of materialising continuities, through the making of new, egalitarian kinship systems, and thus new forms of belonging. Atsa, for instance, ignored the pleas of her clan relatives to seek alternative treatments for her knees. She preferred to follow the advice of her various other contacts - the milkman, the *akhuni* client, a fellow church member, etc. In fact, the traditional healer she consulted during the time of my research, was recommended through this network, and she seemed pleased by her 'alternative' course of action. Her clan relatives did not discouraged her from seeing the healer, but often remarked in her presence that only proper medical treatment could help her. This would make Atsa frown, as it seemed obvious to her that it was precisely the 'experts' that had killed Roko - her only daughter. Indeed, caught up in a medicalised landscape, Atsa believed the experts were just unknown, and untrusted salesmen. Within the pragmatism of her new horizontal collective, there was a more ambivalent stance always at-play, the kind of ambivalence deployed in the facial expressions in everyday petty bargaining in the market place. Indeed, this operative stance, of pragmatism and ambivalence, was underwritten by the knowledge that, as Harper (2014: 71) suggests, 'other orders and rationalities exist and circulate', and an over reliance on the 'best' is simply too high a risk to take, and possibly fatal.

The idea of the extended domestic sphere here is about constructing continuities in places where one is continually reminded of non-citizenship. Everyday interaction with human and non-human persons, in food preparation, and in being attentive to one's surrounding, are processes of materialising continuities. These are formations that birth subjective dispositions of emplacement amid displacement. Atsa's mother and daughter, though now deceased, are 'non-absent' persons; 'present' and in important ways accompanying Atsa in her everyday search for belonging. By the same token, the pain in her knee is a corporeal manifestation of these processes of materialisation; a bodily weather-vane registering the confluence of visible and invisible. But it is in her dreams where these ambiguities begin to disappear. It is here that non-absent kin relations become 'real' and tactile, reflecting the complex entanglement of presences and absences that make up Atsa's personhood - a jumble of disjointed times, places, and peoples that are constitutive of her community of belonging, and the point of departure from which she also turns to experience the world.

SITES OF RELATEDNESS

Atsa is good at concealing her thoughts behind a quiet demeanour and measured movements. Despite this, she has always appeared to me to be intensely perceptive of her surroundings. She can also be light-hearted and is known for her vicious under-the-breath comments regarding one's personal appearance, particularly among her grandchildren when they sit inside her kitchen for a meal and a story: - 'oh, you didn't shave'; 'you should cut your hair'; or 'you are thin – is your wife not feeding you properly? I will speak to her'. One by one each person present will hunch towards the collection of kettles on the wood fire, and serve themselves rice, and Atsa's famous pork curry. Invariably, she will share an incident of that day, and sometimes insert a dream experience she remembers from the previous night. In one such occasion, I jotted Atsa's comments in my notes:

> This knee aches more than the other, but right now I am alright. I had a silly dream last night. I was visited by a man that told me I could make some extra money if I put photographs of myself in one of those calendars. But this man said I would have to dance too. How funny, imagine me dancing - I can hardly walk up those steps.

Atsa feels strongly about her faith in God, and spends several hours every day reading the Bible and praying, but is at the same time increasingly weary of the revivalist rhetoric at her church which would have her renounce her 'worldly condition' - her day-to-day struggle. After all, though it is an existence largely caught up in a thankless routine of cooking, hauling water, cleaning floors, and washing clothes, these are aspects of her life over which she is mostly in control. Her orientation away from influential community or state institutions was accentuated following a string of recent, and successive tragedies in her life: the death of her son-in-law to alcoholism in 2011, the death, only four months later, of her only biological child Roko, and then the sudden death of her dear sister and next door neighbour the following year to cancer. These are unbearable losses, contributing to her increasing insularity, and pessimistic attitude towards the world. While conducting fieldwork, I found she would leave her home only in the most exceptional circumstances. Her sliding, rented home, with a small bedroom, a room to receive guests, a second bedroom which I sometimes use as an office, and a little outdoor kitchen, is a space she understands and can muster the strength every day to manage.

In August 2013, as the monsoon rains subside, the pain in Atsa's knees worsens, and she consults the old Ao healer. Reclining in her room, the slightly built man gently massages her knee and encourages her to be careful not to stress her sensitive joints by climbing the steps. I am surprised to see Atsa consulting a traditional healer given her strong loyalty to her local church, a more or less conservative Baptist Church in the centre of town. She has been a member of the same church for most of her life, and always refuses to entertain invitations to attend other churches with virtually identical services situated nearer her home. Moreover, Apfutsa is a strict Seventh Day Adventist, even more strict than her own church, prohibiting consultation with traditional divinatory practices. This makes the massage session all the more perplexing. But Atsa frequently expresses interest or curiosity about spirit activity, particularly in the nearby forests, and about the power of spiritual forces generally.

As mentioned earlier, Atsa's friendship with vendors, and other individuals with no kinship ties to Kohima clans, revolves around her traditional food preparations, and especially her production of *akhuni*, a fermented and smoke-dried soybean paste used as a condiment in Angami food, and a variant of a product made in kitchens throughout Asia. Atsa's *akhuni* is legendary according to some of her customers. And though in recent years she has shifted to using a pressure cooker and a gas burner to save on the cost of wood and time (boiling takes 30 to 40 minutes), any change in taste has gone unnoticed by her loyal clientele in the village. The small packets of lemon-yellow coloured paste, which she stores inside the chimney or behind the fire within the hearth, she sells for 10 rupees each. Through word of mouth she often receives orders from customers outside the village, and in large quantities of ten to twenty packets.

The process is simple. Atsa washes and then soaks locally available soybeans in water, and boils them until they are soft. She then drains and wraps them in banana leaves in a bamboo basket placed near the hearth to dry and ferment. After three days, she tastes them, and if ready, mashes them with a wooden pestle and tightly wraps them in banana leaves or paper tied with a thin strand of bamboo. The income she receives, however, is not enough to make any significant home improvements or help her grandchildren with school expenses. In fact, the cost of living in Kohima exceeds the income capacity of many poor households. All meals, therefore, are simple and vary little - rice, dal, mustard greens, and occasionally chicken or pork, often brought by a relative. Indeed, 'living simply' is a matter of pride for Atsa. As I sometimes rent a room from Atsa for writing, I feel it is appropriate to offer my handyman skills - to fix the broken window, to mend the sidewalk with a few bricks, etc. But these offers are always brushed aside: 'oh, no need'. There are times when Atsa uses her earnings to purchase rice beer, which helps to numb the pain in her knees, and generally helps her and her husband sleep. Throughout fieldwork I popped into her small kitchen to share a cup or two with Apfutsa, and get an update on any interesting dreams she might share.

But the true value in the *akhuni* is in maintaining her linkages - with her neighbours in the clan, her home village of Khonoma, and her suppliers and traders. These interactions oscillate with the changing rhythms and circulation of the seasons and seasonal ingredients coming from rural villages that are far too costly, if available at all, in the Kohima market. Traders that she has not seen in a long time are greeted as old friends. When someone visits, she might get fresh mushrooms picked from the forest above Khonoma, or home grown Raja chilli peppers from Peren, south west of Kohima, or fresh bamboo shoots from Tuli, further north. These are highly sought-after, and occasionally brought by her birth clan relatives in Khonoma, but more often by relatives of her neighbours or clients who came carrying a bundle and stop first at Atsa's kitchen. Sometimes these are simply gifts, sold for a minimal price, or exchanged for a fresh packet of *akhuni*. With these exchanges, Atsa is able to recreate the traditional dishes she and Apfutsa are accustomed to, that are reminiscences in themselves, with ingredients that are scarce. The best of these special dishes are reserved for weekends when nieces, nephews and grandchildren visit. What is possible on weekends with family visitors is a re-experience of familial gatherings of the past; old recipes served up for at least two generations that have few other ways of relating to the village practices that closely follow the changing seasons.

One of Atsa's many customers, Kezevinuo, is a widow who tends a large garden and sells much of its produce to villagers. Her husband was a heavy drinker and eventually died of liver disease roughly five years prior to my arrival. Kezevinuo rears pigs, which is technically prohibited by the village council due to its generally unpleasant smell. She has moved the pig enclosure away from the road, shifted it around the compound several times, but relies on the sale of piglets for income. Her vegetables and herbs, and small shop help, but the high school fees for her son and daughter are a constant worry. She is a survivor, and had she not had a son the property her home is built on would revert to the clan. Her son, a shy eight-year-old boy, studies before and after school, and somehow the monotony of work seems to lighten when he arrives back home to feed the pigs and help cook dinner.

Unlike Atsa, Kezevinuo lives inside the village boundary of the clan, and inside a clan compound. She is therefore protected from the harassment and taxation by underground insurgents that accompanies owning a small shop or convenience store in Kohima town. But at the same time, she is doubly-bound. With her husband dead, she is stuck in an in-between place where she has little say in how the world around her is organised. She shares her dreams with the other women in the vicinity, believing that they will come true. She shares them frequently while watering the garden and boiling food scraps for the pigs. Her busy day of buying and selling food items, her pig rearing, and great interest in omens and dreams seems to come together as a form of struggle, but also of gentle but unyielding resistance to clan restrictions.

This notion of survival, of getting through, tends to emphasise both the present and the need to understand what is next – that which is forthcoming. The anxiety is to understand the future, what it might bring, since memories and dwelling on the past are not things any of the married women living within the clan have the luxury to worry about at any rate. But this is not to say that memories – memories of childhood, of familial relations in the father's clan – are not intensely felt, and continuously a strongly felt absence. The past creeps in and disturbs wake-time and sleep-time, and is thus ever-present. The consequences of the past haunt their existence and shape their every capacity to act in the unfolding present. The confined spaces, though offering room to work, to plan, and perhaps to contrive, are also spaces that make them aware of their limitations (Merleau-Ponty 2006; cf. Trigg 2013).

TALKING ABOUT THE PAST

For Atsa, despite her appearing not to care very much whether her guests mind hearing her complain about her knee, or about some piece of news she heard from a neighbour, nonetheless cherishes fellowship. However, she does not simply offer to share about her past unless asked specifically about specific years or life events. It is not because she cannot remember, or does not want to relive painful memories, but because she does not want to overstate her own agency in her past – she indeed seeks constantly to depersonalise her own story. Very often, Atsa reveals in her retelling of her own stories of survival, the processes she undertook of absorbing, negotiating, and transforming personal loss and separation into fragments of experience that then could be the ingredients for a kind of 'citizenship'. Carsten (2007: 24) articulates this construction of belongingness as 'creative refashionings, in and through everyday processes of relatedness'. Her generally light-hearted demeanour speaks volumes of her capacity to cope with loss, and dislocation from close kinship times, and instead to divert her attention to her Christian faith, her grandchildren, her friends, and the vegetable vendors and other workers that she welcomes regularly to sit for tea and conversation.

I regularly asked Atsa to talk about her past, about her childhood in Khonoma, and perhaps about such things as seeing the British or the Japanese in her village, prior and during the Second World War. One of Atsa's nieces, seventeen-year-old Zaza, would listen in while playing games on her smartphone, and on occasion showed interest, asking follow-up questions, and then stating that she had never heard these things before. In such situations, Atsa simply chuckles and shifts to the next activity. But Atsa's experiences seem, at times, entirely foreign to Zaza and the younger generation. Though Atsa's dramatic escape from her village under attack, suggests she likely experienced some of the worst horrors of the war, Zaza's age-group appear scarcely aware that there has been a war at all. Certainly indicative of the way different generations converge and diverge in terms of their own constructions of identity in relation to close age-groups, family, and neighbours, there is a sense in which the different generations 'embody different temporal dispositions' (Carsten 2007: 24). Atsa's sharing, including her sharing of dreams, albeit often fragmentary, is done recognizing that loss can be productive in sourcing restorative reconfigurations in day-to-day relatedness (ibid.). Atsa's ability to develop new relationships wherever she shifts next is predicated on her ability to consciously acknowledge loss. As noted earlier following Carsten (2007: 24), this suggests that 'in this sense, we might say that a work of memory is the necessary counterpoint to kinship relations in their broadest sense'. However, as with many in the community that reside at the margins of belonging in relation to patrilineality, enmeshed in repetitive, often arduous routines, Atsa is also attentive to knowledge that may transform her condition, whether in teachings and consolations she receives through prayer and in her Bible reading, in the everydayness of her broader domesticity, or indeed in her relatedness with other-than-human kin in her dreams.

CONCLUDING REMARKS

Atsa lives at the tail end of a complex history of personal and familial challenges. Though her birth clan in Khonoma is Christian, the very first Christian converts were excommunicated, and their houses burned. Their homes were reconstructed and then burned again in the Indo-Naga war given the clan's kinship proximity to Phizo, the leader of the underground nationalist movement. Apfutsa served as a government servant for most of his adult life, so Atsa's clan would not have been openly accepting. Clan members working in the Nagaland Government were often viewed and treated as traitors of the national cause. Ironically, though Phizo was technically Atsa's maternal uncle – she is landless, and rents a home on land far from the village of her birth. Atsa's contingency can be said to contribute to the openness of her lived experience, and to her willingness to relate to members of the broader domestic economy of relations - individuals that do not find the same reception within the clan. Atsa and many of her neighbours express a unique ethical disposition, not because it is sacrificial, nor even intentional, but because otherness is at the heart of the human need for belonging. Indeed, as Levinas (1996: 91) suggests: 'this way of being, without prior commitment, responsible for the other (autrui), amounts to the fact of human fellowship, prior to freedom'.

In 2015, Apfutsa died. He had suffered a bad lung infection earlier in the year, and had declined rapidly in the months leading up to his death. Atsa's relatives living in Khonoma village offered to bury Apfutsa on clan land on the outskirts of the village – an offer that struck everyone as both incredibly generous, and of great significance for her closest relatives. Atsa's face, when I asked her about it, was of tearful joy, as this meant that one day, she would not only be reunited with her husband, but she would be returning to her true home. Following the funeral, Atsa asked her relatives to allow her to stay at their old 'leaning' house in Kohima, but she eventually conceded to living with her nieces up the hill. She now lives within the clan boundaries, and in some respects her living conditions have improved. Her relatives set up a makeshift stove outside so she could cook *akhuni*, and she continues to receive her customers, selling the packets for 25 rupees each, often in large bundles.

The pain in her knees has also subsided, and the last time I met her, her family had not pressed her so much on getting an operation, or taking pain killers. Her nieces say her knee sometimes flares up and she says she feels someone is either very sick or going to die. In many ways, I have come to interpret her pain as an omen, her body extending outward, and absorbing and becoming absorbed into the sentient landscape.

Atsa's continued participation in the domestic economy of relations also allows her to distribute her marginality. She shares her dreams, her daily annoyances with a physical handicap, and by doing so she joins an anonymous multitude of other individuals negotiating day to day uncertainty and unpredictability. By inviting non-clan and very often non-Naga vendors and shop owners to join her the kitchen by the hearth for hot tea or a meal, she decides not to participate in the kind of exclusionary practices that seem to pervade in the village. By hosting guests generally unwelcome beyond their labouring hours, she lifts her chin in defiance, and, in some respects, assumes part of her guests' marginality by not pretending to be anyone except a guest herself.

When the entourage of non-Naga labourers and traders appeared in the early morning hours to carry a few large boxes, kitchen pots and kettles, and cabinets on their heads to help her move house, they walked steadily up the hill and into the heart of the clan neighbourhood with an air of pride. They were giving back the way they could, and this move was a testament to her capacity to materialise her own form of belonging among a motley group of ragged men, and in this way showed her own air of pride in the face of what she felt to be unnecessary snobbery. Her challenge to boundaries, to what seem like unfettered and unnecessary levels of consumerism within the village, and her more recent ambivalence with regards to the morality of the church, do not preclude her from a deeply felt responsibility for everyone she receives in her kitchen. According to one of her nieces, the pain in her body, and the signs and omens that appear to her in her dreams and in her increasingly fragile, tactile environment, only become more acute with old age. The insights - *kesi* - that she gleans are not simply warnings of impending events or troubles, but are a much more dynamic patterning of aspects of the unfolding present that may yet be in a fragile assemblage, malleable, and not-irreversible. These pathways are not foregone conclusions, or resistant to re-direction, but exist in an expanded temporality, emerging from a broader universe of hidden possibilities, which can be potentially apprehended or altered through one's own creative intervention. The more attentive she is, the more capacity she has to think through the patterns - in dream-time and wake-time - that emerge and inform her. These very 'real' absences, as Fowles (2010: 27) suggests 'perform labor, frequently intensifying our emotional or cognitive engagement with that which is manifestly not present'. When Atsa shares her dreams or the signs she has gleaned from her ambit of work and routine, she speaks for and with the messages, because they are not absent or in the past. They are present, and part of a long succession of interpreted, acted upon messages that have altered her life-course. She no longer shares *kesi*, but *kesikele* – 'insights with knowing'.

■ ■■ ■■

13

'EQUALITY OF TRADITION' AND WOMEN'S RESERVATION IN NAGALAND

Kham Khan Suan Hausing

INTRODUCTION

One of the most common presumptions about tribal societies in the North East India or elsewhere is their 'egalitarianism'. Although it is taken as a given and frequently used as a staple justification to mark out the tribal 'others' from inegalitarian caste-Hindu societies in India, egalitarianism as a hallmark of 'equality as tradition' of tribal societies sits uneasily with the inegalitarian discourse and unequal treatment meted out to tribal women (Shimray 2002). This becomes glaringly evident in the controversy surrounding attempts by the Nagaland Legislative Assembly (NLA) to give 33% reservation to women in urban local bodies (ULBs) since 2006 when it inserted Section 23A to the Nagaland Municipal Act, 2001 by bringing about an amendment to this act.

ULBs, encompassing three municipalities — Dimapur, Kohima and Mokokchung — and 19 town councils in Nagaland, became controversial with this amendment as antagonists — constituted by a melange of frontal Naga tribal bodies like Naga Hoho and Eastern Nagaland People's Organisation (ENPO) — contend that this amendment amounts to imposition of 'alien' rules like 'reservation' and 'tax' on 'land and buildings' which violate the Naga 'way of life', social tradition and customary laws of equal treatment (Amer 2013; *Eastern Mirror* 2017; GoN 2012, Wouters 2017c). These arguments were effectively used to mobilise public opposition to implementation of the amended 2001 act and holding of ULB elections since October 2008. Caving into the pressure of these antagonists, NLA invoked its special plenary power under Article 371(A)[1] which protects, inter alia, Naga customary law, land and resources, and passed a resolution on 22 September 2012 exempting the state from Part IX(A) (dealing with municipalities) of the Constitution.

Protagonists of the amended act, the Naga Mothers' Association (NMA) and the Joint Action Committee for Women Reservation (JACWR), consistently argued for holding of ULB elections and implementing the 33% reservation to bring about women's empowerment. They contend that NLA's resolution and the oppositional stand taken by antagonist Naga tribal bodies seek to perpetuate inegalitarian patriarchal societal culture and customary practices (Changkija 2017; Dzuvichu 2011, 2016). Protagonists also considered deeply problematic attempts to invoke Article 371(A) to forestall women's reservation because 'municipalities' are 'modern entities' that lie outside the ambit of Naga's customary laws (Dzuvichu 2016).

Consistent pressure from New Delhi and multilateral aid agencies that increasingly tie up development aid to inclusive democracy at the grass roots, and representations by the protagonists of this act to the Supreme Court led the court to direct the GoN on 20 April 2016 to immediately hold ULB elections. Following this directive, NLA passed a resolution on 22 November 2016 whereby it revoked its September 2012 resolution. In order to pave the way for holding of ULB elections, NLA enacted the Nagaland Municipal (Third Amendment) Act on 24 November 2016 and removed two major grounds of opposition by tribal bodies to ULBs, namely (i) Section 121(1)(a) of the 2001 act pertaining to ULBs' power to impose 'tax on lands and buildings', and (ii) reservation to Scheduled Castes in the state under Sections 23(A) and 23(B) of the act.

However, when GoN fixed ULB elections for 1 February 2017 and initiated the electoral process, frontal Naga tribal bodies vehemently opposed the move and intimidated prospective candidates not to contest

---

[1]NLA, by passing a 'resolution' under Article 371(A) (1), can make inapplicable any law made by the Parliament in matters pertaining to, inter alia, Nagas' 'religious or social practices', 'customary law and procedure', 'ownership and transfer of land and its resources'.

elections. Several candidates withdrew their nomination papers as a result. The opposition to ULB elections reached a climax on 1 February 2017 when two of the violent protesters were killed by alleged police firing in Dimapur and the headquarter building of the municipal council in Kohima was razed to the ground. Although the failure of GoN to honour its agreement on 30 January 2017 with the Joint Coordination Committee — the umbrella tribal bodies which frontally opposed ULB elections — to postpone ULB elections for two months and hold wider consultations, provided the immediate spark to this violent protest, a nuanced examination of the opposition to extend 33% reservation to women and hold ULBs accordingly underscores the complexity of the issues and concerns raised by different segments of Naga society.

QUESTION OF WOMEN'S RESERVATION

It is a truism that despite making significant progress in education, employment and health sectors, women around the world have negligible presence in legislative and executive bodies. Since 1893 when New Zealand extended franchise to women, the entry and presence of women in representative bodies have been incremental (Norris 1996). The British parliament, considered as the mother of modern parliaments, for example, made halting progress as hardly two dozen women found entry as Members of Parliament (MPs) between 1945 and 1983 (Norris 1996: 89). From constituting about 5% in this period, their representation increased to 60 MPs in 1992, accounting for 9.2%, before it eventually reached a high of 32% in 2017 (Norris 1996: 89; IPU 2017). The Scandinavian countries were considered role models in the 1970s and 1980s, yet women barely constituted around 20%–30% of the elected representatives during this period.

The negligible presence of women in representative bodies was somehow rectified since the 1990s when major international aid donors began to link aid with inclusive governance. This arguably sets in what is popularly known as the 'fast track' mode of women's representation in elected bodies even as these donors mandated statutory provisions to secure fixed women's quotas in these bodies as a necessary condition to extend developmental aid (Bush 2011; Dahlerup and Freidenvall 2005; Reynolds 1999). The upshot of this is extensive constitutionally and party-mandated electoral reforms undertaken by aid-dependent developing countries around the world, a phenomenon which had ripple effects on industrially developed democracies as well. Not surprisingly, these countries witnessed increased presence of women in parliaments by introducing the quota system.

Some of the glaring beneficiaries of these reforms include Rwanda with 48.8% in 2003, Costa Rica with 35.1% in 2002, Argentina with 34.1% in 2003, South Africa with 32.8% in 2004—all of which introduced the list proportional system of representation to secure greater presence of women in their parliaments (Dahlerup and Freidenvall 2005: 36). While Costa Rica maintained its 2003 level, Argentina and South Africa have since increased women's representation to their parliament by over 4% in 2017. Rwanda with 61.3% women in its lower house of parliament is currently the world's leader in giving representation to women (IPU 2017).

It is being held that increasing presence of women in elected legislative and executive bodies caters to the demands of justice by securing equal participation right to them in the deliberative and decision-making process. Indeed, the question of representation and giving voice to disenfranchised groups like women has engaged modern liberal political thinkers and activists alike for a long time now. Writing almost a century and a half ago, John Stuart Mill underscored the imperative to have intellectual and social diversity in governments by including representatives of both majority and minorities, including women, if they were to be effective and legitimate (Mill 1975; Phillips 1995; Reynolds 1999). Making a forceful plea for enfranchising women, Mill considered that attempts to deny franchise to half of the population and losing their talents represented nothing but an exercise in 'nonutilitarian idiocy' (cited in Reynolds 1999: 548). He contended that the 'subjection of women' was based on 'theory only' and also that the 'system of inequality' wherein the 'weaker sex' is subordinated to the 'stronger' was 'never ... the result of deliberation, or forethought, or any social ideas, or any notion whatever of what conduced to the benefit of humanity or the good order of society' (Mill 1975: 431, compare with Reynolds 1999: 548).

Normatively, women's presence in elected bodies is considered as a necessary but insufficient condition to cater to the demands of justice as it gives them 'equality of opportunity' to participate in democratic deliberations. Studies have shown that the incremental process of giving 'equal opportunity' to women to get represented in elective bodies has not been effective in ensuring 'equality of outcomes' (Phillips 1995). For one, equal opportunity has not sufficiently led to 'mirror' the actually existing social or gender diversity because not many women could effectively compete and win against men, and also because the category 'women' is not a monolith but heterogeneous, drawn as it were from different caste, class, ethnicity, race, religion, sexual orientation, etc. For another, the roles of ideology, nature of regime and culture, among others, are considered to have important bearings on the 'outcomes' of representation.

Empirically, it is found that while states dominated by the left and Green Party are more favourable to extend reservation/quota, the conservative/

right dominant states are not favourable. Again, the odds of democratic regimes introducing statutory electoral and party reforms to effectuate women's representation in democratic regimes is considered to be higher than authoritarian regimes. A cross-country study by Pippa Norris and Ronald Inglehart (2001) also conclusively showed that the societal culture in a state can either impede or give impetus to women's representation. Despite entailing differential outcomes, there is unanimity among scholars that giving women greater representation enhances legitimacy, diversity and inclusiveness of elective bodies. Studies on increasing representation of women in Scandinavian countries, for example, have shown that it gives impetus to their parliament's responsiveness towards health, childcare and environmental issues which are traditionally considered to be women friendly (Dahlerup and Friedenvall 2005).

When developing and developed countries, including mainland India,[2] made a concerted effort to secure greater presence of women in their legislative and executive bodies, women in Nagaland continued to remain largely invisible in elected public offices. Despite allocating 25% of the seats of Management Committee of Village Development Board for women since 1980,[3] not a single woman has ever got elected in the 12 NLA's elections held so far between 1964 and 2013. This is remarkable given that the average voter turnout of women in the 12 assembly elections during this period stands at 78.3%, which is just 0.2% below the 78.5% turnout of male voters. Interestingly, women have exceeded men's electoral participation in eight of the 12 assembly elections held so far.[4] This is puzzling given that Nagaland is one of the most progressive states of India in terms of key gender indicators.

In fact, Nagaland's child sex ratio of 943 against an all-India average of 914 in 2011 indicates a favourable attitude to gender issue. While its female literacy rate of 76.11% is more than 10 percentage points above the all-India average, a recent report by the National Crime Records Bureau (NCRB) put the state as the 'safest' for women recording only '67 incidences of crime against women, which includes 30 cases of rape' (Singh 2015). Such articles can, as Wouters (2017c) rightly put it, 'conceal more than what they reveal',

---

[2]The Constitution of India [Seventy-third (1993) and Seventy-fourth Amendment (1994)] Acts mandated 33% women reservation respectively in panchayats (rural) and municipalities (urban) bodies.

[3]This was made vide Clause 4(b) of the Village Development Board Rules, 1980 framed under Section 50(1) of the Nagaland Village and Area Council Act, 1978.

[4]Based on my calculations from Election Commission of India's data. www.eci.gov.in.

especially given that actually existing Naga practices of settling criminal cases by customary law considerably reduced the chance of such cases being reported to the police. The state's cognisable crime rate per lakh population of 49.5 against the national average of 220.5 is nonetheless significant (Singh 2015). That Naga women have made significant societal and educational progress is evident from the fact that out of the top 59 bureaucrats currently listed in Nagaland from and above the level of secretary, 14 are women.[5]

The case of Nagaland reaffirms that there is no robust correlation between modernisation and democratisation, a correlation which has been taken as a given by the thesis of 'revised modernisation' (Inglehart and Norris 2003 cited in Bush 2011: 108). In other words, higher level of socio-economic and educational development that accompanied modernisation do not necessarily translate into greater democratic participation of women and gender justice in Nagaland. What is also more puzzling about the case of Nagaland is that favourable attitude towards giving reservation to women in ULBs does not actually translate into actual implementation of reservation policy, a fact underlined by an important survey conducted in the three districts of Kohima, Mokokchung and Mon in 2008 under the joint auspices of GoN and the United Nations Development Programme (UNDP). This survey showed an overwhelming support for women's reservation across gender divide: while 83.38% and 59.74% of rural men and women respectively in the three districts favoured giving 33% reservation for women, an overwhelming section of urban men (88.62%) and women (70.46%) supported this move (GoN 2011: 100).

What then explains the puzzle that increasing electoral participation (voter turnout), socio-economic and educational progress, and favourable attitude to women reservation do not actually translate into women's empowerment and further the cause of gender justice? In the sections below, I offer a twofold explanation to this puzzle by problematising (i) the patriarchally structured deliberations, consultations and decision-making procedures pertaining to the question of women's reservation, and (ii) the claim and presumption of 'equality as tradition' as the hallmarks of 'egalitarian' Naga society.

---

[5]Accessed online at https://www.nagaland.gov.in/portal/portal/StatePortal/Government/Secretaries on 26 July 2017.

PATRIARCHAL PROCEDURES

One compelling reason 33% women's reservation in Nagaland ULBs could never see the light of day is the deeply problematic ways in which patriarchally structured deliberations, consultations and decision-making procedures decide the fate of women's reservation. The fact that these procedures give undue leverage to men, who also constitute brute political majority in NLA, to determine the outcomes of reservation means that women's voice and the substantive concerns of women's empowerment and gender justice are conveniently marginalised at the expense of contingent concerns of land and tax, Naga culture and way of life, law and order, and Nagaland's exceptional status under Article 371(A) of the Constitution. These procedures also fail the test of procedural fairness and democratic justice, which requires that segments of the society (women) that are being affected by the outcomes of these procedures must have equal participation and effective voice in the deliberation, consultation, and decision-making on the question of women's reservation (Hausing 2014).

A critical perusal of what I may call the three moments of controversy surrounding women's reservation in Nagaland ULBs, clearly bears this out. While the initial opposition to the 2006 amendment act from 2008 to 2011 by various tribal bodies exemplifies the first moment of the controversy, the second moment encompasses two waves of consultations held by GoN with various Naga tribal bodies and professional organisations during April–May 2011 and February–March 2012. The third moment of controversy includes the deliberation and decision-making procedures adopted both by the Kohima and Guwahati bench of the Gauhati High Court (GHC) between October 2011 and June 2012, and NLA between December 2009 and September 2012.

INITIAL OPPOSITION

The first moment of controversy began sometime in the autumn of October 2008 when elections to 16 municipal wards in Mokokchung were due for the first time under the 2006 amended act and no candidate dared to file nomination. The joint meeting of 'public' of these wards and four landowner villages falling within Mokokchung's jurisdiction convened on 13 September 2008 and predominantly attended by men, threatened to 'exterminate' any women who contest municipal elections.[6] Intimidation as a tactic to pressurise women candidates to withdraw and boycott ULB elections continues in the recent controversy of January–February 2017 when 140 out of the 535 candidates reportedly withdrew their nomination papers following intimidations (Chakravarty 2017). The Mokokchung public was not only against reservation but also vehemently opposed municipality's power to impose tax on land and building. They considered that reservation and tax are not only alien, they have the propensity to distort and disrupt 'Ao's culture'[7] in particular and the Naga way of life in general. A joint representation on 11 August 2008 to GoN by the four landowning village councils on whose land Mokokchung town is located, namely Chuchuyimlang, Khensa, Mokokchung and Ungma, dismissed the need for reservation by contending that reservation 'is meant for underprivileged, minority section or untouchable group, etc' (GoN 2012: 1).

Two apex Naga tribal bodies, namely Naga Hoho and ENPO, again exclusively run by men, joined this chorus of opposition on the same pretext, and made a joint representation to GoN on 12 December 2009 asking the latter not to implement the proposed reservations of seats for women.[8] Despite the fact that municipal elections in Kohima and Dimapur were due between 19 December 2009 and 9 March 2010 following the expiry of their first tenure, the above opposition was used as a pretext by the state's cabinet to indefinitely postpone elections in its meeting on 16 December 2009.

CONSULTING MORE MEN

In order to break this impasse, GoN, under the auspices of the Department of Urban Development and Municipal Affairs, held two waves of consultations with various Naga tribal bodies and professional organisations during April–May 2011 and February–March 2012 which mark the second moment of controversy surrounding women's reservation in ULBs. In the first wave, GoN held consultation in seven places beginning from Mokokchung, the heart of the controversy, on 11 April 2011 and ended at Peren on 2 May

[6]The meeting was exclusively attended by male members of the wards and villages. See *Nagaland Post*, 'Mokokchung Village Firm on Boycotting MMC Polls', Kohima, 15 September 2008.

[7]Ao is the largest tribe in Mokokchung.

[8]GHC (2011:3). The Municipal and Town Council Forum of Nagaland also subsequently joined this opposition.

2011.[9] These consultations by far involved the widest spectrum of Naga societies by engaging overwhelming number of male-dominated and women's organisations across all major Naga tribes, and professional bodies.[10] Unlike the first, the second wave of consultative meetings exclusively involved male-centric tribal bodies and village councils and conspicuously failed to consult a single women's organisation.[11]

Indeed, in the first wave of consultations, women were not given equal participation and effective voice as they were outnumbered by male-dominated tribal and professional bodies. The deliberation was dominated by men as 64 of the total 81 speakers or slightly over 79% who gave their considered opinion were men, and women with 17 speakers accounted for about 20.9%.[12] Interestingly, except one woman representative who could not express her opinion pending the official stand of the women's wing of her tribe on the issue,[13] all 16 women participants were in favour of reservation. Mindful of the 'gender bias' and unequal circumstances which diminished the electoral chance of women if they openly compete against their male counterparts, a woman participant poignantly remarked, 'If women are allowed to contest in election, they may not win and all the seats will be dominated by male'.[14] Giving 33% reservation was therefore seen as a sine qua non for realising not only their constitutional rights but also to 'promote gender equality and empower women to minimise 'gender-gaps and gender-divide'.'[15]

[9]The seven consultative meetings were held in (i) Mokokchung Municipal Conference Hall (11 April 2011), (ii) Deputy Commissioner's (DC) Conference Hall, Kohima (18 April 2011), (iii) Wokha DC Conference Hall (20 April 2011), (iv) Tseminyu ADC Conference Hall (20 April 2011), (v) Mon DC Conference Hall (27 March 2011), (vi) Zunheboto DC Conference Hall (29 April 2011), and (vii) Peren Town Hall (2 May 2011).

[10]Town-specific Chamber of Commerce and various public organisations attended these consultations.

[11] The second wave of consultations were held at Kohima (29 February 2012), Jalukie (5 March 2012), Kiphire (7 March 2012), Oking, Wokha (12 March 2012), Oking, Zunheboto (13 March 2012), Kohima (14 March 2012) and Kohima (with Naga Hoho and ENPO on 16 March 2012).

[12]My calculation were based on GoN (2012): Background note.

[13] The woman in question is Tohoni H Kiba, Cultural Secretary of the Sumi Totimi Hoho. She intimated the inability of Sumi Women's Organisation to take its official stand on reservation at the DC Conference Hall, Zunheboto, 29 April 2011.

[14] Yhunsenle Khing, women member of the Tseminyu Town Council, ADC Conference Hall, Tseminyu, 20 April 2011.

[15] The quotation is from the speech of Medovino Phizo, President, Angami

Among male participants, 45 were against a women quota either in the form of reservation or nomination. While 13 out of the 19 male participants, who supported the quota for women, favoured nomination ranging from 20% to 50%, six men clearly favoured extending it to 33% women. While male supporters of women's reservation and nomination of seats gracefully accepted the indubitable fact that gender bias and gender discrimination exist within Naga societies, antagonists categorically denied this and argued that reservation not only does not match but also distorts Naga culture and customs.[16] Antagonists also considered it premature and hasty[17] to implement reservation in the absence of cadastral survey of land and lack of consensus across Naga societies.

Another compelling reason why Naga tribal bodies vehemently opposed holding of ULB elections remains imminent imposition of 'tax on land and building' as one participant unambiguously stated during the first consultative meeting at Mokokchung: 'unless section 120(1) of the Act is kept in cold storage/omitted, we will not comply or cooperate for holding of municipal election in Mokokchung area'.[18] In their overweening attempt to underscore the principles of equality and non-discrimination as the hallmarks of Naga customary practices and culture, they also foreground the unwritten patriarchal cultural code which discourages active participation of women in the public space. One member has, by reference to a Spanish proverb, sought to reinforce this code: 'Sat (d)[sic] is the home where the hen crows and the cock remain silent'.[19]

As the matter remained inconclusive and women bodies increasingly saw in NLA's indefinite postponement of ULB elections a deliberate attempt to deny justice to women, the NMA, represented by Rosemary Dzuvichu and Meru Meru, took the matter to the Kohima bench of the GHC between the first and second wave of consultations. Heard as a civil suit on 14 October

---

Women's Organisation at DC Conference Hall, Kohima, 18 April 2011.

[16] See the intervention of Sovenyi, President, Chakhesang People's Organisation at DC Conference Hall, Kohima, 18 April 2011, GoN (2012). Also see Ao Sendan's resolution on 2 November 2010.

[17] Zukeya Woch, member, Rengma Hoho at ADC Conference Hall, Tseminyu, 20 April 2011.

[18] Intervention of Puryabang, Secretary, Land Owners Union of four Naga villages of Chuchuyimlang, Khensa, Mokokchung, and Ungma at Mokokchung Municipal Conference Hall, 11 April 2011.

[19] Quotation reproduced in the original. The proverb was cited by R Ezung, Central Executive Committee member of the Nagaland People's Front at DC Conference Hall, Wokha, 20 April 2011. See GoN (2012).

2011 by a single-judge bench of Justice A K Goswami, the judgment was promptly delivered on 21 October 2011.

JUDICIAL PROCEEDINGS

As the controversy entered its third moment with this case, there were remarkable twists in arguments presented by GoN, pressurised and unduly influenced as it were by patriarchal tribal bodies, before the Kohima bench in October 2011 and subsequently before GHC in June–July 2012. Under this rubric, the audacious claim of equality and non-discrimination gave way to concerns that reservations would not only 'destroy the very fabric of the Naga society'[20] but also 'divide the society and weaken the strong administration of the Naga way of life'[21] when GoN represented its case before the Kohima bench. Subsequently, the special powers of NLA under Article 371(A) of the Constitution was invoked by GoN before the high court to trump women's reservation. Interestingly, both the benches limited their hearing and decision-making (judgments) on these set of contingent concerns and shelved the substantive concerns of women's empowerment and gender justice in the process. Sidelining the substantive concerns and making the court and Naga public preoccupied with contingent concerns not only help entrench patriarchal interest in the power structure but also perpetuate gender injustice.

Indeed, the respondents representing GoN maintained before the Kohima bench that the state cabinet decided to indefinitely postpone elections because of 'the need to maintain harmony in the society' given 'the delicate situation in the state and the on-going reconciliation and peace process' (GHC 2011: 9), contingent concerns which were never raised in the first wave of consultations. They also maintained that since a committee of secretaries constituted by Gon to examine the 'shortcomings' of the 2001 act is yet to give its report, the state could not hold elections in time. However, the court was not convinced by this and was willing at the most to accept only a 'tenuous link', if at all it exists, between 'issue of reservation of seats for women ... and the ongoing peace process in the state' (GHC

---

[20]View of the Kohima Village Council consulted by GoN at Kohima on 29 February 2012.

[21]The unanimous resolution taken by 48 participants who were consulted by GoN at Kiphire Town, 7 March 2012.

2011: 21). Contending that there were no 'exceptional circumstances or special, emergent and unforeseen circumstances' that prevented the state from holding elections, it directed GoN to immediately initiate the electoral process and hold elections by 20 January 2012 (GHC 2011: 21-24).

After having secured permission to further postpone the elections till 30 April 2012, GoN made an announcement for municipal elections with due provision for reservation of seats for women on 14 March 2012. But this announcement was met with opposition, several representations were made by Naga Hoho, ENPO and several tribal bodies to this effect (GHC 2012: 8). They contended that reservation of seats for women is unsuitable and 'would disintegrate the Naga society and strong administration of the Naga way of life' (GHC 2012: 30), and this must be done away with 'to obviate the possibility of disharmony and mistrust in the Naga society' (GHC 2012: 48). Bowing to increasing public pressure, NLA invoked the special powers it enjoys under Article 371(A) of the Constitution and passed a resolution on 22 March 2012 to constitute a select committee 'to examine whether the State should be exempted from Part IXA of the Constitution of India' and to report back to it in six months (GHC 2012: 26). It resolved to suspend electoral process till the committee submitted its report. When GoN approached the Kohima bench of GHC to postpone elections the latter declined on 27 April 2012 by contending that the matter cannot be reopened as it had been 'elaborately dealt with' in an earlier judgment (GHC 2012: 27).

GoN then filed a writ petition to the Guwahati bench. The matter was heard by a two-judge bench of Justices Amitava Roy and P K Musahary on 27 June 2012 and the judgment was delivered on 31 July 2012 (GHC 2012: 3). Noting that 'the emphatic opinion opposing reservation did have resonating undertones of strong disapproval and resentment in some prominent quarters' (GHC 2012: 48), the court did not find any 'want of bonafide or actuation by oblique objectives' of NLA when it resolved to constitute a select committee to 'survey whether Part IXA would be applicable' to the state (GHC 2012: 57). Based on this premise, the bench allowed the writ appeal to postpone elections till the select committee submits its report.

Meanwhile, the seven-member select committee of NLA headed by T R Zeliang after 'thorough deliberation' was of 'the strong opinion that Part IX(A) of the Constitution of India contravenes the provisions of the Article 371(A)', recommended the NLA not to implement Part IX(A) and asked NLA to pass a resolution to frame its 'own laws for conduct of Municipal and Town Council Act' (Sagar 2012). On the basis of this 'strong opinion', NLA accepted the recommendation and passed a resolution to this effect on 22 September 2012 exempting Nagaland from Part IX(A).

Not surprisingly, NMA brought the matter to the Supreme Court in the winter of 2012. After sitting over the case for over four years, the Supreme Court admitted the special leave petition of NMA on 20 April 2016 and directed GoN to hold ULB elections. In order to pave the way for ULB elections, NLA revoked its 22 September 2012 resolution on 22 November 2016 and cleared two major stumbling blocks on 24 December 2016 by enacting the Nagaland Municipal (Third Amendment) Act which omitted reference to municipalities powers to impose tax on land and building (Section 121(1)(a)) and removed reservation for Scheduled Castes. These overtures however could not satisfy various Naga tribal bodies. They demanded wider consultations and deliberations. When these demands were not met and elections sought to be held on 1 February 2017, violent protests erupted in various parts of Nagaland, which again forestalled ULB elections.

LAND AND TAXATION

In hindsight, the relationship between municipalities, land and tax are indubitably complex and sensitive. Writing in the wake of the recent controversy, scholars like Charles Chasie (2017) and Jelle J P Wouters (2017c) contended that it is not opposition to women's reservation per se, but rather a broader opposition to allow modern institutions like ULBs to encroach on Nagas' land and resources, the pivot around which Naga's idea of sovereignty revolves, that lies at the heart of this controversy. Wouters (2017c: 21) elegantly put it:

> For A Z Phizo, who captained the Naga National Council (NNC) into its struggle for independence, the idea of sovereignty itself was always less about state, courts, and a Weberian monopoly on violence, but crucially hinged on Nagas' unconditional ownership over their land and its resources, cattle and other possessions, and communitarian ethics.

Contending that land and tax are central to the Naga nationalist imagination and political project which is best encapsulated in the vernacular axiom, 'Ura Uvie' (our land is ours), this perspective holds that tax is an 'abhorrent issue' which drove the Nagas to rise against the British in 1879 and which continues to sustain the Naga nationalist and resistance movement against the colonial and postcolonial state (Chasie 2017). Given the sensitivity of the issue, the onus is on the genius of the Naga to deliberate and decide on ways and means of overcoming the controversy (Wouters 2017c).

This perspective captured the Naga public mood very well, a point put in sharp focus by the editorial column of *Eastern Mirror*, one of the influential newspapers of Nagaland, on 27 January 2017. Provocatively titled, 'Why Every Naga Should Object to the Nagaland Municipal Elections', the column was agitated at the prospect of imposing 15% tax on the actual value of land and property, which it considered tantamount to paying income tax. This, it avers, not only violates the protection given to Nagaland in relation to income tax, but also entails the possibility of rendering the Naga 'a homeless refugee' in the land of his ancestors as ULBs have the power to seize and auction off land or property if the owner could not pay up his tax. Considering that GoN has omitted ULBs' power to impose tax and given that the contingent concerns that ULBs have bearings on land and tax can be addressed and resolved by simplifying the tax and complex bureaucratic procedure it entails, it would be 'illogical and unfair' as Meru Meru[22] argued since the initial days of the controversy, to perpetually deny the right of the modern state to impose tax and use it as a ruse to deny empowerment and justice to women.

Although there is no institutional rules which prevent women from entry into NLA and ULBs, it is a particular understanding of Nagas' culture and way of life which continues to impose gridlock on women's empowerment in Nagaland. As Monalisa Changkija lamented, 'it is the patriarchal structure, the patriarchal mindset'[23] that prevented women from entry into NLA and ULBs. I shall now examine how equality and non-discrimination which have been claimed as the hallmarks of Naga culture and way of life sit uneasily with the actually existing gender inequality and inegalitarian discourse in Naga society.

---

[22]Personal interview with Meru Meru, President of the Naga Mothers Association, Kohima, 24 June 2012.

[23]Personal interview with Monalisa Changkija, Editor of the *Nagaland Page*, Dimapur, 13 June 2012.

REVISITING 'EQUALITY AS TRADITION'

After conducting an intensive field study of the Konyaks in the Naga Hills over eight decades ago, Christoph von Furer-Haimendorf (2004: 96), one of the most well-known ethnographers on the Nagas, underscored what has now become a quintessential description of 'egalitarianism' of the Naga in particular, and that of tribal societies in general, in the following words:

> The spirit of *camaraderie* and equality which prevails between the young girls and boys colours [also] the relations between husband and wife. A girl who enjoyed for years almost complete independence and was used to be courted by a number of youths, is not likely to turn into a meek wife, and whoever watches the Konyaks at work, in their houses and at feasts realises that there is an essential equality of men and women.

Fürer-Haimendorf (2004: 96) went on further to note that

> Many women in more civilised parts of India may well envy the women of the Naga Hills their high status and their free and happy life; and if you measure the cultural level of a people by the social position and personal freedom of its women, you will think twice before looking down on the Nagas as 'savages'.

Indeed, most ethnographic studies on the Nagas and other tribal societies in North East India or elsewhere are eloquent in their encomium about the equality, freedom and non-discrimination enjoyed by tribal women in their social, cultural and religious affairs. Egalitarianism and non-discrimination are almost taken as givens and are often used as a yardstick to mark out the tribal others from inegalitarian and discriminatory caste-Hindu society. These have been pervasively internalised so much so that U A Shimray (2002), the late Naga scholar, even wrote an article titled, 'Equality as Tradition: Women's Role in Naga Society'. Although Shimray admitted that the Nagas by tradition follow patriarchal social norms, he contended that the idea of man dominating over nature and women is a 'white man's beliefs system' which is 'alien to Nagas' (Shimray 2002: 376). He underscored the important traditional roles Naga women play in peace-making, in running the economy by engaging in economically productive works like weaving and in sustaining a culture of self-reliance and self-independence (Shimray 2002: 376–77). Nagas, he averred, have equal rights in social, cultural and religious matters. On this premise, Shimray (2002: 376) went on to the extent of claiming that 'Naga society is casteless and classless' as 'the rigid hierarchical structure as in Hindu society, based on caste and class is non-existent'.

On close examination, however, the claims of egalitarianism, freedom and non-discrimination as the hallmarks of Nagas' egalitarianism sit uneasily with the emerging class division and persistent sexual division of labour, which continue to relegate Naga and other tribal women to subordinated positions in society (Hausing 2015). In analysing the status of women in tribal society the distinction drawn by Virginius Xaxa (2004: 348) between role and position of women on the one hand, and status understood in terms of their prestige and honour on the other hand, is helpful. While Verrier Elwin (1961: 104) noted the important role Naga women played in the *jhum* fields and in the village councils in 'equal terms' with their male counterparts, J H Hutton (1921: 183), was particularly struck by the freedom of choice that Sema women have in selecting their life partner. The important role and freedom of choice exercised by women ensured that they are treated well and occupy high position both at home and in the society. Women's freedom of choice could however be circumscribed, say among segments of the Konyaks and Angami tribes where marriage was traditionally arranged (Kelhou 1998, Zehol and Zehol 1998). While polygamy and the ability to develop illicit relations after marriage were valorised as instances of 'male prowess' among segments of the Angami tribe, infidelity among married women invited cruel punishment such as the chopping off of 'the tip of the nose' (Kelhou 1998: 56–57). Given this, the diverse social and customary practices among different Naga tribes need to be borne in mind while examining the role and status of women in Naga society.

Again on close scrutiny, women across the 14 recognised Naga tribes in Nagaland have unequal rights and access to property, in relation to their male counterparts as customary laws governing this continue to impose severe restrictions as they are entitled to inherit only acquired property and not inherited property (Zehol 1998, GoN 2009). Women did not have equal right to the selection and allocation of jhum sites of the village which are still the exclusive preserve of men, although they played very important role in performing rituals like *tsiakrii, liede* and *ki kenyii,* which are respectively associated with inaugurating jhum field works, harvest and sanctification of the harvest in Angami society (Kelhou 1998: 57–58).

Even in the symbolic realm which invests prestige and honour in individuals, Naga society continues to be marked by deeply entrenched patriarchal norms and values. The feast of merit, for example, could be performed only by a male who attained enormous affluence (determined by accumulation of slaves, animals, grains, and property) and prowess in war, considered to be the valorisation of the highest symbolic virtue, of bestowing prestige and honour in Naga society. The symbolic sacralisation of two stone monoliths—the bigger one for the husband and the smaller one for the wife—to commemorate the feast of merit has a subtle symbolic value: it highlights unequal status and prestige that women occupy in Naga society.[24]

Although the advent of Christianity abolished the feast of merit principally because of its opposition to invocation of spirit and alcoholic indulgence associated with the rituals, Christianity also brought with it what Moamenla Amer (2013) in a different context calls a new pattern of 'gendered socialisation' in the church and Naga public sphere constituted by the educated middle class. In this context, the role of Christianity can be both liberating and constraining. While Christianity liberates both men and women in ways that enable them to have equal access to education and the new public sphere, it reproduces social conservatism and entrenched patriarchal norms and values.

CONCLUSIONS

The controversy surrounding the purported attempts to extend 33% reservation to women in Nagaland ULBs have thrown up unsettled and complex issues of land, tax, and the question of women's reservation. While these issues are unmistakably interrelated and contingent, the failure to jettison each of these complex issues and address them separately on the merit of their case have important bearings on the question of women's empowerment and gender justice in Nagaland. Given that NLA, the custodian of this special autonomy, could make inapplicable a progressive law like 33% reservation for women in ULBs under the cover of Article 371(A) is of particular concern, as no woman has ever got elected to NLA since its inception in 1964. The patriarchal procedures adopted by GoN in the deliberations, consultations and decision-making of extending 33% reservation of ULB seats to women in Nagaland was particularly unhelpful as it resulted in the entrenchment of patriarchal norms and values. These procedures and the GHC's judgment shelved the substantive questions of women's empowerment and justice by leveraging contingent concerns of law and order, distortion and disruption of Naga culture and way of life.

What is more disconcerting is the violent boycott of ULBs elections by tribal bodies on 1 February 2017 even after GoN addressed their

---

[24] See Fürer-Haimendorf's (1976: 16-24) discussion of the 'feast of merit' to understand this nuance.

concerns and grievances. This controversy reinforces the fact that behind the tall claims of equality as tradition, freedom and non-discrimination of Naga women, lies a deeply entrenched inegalitarian gender discourse and social conservatism which continues to impose cultural barriers to women's reservation and the cause of justice. It also brought to sharp focus one of the great dilemmas confronting the grant of territorial autonomy to minorities around the world—the protection of autonomy of minority groups. It is about time that Naga tribal bodies and GoN seriously heard the increasingly strident voice of women's empowerment by reflecting and learning from the insights of liberal nationalists that territorial autonomy is defensible so long as it promotes democracy and justice within and across its constituents, including women and minority tribes/communities (Kymlicka 1995). The fact that increasing voter turnout and support for women's reservation did not result in women's entry into NLA and making ULBs work would continue to be a sore spot in the tall claim and presumption of 'equality as tradition' in Naga society.

To break the impasse, the collective wisdom of the Nagas needs to seriously think of means and ways to promote democracy and justice where women are given equal participation and voice. In the meantime, Naga women's groups need to make course-correction by forging more effective networks and linkages across the social and political divide in Naga society to fructify their demand.

The unmistakable influence of St Paul's teaching of women church members of Corinth to be 'submissive' and 'not to speak in the church' on faithful Naga women Christians is evident in the gendered socialisation, a point that resonated in the invocation of the Spanish proverb that I have already alluded to earlier.[25] While St Paul's teaching had particular traction for the Corinthian women in the first century CE because of the widespread debasement in morality, his teaching was taken out of the leaf by Christian Naga women in particular and Naga society in general so much so that no woman has ever been elected as an executive member of the Nagaland Baptist Church Council, the largest conglomerations of churches in Nagaland since its inception in 1937.

That an unwritten gender and cultural code is imprinted into church practices is evident from the fact that women's 'public' engagements continue to be largely confined within the 'Ladies Department' of the churches in

---

[25]Saint Paul wrote the epistles to the Corinthians when he was in Ephesus from 53–55 CE. Not surprisingly, the same message which urged women to be submissive to their husbands, the symbolic heads of the family, was relayed to the Ephesians as well. See the first epistle to the Corinthians in chapter 14, verses 34–35 in the Bible, and Ephesians 5: 22–23.

Nagaland, again affirming the entrenched sexual division of labour in the church. In common church congregations and social ceremonies while men would continue to play the more 'prestigious' role of the main speaker/ preacher, women continue to be given subordinated and decoratory roles like singing solos and dancing, performing prayers (opening and closing ceremonies), members of the choirs, and so on. These practices underscore the subordination and discrimination of Naga women in the church and society.

Research has highlighted the traditional role played by Naga women in conflict-mediation and peace-making (Dzuvichu 2011; Manchanda 2001). From a situation where 'women's voices were often silenced in the midst of war and chaos' (Vamuzo 2011: 141) and where they were largely seen as victims of armed conflicts and domestic violence, Naga women have begun to play important 'agency' roles by mediating between warring armed factions—state and non-state actors—and forging peace. The stellar role of NMA in setting up a peace team under the banner of 'shed no more blood' in October 1994 and their continued involvement in the Naga reconciliation process are noteworthy (Banerjee 2000; Dzuvichu 2011; Vamuzo 2011: 139– 41). Despite playing a helpful role in setting up the peace agenda during the various ceasefire negotiations between GoI and NSCN-IM, women's groups do not have effective voice in the official high table of peace-talks between GoI and NSCN-IM. The fact that the Framework Agreement entered into by GoI and NSCN-IM in August 2015 was not revealed to any Naga tribal organisations, including women's groups, is also a telling testament to this and the subordinated peace-making role that women play in Naga society.

■ ■■ ■■

REFERENCES

Abramson, D. 2002. The soviet legacy and the census in Uzbekistan. In *Census and Identity: The Politics of Race, Ethnicity, and Language in National Censuses*, edited by D. Kertzer and D. Arel, 176-201. Cambridge: Cambridge University Press.

Acharya, K. 2017. Nagaland Civil Polls: Naga tribes to boycott elections to protest 33% reservation for women. *Firstpost.* Url: http://www.firstpost.com/india/nagaland-civic-polls-naga-tribes-to-boycott-elections-to-protest-33-reservation-for-women-3190086.html.

Adepoju, A. 1981. Military rule and population issues in Nigeria. *African Affairs* 80(318): 29-47.

Agarwal, B. 1997. Bargaining and gender relations: within and beyond the household. *Feminist Economics* 3(1): 1-51.

Agrawal, A. and V. Kumar 2012. *An investigation into changes in Nagaland's population between 1971 and 2011.* IEG Working Paper No 316. New Delhi: Institute of Economic Growth.

Agrawal, A. and V. Kumar. 2013. Nagaland's demographic somersault. *Economic and Political Weekly* 48(39): 69-74.

Agrawal, A. and V. Kumar. 2017a. Cartographic conflicts within a union: finding land for Nagaland in India. *Political Geography* 61: 123-47.

Agrawal, A. and V. Kumar. 2017b. *NSSO Surveys along India's Periphery: data quality and implications.* Working Paper No 9. Bengaluru: Azim Premji University.

Agrawal, S.P. and Datta Ray 1994. *Reorganisation of North-East India since 1947.* New Delhi: concept Publishing House.

Alesina, A., W. Easterly. and J, Matuszeski. 2006. *Artificial States.* NBER Working Paper No 12328. Cambridge: National Bureau of Economic Research.

Alibe, K.D. 2014. *Kuzhami Naga Dze.* Kohima: published by author.

Almond, G. and S. Verba. 1963. *The Civic culture: Political attitudes and democracy in five nations.* London: Sage Publications. Amer, M. 2013. Political status of women in Nagaland. *Journal of Business Management and Social Sciences Research* 2(4): 91–95.

Amer, M. 2014. Electoral dynamics in India: a study of Nagaland. *Journal of Business Management & Social Science Research* 3(4): 6-11.

Angeles, L. and K.C. Neanidis 2010. *Colonialism, elite formation and corruption.* Url: https://www.gla.ac.uk/media/media_186044_en.pdf . 8th June.

Ao, L. 1993. *Rural development in Nagaland.* New Delhi: Har-Anand Publications.

Ao, L. 2002. *From Phizo to Muivah: The Naga national question in Northeast India.* New Delhi: Mittal Publications.

Ao, L. 2013. Indo-Naga political conflict, resolution and peace-process: A critical review. Delhi: *Delhi Naga Students Union.*

Ao, T, N. 1997. *Ao-Naga Cultural Heritage.* Mokokchung: Arkong.

Ao, T. 2014. *Once Upon a Life: a memoir.* New Delhi: Zubaan.

Aram, M. 1974. *Peace in Nagaland: eight year story, 1964-1972.* New Delhi: Arnold-Heinemann Publishers.

Archer, M. 1947. Journey to Nagaland: an account of six months spent in the Naga Hills in 1947. *Naga Video Disc.* Url: http://himalaya.socanth.cam.ac.uk/collections/naga/coll/81/records/detail/all/index.html

Argenti, N. & K. Schramm. 2010. *Remembering violence: Anthropological perspectives on intergeneration transmission.* Oxford: Oxford University Press.

Aristotle 1976. *Politics.* Middlesex: Penguin Books.

Asian Tribune. Nagaland heading for opposition-less government; not healthy in democratic government. 21st March.

Bachani, D., R. Sogarwal, and K.S. Rao. 2011. A Population based Survey on HIV Prevalence in Nagaland, India. *SAARC Journal of Tuberculosis Lung Diseases and HIV/AIDS* (1): 1-11.

Baker, K. 2012. Identity, Memory and Place. Url: http://ir.lib.uwo.ca/wordhoard/vol1/iss1/4

Banerjee, P. 2000. The Naga Women's Intervention for Peace. *Canadian Women Studies* 19(4): 137-42.

Bareh, H. M. (ed.) 2001. *Encyclopedia of North-East India, volume 6.* New Delhi: Mittal Publications.

Barrier, N. Gerald. 1981. *The census in British India: new perspectives.* New Delhi: Manohar Publications.

Barro, R.J. and X. Sala-i-Martin 2004. *Economic Growth.* Cambridge: The MIT Press.

Baruah, S. 2002.Governors as generals. Url: http://mail.sarai.net/pipermail/reader-list/2002-june/001600.html.

Baruah, S. 2003. Nationalizing space: Cosmetic federalism and the politics of development in Northeast India. *Development and Change* 34(5): 915-39.

Baruah, S. 2004. Unscheduled Matters. *The Telegraph.* 26th May. Url: http://www.telegraphindia.com/1040526/asp/opinions)

Baruah, S. 2007. *Durable disorder: Understanding the politics of northeast India.* Delhi: Oxford University Press.

Bear, L. 2007. Ruins and Ghosts: the domestic uncanny and the materialization of Anglo-Indian genealogies in Kharagpur. In *The Ghosts of Memory,* edited by J. Carsten. London: Routledge Press.

Begum, S. and A. Miranda. 1979. The Defectiveness of the 1974 population census of Bangladesh. *Bangladesh Development Studies* 7(3): 79-106.

Bendangjungshi. 2012. *Confessing Christ in the Naga context: towards a liberating ecclesiology.* Berling: Lit Verlag.

Bennett, T et al. 2009. *Culture, Class, Distinction.* London: Routledge.

Berliner, D. 2005. The Abuses of Memory: reflections on the memory boom in anthropology. *Anthropological Quarterly* 78(1): 197-211.

Bhagat, R.B. 2001. Census and the construction of communalism in India. *Economic and Political Weekly* 36(46/47): 4352-56.

Bhasin, K. 2003. *Understanding gender*. New Delhi: Women Unlimited.

Bhat, P., N. Mari and A.J. Francis Zavier 2005. Role of religion in fertility decline: The case of Indian Muslims. *Economic and Political Weekly* 40(5): 385-402.

Bhowmik, K.L., M.K. Chowdhuri, P. Das, and K.K. Chaudhuri 1971. *Fertility of Zemi women in Nagaland*. Calcutta: Institute of Social Studies.

Biswas, P. and C. Suklabaidya 2008. *Ethnic life-worlds in Northeast India: an analysis*. Delhi: Sage Publications.

Bose, A., D.B. Gupta, and G. Raychaudhuri (eds) 1977. *Population statistics in India (database in Indian Economy Volume III)*. New Delhi: Vikas.

Brass, P.R. 1974. *Language, Religion and Politics in North India*. Cambridge University Press: New York.

Burling, R. 2003. The Tibeto-Burman Languages of North-Eastern India. In *The Sino-Tibetan Languages*, edited by G. Thurgood and R. J. LaPolla. London: Routledge. Bush, S, S. 2011. International politics and the spread of quotas for women in Legislatures. *International Organisation* 65(1): 103–37.

Butler, J. 1875. Rough notes on the Angami Nagas and their Language. *Journal of the Asiatic Society Bengal* 44 (1): 307-46.

Calhoun, C. 2002. Imagining solidarity: Cosmopolitanism, constitutional patriotism, and the public sphere. *Public Culture*. 14(1): 147-171.

Carole, S. 2014. Women candidates and party nomination trends in India – evidence from the 2009 general election. *Commonwealth and Comparative Politics* 52(1): 109-138.

Carsten, J. 2007a. *The ghosts of memory*. London: Routledge Press

Carsten, J. 2007b. Connections and disconnections of memory and kinship in narratives of adoption reunions in Scotland. In *The Ghosts of Memory*, edited by J. Carsten. London: Routledge Press.

Census of India 2001. *Series 1 – India, migration tables (Table D-2)*. New Delhi: Office of the Registrar General and Census Commissioner.

Census of India 2001. *Series 13 – Nagaland, migration tables (Table D0302)*. New Delhi: Office of the Register General and Census Commissioner.

Chakravarty, I. 2017. Municipal polls in Nagaland have pitted gender equality against tribal customary laws. Url: https://scroll.in/article/828203/why-municipal-polls-in-nagaland-have-pitted-gender-equality-against-tribal-customary-laws

Chandhoke, N. 2003. *The conceits of civil society*. New Delhi: Oxford University Press.

Chandra, K. 2004. *Why ethnic parties succeed: Patronage and ethnic headcounts in India*. Cambridge: Cambridge University Press.

Changkija, M. 2017. Pride as well as prejudice. The *Hindu*, 8th February.

Chasie, Charles 2001. 'Nagaland – land and people'. Url: www.ide.go.jp/English/Publish/Download/Jrp/pdf/133_9.pdf.

Chasie, C. 2005. *The Naga imbroglio (a personal perspective)*. Kohima: City Press.

Chasie, Charles. 2005. Nagaland in Transition. *India International Centre Quarterly* 32(2/3): 253-264.

Chasie, C. 2017. Naga society lies wounded again. *Morung Express*, 5th February.

Chaudhury, P. 2005. Does caste indicate deprivation? *Seminar* No. 549. Url: http://www.india-seminar.com/2005/549/549%20pradipta%20chaudhury.html.

Chaurasia, A.R. 2011. Population growth in India during 2001-2011: an analysis of provisional results of 2011 population census. *Studies in Population and Development No 11-02*. Shyam Institute: Bhopal.

Clark, M. 1907. *A corner in India*. Philadelphia: American Baptist Publication.

Cohen, J, L. and Arato, A. 1992. *Civil society and political theory*. Cambridge, MA: MIT Press.

Cohn, B.S. 1987. The census, social structure and objectification in South Asia. In *An Anthropologist among the Historians and Other Essays*, edited by B.S. Cohn, 224-254. Delhi: Oxford University Press.

Connerton, P. 1989. *How societies remember*. Cambridge: Cambridge University Press.

Connerton, P. 2009. *How modernity forgets*. Cambridge: Cambridge University Press.

Cornwall, A. and A.M. Goetz 2005. Democratising democracy: Feminist perspectives. *Democratization* 12(5): 783–800.

Crenshaw, K. 1991. Mapping the margins: Intersectionality, identity of politics and violence against women of color. *Standford Law Review 33* (6): 1241-1299.

Dahl, R. 1989. *Democracy and its critics*. Berkeley: Yale University Press.

Dahlerup, D. and L. Freidenvall. 2005. Quotas as a fast track to equal representation for women. *International Feminist Journal of Politics* 7(1): 26–48.

David, H. 1981. Political culture on female political representation. *Journal of Politics* 43(1): 159- 65.

Davis, A.W. 1891. 'The Lhotas in 1891'. In: *Nagas in the nineteenth century*, edited by V. Elwin (1969), 350-352. Oxford: Oxford University Press.

De Tocqueville, A. 1969 *Democracy in America* (translated by G. Lawrence). New York: Doubleday Anchor.

Delimitation Commission of India 2008. *Changing face of electoral India: Delimitation 2008, volumes I & II*. New Delhi: Delimitation Commission of India

Deng, F, M. 1987. Myths and reality in Sudanese identity. In *The search for peace and unity in Sudan*, edited by F.M. Deng and P. Gifford. Washington: Wilson Centre Press.

Dev, R. 2006. Ethnic self-determination and electoral politics in Nagaland. In *Ethnic identities and democracy: Electoral politics in India's Northeast*, edited by A.K. Baruah and R. Dev, 68-92. New Delhi: Regency Publications.

Dev, S.C. 1988. *Nagaland: The untold story*. Calcutta: Calcutta: Regent Publications.

Dhillon, A. 2017. Nagaland: Where men are on strike until women go back to the kitchen. *The Sydney Morning Herald*. Url: http://www.smh.com.au/

world/nagaland-where-men-are-on-strike-until-women-go-back-to-the-kitchen-20170214-gucdtw.html

Dzuvichu, R. 2011. Peace is possible by empowering women. In *Walking the Path of Despair and*

Hope: Understanding and Justifying the Ways of God, edited by K. Longchar. Kohima: Nagaland Baptist Church Council.

Dzuvichu, R. 2016. Unpacking reservation: The Nagaland gender equity question. *Eastern Mirror*, 15th January.

Eastern Mirror 2016. Women reservation not the issue but land tax: Naga Hoho. 13th September.

Eastern Mirror 2017. Zeliang and Acharya deliver anti-corruption messages. 29th October.

Eastern Mirror. 2017. Why Every Naga Should Object to the Nagaland Municipal Elections. 27th January.

Eastern Panorama. 2011. Nagaland Census 2011 Begins. Url: http://www.easternpanorama.in/index.php/cover-story/59-2010/july/1065-nagaland-census-2011-begins.

Economic Times. 2015. NITI Aayog's flexible fund may benefit special category states. Url: http://articles.economictimes.indiatimes.com/20150520/news/62413535_1_nitiaayogcategorystatusspecialcategorystates/

Election Commission of India 2014. State-wise voter turnout in general elections.

Election Commission of India. 2013. Statistical report on general election to the Legislative Assembly of Nagaland.

Elwin, V. 1961. *Nagaland*. Shillong: Government Press.

Empson, R. 2007. Enlivened memories: Recalling absence and loss in Mongolia. In *Ghosts of memory*, edited by J. Carsten. London: Routledge Press.

Ezung, T. 2012. Corruption and its impact on Nagaland: A case study of Nagaland. *International Journal of Rural Studies* 19(1): 1-7.

Farmer, P. 2004. An Anthropology of structural violence. *Current Anthropology 45* (3): 305-325.

Fowles, S. 2010. People without things. In *An Anthropology of Absence: materializations of transcendence and loss* edited by M. Bill, T. Sørensen, and F. Hastrup, 23-41. New York: Springer.

Franke, M. 2011. *War and nationalism in South Asia: The Indian State and Nagas*. London: Routledge.

Franklin, M. 2004. *Voter turnout and the dynamics of electoral competition in established democracie since 1945*. Cambridge : Cambridge University Press.

Fürer-Haimendorf, C. V. 1939. *The naked Nagas*. London: Methuen & Co Ltd.

Fürer-Haimendorf, C. Von and J.P. Mills 1936. The sacred founder's kin among the Eastern Angami Nagas. *Anthropos* 31 (5/6): 922-933.

Fürer-Haimendorf, C. Von. 1973. Social and cultural change among the Konyak Naga. *The Highlander* 1(1): 3-12.

Galtung, J. 1969. Violence, peace, and peace research. *Journal of Peace Research* 6 (3): 167-191.

Gauhati High Court 2012. *Writ appeal no 116/2012*. Url: http://ghconline.gov.in/Judgment/WA116-2112012.pdf

Gauhati High Court 2011. *Writ petition No. W.P.(C) No. 147(K)/2011*. Url: http://www.hrln.org/hrln/womens-justice-/pils-a-cases/732-naga-women-file-writ-petition-in-high-court-regarding-womens-reservations-in-nagaland-municipal-council-elections.html#ixzz51joUuOZV

Gauhati High Court 2012. *Writ petition CMC No. 40(K)/2012*. Url: http://www.hrln.org/hrln/womens-justice-/pils-a-cases/886-kohima-high-court-orders-district-municipal-elections-within-one-month-with-33-reservation-for-women.html#ixzz51jTRZ2vZ

Geertz, C. 1973. *The Interpretation of cultures – selected essays*. New York: Basic Books.

Gellner, D, N. 2010. Introduction: Making civil society in South Asia. In *Varieties of activist experience: Civil society in South Asia*, edited by D.N. Gellner. New Delhi: Sage Publications.

Gellner, E. 1977. *Patrons and clients in Mediterranean societies*. London: Duckworth.

Gellner, E. 1983. *Nations and nationalism*. Ithaca: Cornell University Press.

Gill, M.S. 2007. Politics of population census data in India. *Economic and Political Weekly* 42(3): 241-49.

Gorringe, H. 2011. Party political panthers: hegemonic Tamil politics and the Dalit challenge. *South Asia Multidisciplinary Academic Journal*. http://samaj.reveues.org/3224.

Government of India 1954. *Census of India, Paper No. 6, Estimation of birth and death rates in India during 1941-50–1951 Census*. New Delhi: Registrar General and Census Commissioner.

Government of India 1975. *Census of India 1971, series 1, India, Part II-A (i) general population tables*. New Delhi: Registrar General and Census Commissioner.

Government of India. 1976. Census of India 1971, Series 15, Nagaland, Part II D, migration tables. New Delhi: Director of Census Operations, Nagaland.

Government of India. 1977. *Census of India 1971, Series 1 - India, Part II - D (i), migration tables (tables D-I to D-IV)*. New Delhi: Registrar General and Census Commissioner.

Government of India 1978. *Census of India 1971, India, Series 1, paper 1 of 1979, report of the Expert Committee on Population Projections*. New Delhi: Office of the Registrar General of India.

Government of India 1985. *Census of India 1981, Series 15, Nagaland, Part - Volume A & B, migration tables*. New Delhi: Director of Census Operations, Nagaland.

Government of India 1988. *Census of India 1981, Series 1 - India, Part V-A & B (i), migration tables (table D-1 and D-2)*. New Delhi: Registrar General and Census Commissioner.

Government of India 1996. *Census of India 1991, population projections for India and*

States 1996-2016, *Report of the Technical Group on Population Projections constituted by the Planning Commission*. New Delhi: Registrar General.

Government of India 1997a. *Census of India 1991 Series-1 India, Part V- D Series, migration tables, volume 2 part 1*. New Delhi: Registrar General and Census Commissioner.

Government of India 1997b. *Census of India 1991 Series 1 India, Part V- D Series, migration tables, volume 2 Part 2*. New Delhi: Registrar General and Census Commissioner.

Government of India 1997c. District level estimates of fertility and child mortality for 1991 and their inter-relations with other variables. *Occasional Paper No 1 of 1997*. New Delhi: Registrar General.

Government of India 1999. *Compendium of India's fertility and mortality indicators 1971-1997 based on the sample registration system (SRS)*. New Delhi: Registrar General.

Government of India 2005. *General population tables: India, states and union territories (tables A-1 to A-3), Part-1*. New Delhi: Office of the Registrar General and Census Commissioner.

Government of India 2006. *Population projections for India and states 2001-2026, report of the Technical Group on Population Projections constituted by the National Commission on Population*. New Delhi: Office of the Registrar General & Census Commissioner.

Government of India 2008. *The gazette of India extraordinary, Part II - Section 3 - subsection (ii), no 189*. New Delhi: Legislative Department, Ministry of Law and Justice.

Government of Nagaland 2009. List of recognised Naga/Scheduled Tribes certification. Url: http://dpar.nagaland.gov.in/list-of-recognized-nagascheduled-tribes-certificate/

Government of India 2010. HIV declining in India; New infections reduced by 50% from 2000-2009; Sustained focus on prevention required. *Press Release*. Release ID: 67983.

Government of India 2011a. *Census of India 2011, provisional population totals, paper 1 of 2011, Series 1 India*. New Delhi: Office of the Registrar General and Census Commissioner: India.

Government of India 2011b. *Census of India 2011, provisional population totals, Paper 1 of 2011, Series 14 Nagaland*. New Delhi: Directorate of Census Operations.

Government of India 2011c. *Census of India 2011, provisional population totals, paper 2, volume 1 of 2011, rural-urban distribution, series 14 Nagaland*. New Delhi: Directorate of Census Operations.

Government of India 2011d. *Economic Survey 2010-11*. New Delhi: Ministry of Finance.

Government of India 2013. *Census of India. 2011, Primary census abstract data tables (India & States/UTs - district level)*.

Government of Nagaland 2001. *The Nagaland Municipal Act*. url: http://kmc.

nagaland.gov.in/

Government of Nagaland 2010. *District human development report Kohima 2009.* Kohima: Department of Planning and Coordination/UNDP.

Government of Nagaland. 2011. *District human development report Mon, 2009.* Kohima: Department of Planning and Coordination/UNDP.

Government of Nagaland. 2012. *Background note relating to the 33% reservation for women in the Municipality/Town Councils in Nagaland.* Kohima: Department of Urban Development.

Government of Nagaland. 2013. Report on the tenth general election to the Nagaland Legislative Assembly.

Guha, S. 2003. The Politics of identity and enumeration in India c. 1600-1990. *Comparative Studies in Society and History* 45(1): 148-67.

Guilmoto, C.Z. and S. I, Rajan. 2002. District level estimates of fertility from India's 2001 Census. *Economic and Political Weekly* 37(7): 665-72.

Guilmoto, C.Z. and S. I, Rajan. 2013. Fertility at the district Level in India: lessons from the 2011 census. *Economic and Political Weekly* 48(23): 59-70.

Gundevia, Y.D. 1975. *War and peace in Nagaland.* New Delhi: Palit & Palit publishers

Gupta, A. 1995. Blurred boundaries: The discourse of corruption, the culture of politics, and the imagined state. *American Ethnologist* 22(2): 375-402.

Habermas, J. 1991. *The structural transformation of the public sphere: An inquiry into a category of bourgeois society.* Cambridge, Massachusetts: MIT press.

Habermas, J. 1996. *Between facts and norms: Contributions to a discourse theory of law and democracy* (translated by W. Rehg). Cambridge, Massachusetts: MIT Press.

Harper, I. 2014. *Development and public health in the Himalaya: Reflections on healing in contemporary Nepal.* London: Routledge.

Harries, J. 2010. Of bleeding skulls and the postcolonial uncanny: Bones and the presence of Nonosabusut and Demasduit. *Journal of Material Culture* 15: 403-421.

Harriss, J. 2011. Civil society and politics: An anthropological perspective. In *An compendium to the Anthropology of India,* edited by I. Clark-Decès, 389-406. Oxford: Blackwell.

Hausing, K, K, S. 2014. Asymmetric federalism and the question of democratic justice in Northeast India. *India Review* 13(2): 87–111.

Hausing, K, K, S. 2015. Framing the Northeast in Indian politics: Beyond the integration framework. *Studies in Indian Politics* 3(2): 277–83.

Hazarika, S. 2005. Rio tosses interim solution idea. *The Statesman,* 24th December.

Hazarika, S. 2011 [1994]. *Strangers of the mist: Tales of war and peace from India's Northeast.* New Delhi: Penguin.

Hilde, C. and C. Bolzendahl. 2011. Gender gaps in political participation across Sub-Saharan African Nations. *Social Indicators Research* 102(2): 245–264

Hirsch, M. 2008. The generation of postmemory. *Poetics Today* 29(1): 103-128.

Ho, K. 2007. Structural violence as a human rights violation. *Essex Human Rights*

Review 4(2): 1-7.

Horam, M. 1988. *Naga Insurgency: the last thirty years.* New Delhi: Cosmo Publications.

Horam, M. 1992. *Naga Polity.* Delhi: D K Fine Art Press.

Horowitz, D. L. 2000. *Ethnic groups in conflict.* Berkeley: University of California Press.

Hoshi, K. 2014. Election malpractices in Nagaland. *Eastern Mirror*, 25th April.
Hunnam, H. 1990. *Autonomy, sovereignty, and self-determination: The accommodation of conflicting rights.* Philadelphia: University of Pennsylvania Press.

Hutton, J H. 1921a. *The Angami Nagas: With Some Notes on Neighbouring Tribes.* London: Macmillan.

Hutton, J. H. 1921b. *The Sema Nagas.* London: Macmillan.

Hutton, J.H. 1928. The significance of head-hunting in Assam. *Journal of the Royal Anthropological Institute.* 58: 399-408.

Hutton, J. H. 1965. The mixed culture of the Naga tribes. *The Journal of the Royal Anthropological Institute of Great Britain and Ireland* 95(1): 16-43.

Inglehart, R. and P. Norris .2003. *Rising Tide: gender equality and cultural change around the world.* New York: Cambridge University Press.

International Institute for Democracy and Electoral Assistance 2005. *Women in parliament: Beyond numbers.* Stockhold: IDEA.

International Institute for Population Sciences 2007. *National family health survey (NFHS-3), 2005–06: India: vols I and II.* Mumbai: IIPS.

International Institute for Population Sciences 2007. *National family health survey (NFHS-3), India, 2005-06: Nagaland.* Mumbai: IIPS.

Inter-Parliamentary Union 2017. Women in national parliament. Url: http://www.ipu.org/wmn-e/classif.htm. 1st July.

Jacobs, J., A. Macfarlane, S. Harrisan, and A. Herle 1990. *The Nagas: Hill peoples in North-East India.* London: Thames and Hudson.

Jaffrelot, C. 2002. *The silent revolution.* New York: Columbia University Press.

Jamir, A. 2002. 'Keynote address'. In *Dimensions of development in Nagaland*, edited by C.J. Thomas and G. Das, 1-8. New Delhi: Regency Publications.

Jamir, S.C. 2016. *A Naga's quest for fulfillment.* Bhubaneswar: Apurba.

Jamir, S.C. nd1. *Speeches of Mr. S. C. Jamir Chief Minister Nagaland, 1999.* Kohima: Department of Information & Public Relations.

Jamir, S.C. nd2. *Speeches of Mr. S. C. Jamir Chief Minister of Nagaland, 2000.* Kohima: Department of Information & Public Relations.

Jerven, M. 2013. *Poor numbers: How we are misled by African development statistics and what to do about it.* Ithaca: Cornell University Press.

Jimomi, V.H. 2009. *Political parties in Nagaland.* Kohima: Graphic Printers.

Joshi, V. 2012. *A matter of belief: Christian conversion and healing in North-East India.* Oxford: Berghahn Books.

Jullie, B. 2012. *Empowering women for stronger political parties: A guide book to promote women's political participation.* UNDP: National Democratic Institute for International affairs.

Kaviraj, S. 1984. On the crisis of political institutions in India. *Contributions to Indian Sociology* 18(2): 223-43.

Kaviraj, S. 2011. *The enchantment of democracy and India: Politics and ideas.* New Delhi: Permanent Black.

Kelhou 1998. Women in Angami society. In *Women in Naga society,* edited by L. Zehol, 55-61. New Delhi: Regency.

Kertzer, D. and D. Arel. 2002. Censuses, identity formation, and the struggle for political power. In *Census and identity: The Politics of Race, Ethnicity, and Language in National Censuses,* edited by D.

Kertzer and D. Arel,1-42. Cambridge: Cambridge University Press.

Khiamniungan, T. L. 2013. Gender and democracy: Disparity in women's political representation in Nagaland *Eastern Quarterly* 9(1&2): 107-118.

Khilnani, S. 1997. *The idea of India.* London: Penguin.

Khilnani, S. 2009. Arguing democracy: Intellectuals and politics in Modern India. *CASA Working Paper Series* 9(2): 1-34.

Khutso, R. 2013. *English Language and the formation of public sphere in the colonial Naga Hills.* Hyderabad University: Unpublished MPhil thesis.

Kiewhuo, K. 2002. Constructive political agreement and development. In *Dimensions of development in Nagaland* edited by C.J. Thomas and G. Das. New Delhi: Regency Publications.

Kikon, D. 2002. Political mobilization of women in Nagaland: A sociological background. In *Changing women's status in India: focus on the Northeast,* edited by W. Fernandes and S. Barbora, 174-182. Guwahati: North-Eastern Social Research Centre.

Kishwar, M. 1996. Women and politics: Beyond quotas. *Economic and Political Weekly* 31(43): 2867-2874.

Koijam, R. 2001. Naga ceasefire and Manipur. *The Hindu,* 13th July.

Krocha, V. R. and R.D. Rekha 2013. *Chakhesang: A window to Phek district.* Kohima: Chakhesang Student Union.

Kulkarni, S. 1991. Distortion of census data on Scheduled Tribes. *Economic and Political Weekly* 26(5): 205-08.

Kumar, B.B. 2005. *Naga identity.* New Delhi: Concept Publishing

Kumar, S. and N.K. Sharma 2006. Riddle of population growth deceleration in Andhra Pradesh during 1991–2001. *Economic and Political Weekly* 41(42): 4507–12.

Kumar, V. 2003. Anatomy of Congress defeat in Tripura. *Mainstream* 41(16): 25-26.

Kumar, V. and A. Agrawal. 2016. Winning censuses. *Paper presented at the Annual Meeting of the European Public Choice.*

Kundu, A. and D. Kundu 2011. The Census and the development myth. *Business Standard,* 8th April.

Kymlicka, W. 1995. *Multicultural citizenship: A liberal theory of minority rights*. Oxford: Clarendon Press.

Lambek, M. & P. Antze. 1996. Introduction: Forecasting memory. In *Tense Past: cultural essays in trauma and memory* edited by P. Antze & M. Lambek. London: Routledge.

Lerner, G. 1986.*The creation of patriarchy*. Oxford: Oxford University Press.

Lijphart, A. 1997. Unequal participation: Democracy's unresolved dilemma. *The American Political Science Review* 91(1) : 1-14.

Lipton, M. 1972. The South African census and the Bantustan policy. *The World Today* 28(6): 57-271.

Longchari, A. 2017. *Self-determination: A resource for just peace*. Dimapur: Heritage Publishers.

Lotha, A. 2016. *The Hornbill spirit: Nagas living their nationalism*. Dimapur: Heritage Publishing House.

Lujan, C. 1990. As simple as one, two, three: Census underenumeration among the American Indians and Alaska natives. *Undercount Behavioral Research Group Staff Working Paper 2*.

Lukes, S. 1975. Political ritual and social integration. *Sociology* 9: 289-308.

Mackenzie, A. 1995. *The North-East Frontier of India*. New Delhi: Mittal Publications. Manchanda, R. (ed.) 2001. *Women, war and peace in South Asia*. New Delhi: Sage.

Manchanda, R. and B. Tapan. 2011. Expanding the Middle Space in the Naga Peace Process. *Economic and Political Weekly* 46(53): 51-60.

Marshall, G. (ed.) 1998. *A dictionary of Sociology*. Oxford: Oxford University Press.

Matthew K. M. 2005. Manorama Yearbook 2005. Kottayam: Malayala Manorama Press.

Menon, N. 2000. Elusive 'woman': feminism and women's reservation bill. *Economic and Political Weekly*. 35(43/44): 3835-3844.

Michelutti, L. 2004. We (Yadav) are a caste of politicians: Caste and modern politics in a North Indian town. *Contributions to Indian Sociology* 38: 43-71.

Michelutti, L. 2007. The Vernacularisation of democracy: popular politics and political participation in North India. *Journal of the Royal Anthropological Institute* 13(3): 639-656.

Michelutti, L. 2008. *The Vernacularisation of democracy: Politics, caste and religion in India*. London: Routledge.

Mill, J, S. 1975 [1893]. *Three essays on liberty, representative government, the subjection of women*. Oxford: Oxford University Press.

Miller, D .1995. *On nationality*. Oxford: Clarendon Press.

Mills, J. P. 1922. *The Lhota Nagas*. London: Macmillan.

Mills, J. P. 1926. *The Ao Nagas*. London: Macmillan.

Mills, J.P. 1935. The effect of ritual upon industries and arts in the Naga Hills. *Man* 35: 132-135.

Misra, J.P. 2004. A.Z. Phizo: as I knew him. Url: http://nagaland.faithweb.com/articles/phizo.html.

Misra, U. 1987. Nagaland elections. *Economic and Political Weekly* 22(51): 2193-2195.

Misra, U. 2000. *The periphery strikes back: Challenges to the Nation-state in Assam and Nagaland.* Shimla: Indian Institute for Advanced Studies.

Mitra, S. and C. James (eds) 1992. *Electoral politics in India: A changing landscape.* New Delhi: Segment Books.

Moffatt-Mills, A.J. 1980[1854] *Report on Assam.* New Delhi: Gian Publications.

Morung Express 2013. CPO statement on clean elections. 19th January.

Morung Express 2017. CM bats for active participation of people to end corruption. 30th October.

Morung Express 2017. Imposition of Aadhar a treat to Naga customary law and identity. 1st November.

Mullik, B.N. 1972. *My Years with Nehru.* New Delhi: Allied Publishers.

Murry, B., M.P. Sachdeva, and A.K. Kalla. 2005. Estimates of fertility and mortality differentials among the Lotha Nagas of Nagaland. *Anthropologist* 7(1): 45-52.

Murry, K.C. 2007. *Nagaland Legislative Assembly and its Speakers.* New Delhi: Mittal Publications.

Nagaland Baptist Church Council. 2012. *Clean election campaign. Engaging the powers: Elections – a spiritual issue for Christians.* Kohima: Nagaland Baptist Church Council.

Nagaland Post 2008. Mokokchung Village Firm on Boycotting MMC Polls. 15th September.

Nagaland Post 2009. Nagaland's inflated census. 21st September.

Nagaland Post 2013. Solo, T. On Extra Constitutional Taxation. 1st June.

Nagaland Post 2015. Centre Examining NE's spl. category status: Minister. 10th October.

Nagaland Post 2016. Jaitley Clarifies Changes in Funding Pattern for NE. 26th November.

Nagaland Post 2017. 18-point agreement inked for clean polls. 22nd June.

Nagaland Post 2017. Aug 25 rally biggest in the state: ACAUT. 27th August.

Nagaland Post 2017. Nagaland public rally – war against corruption. 26th August.

Nagaland Post 2017. Story of Naga Club and Simon Commission Petition. 24th June.

Nagaland Post 2016. Patton asks NCS officers to rededicate themselves. 22nd April.

Nagaland Post 2017. Nagaland Legislative Assembly Revokes Nov 24, 2016 resolution on ULB. 16th December.

Nagaland State AIDS Control Society. *2011. HIV/AIDS Scenario, Nagaland (Till July 2011).* Url: http://www.nagalandsacs.com/main/index.php?option=com_content&view=article&id=128:cmis-july-2011&catid=38:cmis&Itemid=239.

National AIDS Control Organisation and National Institute of Medical Statistics, n.d. India *HIV estimates-2006, technical report.* New Delhi

Natrajan, D. 1972. *Census of India 1971, intercensal growth of population (analysis of extracts from all India Census reports), census centenary monograph No 3.* New Delhi: Office of the Registrar General.

Nibedon, N. 1978.*North-East India: the ethnic explosion.* New Delhi: Lancers Publishing.

Nongkynrih, A K. 2010. Scheduled Tribes and the census: A sociological inquiry. *Economic and Political Weekly* 45(19): 43-47.

Norris, P. 1996. Women politicians: transforming Westminster. *Parliamentary Affairs* 49(1): 89-102.

Norris, P. and R. Inglehart 2001. Cultural obstacles to equal representation. *Journal of Democracy* 12(3): 26–40.

Nugent, D. 2008. Democracy otherwise: struggles over popular rule in the northern Peruvian Andes. In *Democracy Anthropological Approaches,* edited by Julia Paley, 21-62. Santa Fe: School for Advanced Research Press.

Nuh, V.K. 1986. *Nagaland Church and Politics.* Kohima: V.K. Nuh

Nuh, V.K. 2002. *My Native Country: the land of the Nagas.* Guwahati: Spectrum Publications.

Nuh, V. K and L. Wetshokhrolo (eds) 2002. *The Naga chronicle.* New Delhi: Regency Publication.

Oakes, A. and E. Almquist 1993. Women in national legislatures. *Population Research and Policy Review* 12: 71–81.

Ovung, A. 2012. *Social stratification in Naga society.* Delhi: Mittal Publications.

Parashar, U. 2017. Nagaland Crisis: clash of traditional values and women empowerment. *Hindustan Times,* 8th February.

Park, K. 1999. Political representation and South Korean women. *The Journal of Asian Studies* 58(2): 432-448.

Peabody, N. 2001. Cents, sense, census: Human inventories in late pre-colonial and early colonial India. *Comparative Studies in Society and History* 43(3): 819-850.

Peperzak, A. T., S. Critchley & R. Bernasconi 1996. *Emmanuel Levinas: Basic philosophical writings.* Bloomington: Indiana University Press.

Phillips, A. 1995. *The politics of presence.* Oxford: Oxford University Press.

Phizo, A.Z. 1951. *Plebiscite speech.* Url:http://www.neuenhofer.de/guenter/nagaland/phizo.html (Accessed on 13-07-2013).

Phom, H, B. 2003. *Socio-Cultural Issues in Nagaland.* Yingli College: Longleng.

Phom, H, B. 2005. *The Phom Naga Customary Laws.* Longleng: Longleng District Customary Court.

Phom, H, B. 2015. The Phom Naga Indigenous Religion. Dimapur: Heritage Publishing House.

Pierce, S. 2016. *Moral economies of corruption: State formation and political culture in Nigeria.* Durham and London: Duke University Press.

Piliavsky, A. (ed.). 2014. Patronage as politics in South Asia. Cambridge: Cambridge University press.

Pillai, M. S. 2017. *I'm a Naga first, a Naga second, and a Naga last. Livemint,* 19th

August.

Pippa, N. and R. Inglehart 2001. Cultural obstacles to equal representation. *Journal of democracy* 12(3):127-140.

Pisharoty, S, B. 2017. The myth of Nagaland's empowered woman. *The Wire*. Url: https://thewire.in/82254/gender-discrimination-nagaland-northeast/

Population Foundation of India and Population Reference Bureau 2007. *The Future Population of India: a long-range demographic view*. New Delhi.

Prasad, M.M. 2010. Fun with democracy: Election coverage and the elusive subject of Indian politics. In *Elections as Popular Culture in Asia*, edited by C.B. Huat.139-154. London: Routledge.

Preston, S.H., P. Heuveline, and M. Guillot. 2001. Demography: Measuring and modeling population processes. Oxford: Blackwell Publishers.

Rahman, A. 2008. *Social and political development of the Phom tribe of Nagaland since independence*. Dibrugarh University: Unpublished PhD thesis.

Ramunny, M. 1993. *The world of Nagas*. New Delhi: Northern Book Centre.

Reid, R. 1983 [1942]. *History of the frontier areas bordering on Assam from 1883-1941*. New Delhi: Eastern Publishing House.

Reynolds, A. 1999. Women in legislatures and executives of the world: Knocking at the highest glass ceiling. *World Politics* 51(4): 547-72.

Rio, N. 2010. Address at the conference of the Chief Ministers on internal security. New Delhi, 7th February.

Ruud, A.E. and G. Heierstad (eds) 2014. *India's democracies: Diversity, co-optation and resistance*. Oslo: Oslo Academic Press.

Sagar, N, B. 2012. NLA Committees Reject 33% Women Reservation. *Eastern Mirror*, 21st September.

Samaddar, R. 2001. *A biography of the Indian Nation, 1949-1997*. Delhi: Sage Publication.

Sanyu, V. 2003. The rise of the middle class in Nagaland. Url:nhttp://dspace.nehu.ac.in/handle/1/11111

Schlozman, K, L., N. Burns, and S. Verba 1994. Gender and pathways to participation: The role of resources. *The Journal of Politics* 56(4): 963-990.

Schürmann, R. 2003. *Broken hegemonies*. Bloomington: University of Indiana Press.

Sema, H. 1986. *Emergence of Nagaland*. New Delhi: Vikas Publishing House.

Sema, K. 2016. *Encountering life: Antics of a government servant*. Dimapur: Heritage Publishers.

Sema, K. 2017. The Debate on Reservation for Women. *Morung Express*, 15th January.

Sema, P. 1992. *British policy and administration in Nagaland 1881-1947*. New Delhi: Scholar Publishing House.

Sen, A.N. 1974.Operation Election. *Economic and Political Weekly* 9(11): 424.

Shah, A. 2010. *In the Shadows of the State: indigenous politics, environmentalism, and insurgency in Jharkhand India*. Durham and London: Duke University Press.

Sharma, H.N. and B.K. Kar 1997. Pattern of population growth in North-East India.

In *Demographic transition: The third world scenario*, edited by A. Ahmad, D. Noin, and H.N. Sharma, 73-93. Jaipur: Rawat Publications.

Shimray, R.R. 1985. *Origin and culture of Naga*. New Delhi: Somsok Publication. Shimray, U, A. 2002. Equality as tradition: women's role in Naga society. *Economic and Political Weekly* 37(5): 75-77.

Shurhozelie 1992. *Tenyidie Dze*. Kohima: Ura Academy Publication.

Singh, C. 2004. *Naga Politics: A critical account*. New Delhi: Mittal Publications.

Singh, C. 2008. *The Naga society*. New Delhi: Manas Publications

Singh, R.P. 1986. Electoral Politics in Nagaland. In *Electoral Politics in North East India*, edited by

P.S. Dutta, 179-91. New Delhi: Omsons Publications.

Singh, S. S. 2015. Women Are Safest in Nagaland. *The Hindu*, 22nd August.

Smith, A. 2001. *Nationalism: Theory, ideology, history*. London: Polity Publication.

Solo, T. 2011. *From violence to peace and prosperity: Nagaland*. Kohima: NV Press.

Soule, S. and J, Nairne. 2006. Are girls checking out? Gender and political socialisation in transitioning democracies. *Paper Presented at the Midwestern Political Science Meeting, Chicago*. Url : *www.civiced.org/pdfs/research/GenderAndPolitical.pdf*

South Asia Terrorism Portal n.d. Insurgency related Fatalities in Nagaland: 2002-2010. Url:http://www.satp.org/satporgtp/countries/india/states/nagaland/data_sheets/annualreport.htm

South Asia Terrorism Portal n.d. Insurgency related killings 1992-2017. url: http://www.satp.org/satporgtp/countries/india/states/nagaland/data_sheets/insurgency_related_killings.htm.

Srivastava, S.C. 1987. *Demographic profile of North East India*. New Delhi: Mittal Publications.

Steyn, P. 2002. *Zapuphizo: Voice of the Nagas*. London: Kegan Paul Ltd.

Swami, P. 2016. Talks with Andhra Pradesh on special status at fairly advanced stage: Centre. *The Indian Express*, 9th August.

Thomas, J. 2016. *Evangelising the nation: Religion and the formation of Naga political identity*. New Delhi: Routledge.

Thomas, N. & C. Humphrey 1996. *Shamanism, history, and the state*. Ann Arbor: Michigan University Press: 76-89.

Thong, T. 2014. *Progress and its Impact on the Naga: a clash of worldviews*. New York: Ashgate.

Times of India. 2015. Mob drags alleged rapist out of jail in Nagaland, trashes him to death. 6th March.

Tinyi, V. 2017. The headhunting culture of the Nagas: reinterpreting the self. *The South Asianist* 5 (1): 83-98.

Tinyi, Venusa. 2017. Rethinking human rights from a Naga Perspective: In *Human rights in Nagaland: Emerging issues.*, edited by L, Lanusashi and J, Toshimenla, 54-70. Dimapur: Heritage Publishing House.

Transparency International 2017. How do you define corruption? Url: https://www. transparency.org/what-is-corruption#define

Trigg, D. 2013. *Memory of place: A phenomenology of the uncanny.* Ohio: Ohio University Press.

United Nations 2011. *World population prospects: The 2010 revision.* UN: Population Division, Department of Economic and Social Affairs.

Url: http://www.censusindia.gov.in/2011census/population_enumeration.aspx Vamuzo, M. 2011. *Contemporary challenges of Naga women in nation-building.* Trent University: Unpublished PhD dissertation.

Varshney, A. 2002. *Ethnic conflict and civic life: Hindus and Muslims in India.* New Delhi: Oxford University Press.

Vashum, R. 2000. *Nagas' right to self-determination: An anthropological – historical perspective.* New Delhi: Mittal publications.

Venuh, N. 2005. *British colonization and restructuring of the Naga polity.* New Delhi: Mital Publications.

Verba, S., N. Burns, and K.L. Scholozman 1997. Knowing and caring about politics: Gender and political engagement. *The Journal of Politics* 59(4): 1051-1072.

Verba, V. 1996. The Citizen as Respondent: Sample surveys and American democracy presidential address, American Political Science Association, 1995. *The American Political Science Review* 90(1) : 1–7.

Verma, A.K. 2013. Tribal Annihilation and upsurge in Uttar Pradesh. *Economic and Political Weekly* 48(51), 52-59.

Wade, R. 1985. The market for public office: Why the Indian state is not better at development. *World Development* 13(4): 467-97.

Wade, R. 2012. The Politics behind World Bank Statistics: the case of China's income. *Economic and Political Weekly* 47(25): 17-18.

Weber, M. 1978. *Economy and society: An outline of interpretive sociology.* Berkeley: University of California Press.

Williams, S. 2011. Democracy, gender equality, and customary law: Constitutionalizing internal cultural disruption. *Indiana Journal of Global Legal Studies* 18(1): 65-85.

Witsoe, J. 2009. Territorial Democracy: Caste, dominance and electoral practice in postcolonial India. *Polar* 32(1): 64-83.

Witsoe, J. 2013. *Democracy against development: Lower-caste politics and political modernity in postcolonial India.* Chicago: Chicago University press.

Woodthorpe, R.G. 1881. Notes on the wild tribes inhabiting the so-called Naga Hills, on our North-east frontier of India. *The Journal of the Anthropological Institute of Great Britain and Ireland* 11: 56-73.

Wouters, J. J. P. 2014. Performing democracy in Nagaland: Past polities and present politics. *Economic and Political Weekly* 49(16): 59-66.

Wouters, J. J. P, 2015a. Polythetic democracy: Tribal elections, bogus votes, and political imagination in the Naga uplands of Northeast India. *Hau: Journal of Ethnographic Theory.* 5 (2): 121–151.

Wouters, J.J.P. 2015. 2015b. Feasts of merit, election feasts, or no feasts? On the politics of wining and dining in Nagaland, Northeast India. *The South-Asianist* 3(2): 5-23.

Wouters, J. J. P. 2017a. Land tax, reservation for women and customary law in Nagaland. *Economic and Political Weekly* 52(9): 20-23.

Wouters, J. J. P. 2017.b The making of tribes: The Chang and Chakhesang Nagas in India's Northeast. *Contributions to Indian Sociology* 51(1) : 79-104.

Wouters, J. J. P. 2017c. Who is a Naga village? The Naga village republic through the ages. *The South-Asianist:* 5(1), 99–120.

Xaxa, V. 2004. Women and gender in the study of tribes in India. *Indian Journal of Gender Studies* 11(3): 345–67.

Yonuo, A.1974. *The rising Nagas: A historical and political study.* Delhi: Vivek Publishing House.

Zehol, L. (ed.) 1998. *Women in Naga Society.* New Delhi: Regency.

Zhimomi, K.K. 2004. *Politics and militancy in Nagaland.* New Delhi: Deep and Deep Publications.

■ ■■ ■■

INDEX